Culture and Customs
of Mongolia

Mongolia. Cartography by Bookcomp, Inc.

Culture and Customs of Mongolia

TIMOTHY MICHAEL MAY

Culture and Customs of Asia
Hanchao Lu, Series Editor

GREENWOOD PRESS
Westport, Connecticut • London

Library of Congress Cataloging-in-Publication Data

May, Timothy Michael.
    Culture and customs of Mongolia / Timothy Michael May.
        p.   cm.—(Culture and customs of Asia, ISSN 1097–0738)
    Includes bibliographical references and index.
    ISBN 978–0–313–33983–7 (alk. paper)
    1. Mongolia—Civilization.   2. Mongolia—Social life and customs.   I. Title.
    DS798.4.M38   2009
    951.7′3—dc22   2008033801

British Library Cataloguing in Publication Data is available.

Library of Congress Catalog Card Number: 2008033801
ISBN: 978–0–313–33983–7
ISSN: 1097–0738

First published in 2009

Greenwood Press, 88 Post Road West, Westport, CT 06881
An imprint of Greenwood Publishing Group, Inc.
www.greenwood.com

Printed in the United States of America

The paper used in this book complies with the
Permanent Paper Standard issued by the National
Information Standards Organization (Z39.48–1984).

10 9 8 7 6 5 4 3 2 1

For Kelsey, who always listens.

Contents

Series Foreword

GEOGRAPHICALLY, ASIA ENCOMPASSES the vast area from Suez, the Bosporus, and the Ural Mountains eastward to the Bering Sea and from this line southward to the Indonesian archipelago, an expanse that covers about 30 percent of our earth. Conventionally, and especially insofar as culture and customs are concerned, Asia refers primarily to the region east of Iran and south of Russia. This area can be divided in turn into subregions, commonly known as South, Southeast, and East Asia, which are the main focus of this series.

The United States has vast interests in this region. In the twentieth century, the United States fought three major wars in Asia (namely the Pacific War of 1941–45, the Korean War of 1950–53, and the Vietnam War of 1965–75), and each had a profound impact on life and politics in America. Today, America's major trading partners are in Asia, and in the foreseeable future the weight of Asia in American life will inevitably increase, for in Asia lie our great allies as well as our toughest competitors in virtually all arenas of global interest. Domestically, the role of Asian immigrants is more visible than at any other time in our history. In spite of these connections with Asia, however, our knowledge about this crucial region is far from adequate. For various reasons, Asia remains for most of us a relatively unfamiliar, if not stereotypical or even mysterious, "Oriental" land.

There are compelling reasons for Americans to obtain some level of concrete knowledge about Asia. It is one of the world's richest reservoirs of culture and an ever-evolving museum of human heritage. Rhoads Murphy, a prominent Asianist, once pointed out that in the part of Asia east of Afghanistan and south of Russia alone lies half the world, "half of its people and far more than half of its historical experience, for these are the oldest living civilized traditions." Prior to the modern era, with limited interaction and mutual influence between the East and the West, Asian civilizations developed largely independent from the West. In modern times, however, Asia and the West have come not only into close contact but also into frequent conflict: The result has been one of the most solemn and stirring dramas in world history. Today, integration and compromise are the trend in coping with cultural differences. The West—with some notable exceptions—has started to see Asian traditions not as something to fear but as something to be understood, appreciated, and even cherished. After all, Asian traditions are an indispensable part of the human legacy, a matter of global "common wealth" that few of us can afford to ignore.

As a result of Asia's enormous economic development since World War II, we can no longer neglect the study of this vibrant region. Japan's "economic miracle" of postwar development is no longer unique, but in various degrees has been matched by the booming economy of many other Asian countries and regions. The rise of the four "mini dragons" (South Korea, Taiwan, Hong Kong, and Singapore) suggests that there may be a common Asian pattern of development. At the same time, each economy in Asia has followed its own particular trajectory. Clearly, China is the next giant on the scene. Sweeping changes in China in the last two decades have already dramatically altered the world's economic map. Furthermore, growth has also been dramatic in much of Southeast Asia. Today, war-devastated Vietnam shows great enthusiasm for joining the "club" of nations engaged in the world economy. And in South Asia, India, the world's largest democracy, is rediscovering its role as a champion of market capitalism. The economic development of Asia presents a challenge to Americans but also provides them with unprecedented opportunities. It is largely against this background that more and more people in the United States, in particular among the younger generation, have started to pursue careers dealing with Asia.

This series is designed to meet the need for knowledge of Asia among students and the general public. Each book is written in an accessible and lively style by an expert (or experts) in the field of Asian studies. Each book focuses on the culture and customs of a country or region. However, readers should be aware that culture is fluid, not always respecting national boundaries. While every nation seeks its own path to success and struggles to maintain its own identity, in the cultural domain mutual influence and integration among Asian nations are ubiquitous.

Each volume starts with an introduction to the land and the people of a nation or region and includes a brief history and an overview of the economy. This is followed by chapters dealing with a variety of topics that piece together a cultural panorama, such as thought, religion, ethics, literature and art, architecture and housing, cuisine, traditional dress, gender, courtship and marriage, festivals and leisure activities, music and dance, and social customs and lifestyle. In this series, we have chosen not to elaborate on elite life, ideology, or detailed questions of political structure and struggle, but instead to explore the world of common people, their sorrow and joy, their pattern of thinking, and their way of life. It is the culture and the customs of the majority of the people (rather than just the rich and powerful elite) that we seek to understand. Without such understanding, it will be difficult for all of us to live peacefully and fruitfully with each other in this increasingly interdependent world.

As the world shrinks, modern technologies have made all nations on earth "virtual" neighbors. The expression "global village" not only reveals the nature and the scope of the world in which we live but also, more importantly, highlights the serious need for mutual understanding of all peoples on our planet. If this series serves to help the reader obtain a better understanding of the "half of the world" that is Asia, the authors and I will be well rewarded.

Hanchao Lu
Georgia Institute of Technology

Preface

THE VERY NAME "Mongolia" conjures romantic images of blue skies, windswept plains, charging horsemen, and mystery. Indeed, Mongolia remains a mysterious and exotic land to many people, even in the twenty-first century, as until 1990, it was isolated by virtue of the cold war. As the second Communist state, Mongolia was, in all but name, the sixteenth republic of the Soviet Union. Thus very few Westerners were allowed to set foot into it. Today, with the end of the Soviet Union and Mongolia's own Communist government, Mongolia has embraced democracy and a capitalist economy. Mongolia's transition has not been easy. Although life in the shadow of the Soviet Union had many hardships, it also brought many benefits, quality health care and education being among them. Yet now, Mongolia is able to forge its own identity as well as celebrate its culture, which was often repressed under the old regime. While some traditions, such as Buddhism and icons of national heroes like Chinggis Khan, were repressed, Mongolians are now recovering them. Some customs were lost, but others were maintained secretly and waited to be recovered. At the same time, new traditions are being created in twenty-first-century Mongolia.

This book is designed to introduce Mongolia as a country, along with its customs and culture in the modern era. Mongolia is primarily known for one thing: Chinggis Khan, or as most Westerners erroneously know him, Genghis Khan. Without doubt, Chinggis Khan is a large part of Mongolia's identity, but there is much more. Because Mongolia has been isolated and considered somewhat of an esoteric destination just north of China, many people do not realize that Mongolia is an independent country and that the language is not Chinese. Furthermore, being a relatively poor country with a small population, it has not been a major player in international affairs.

Roughly the size of the United States east of the Mississippi, Mongolia has a very small population but is rich in customs and traditions different from those of virtually any other place in the world. While almost 3 million Mongolians live in Mongolia, more Mongolians live in China and Russia, along with small numbers elsewhere.

Since independence from Soviet domination, however, Mongolia has taken significant strides in establishing itself. Although it is not perfect, its government has been one of the few stable democracies to emerge from the Soviet bloc. It has eschewed its traditional ties and difficulties with Russia and China, two countries that comprise 99 percent of its borders, with a third neighbor policy. Who is the third neighbor? Mongolia has showed willingness to be neighbors with Japan, South Korea, the European Union, and the United States. Indeed, Mongolian soldiers have served in Afghanistan and Iraq as part of U.S.-led coalitions. At the same time, Mongolian athletes, musicians, artists, and even movies are gaining international recognition. In addition, it has embraced its heritage of nomadic living and Chinggis Khan, using these to attract curious tourists for a unique experience.

Still, Mongolia faces a number of hurdles. Although Mongolia is the land of the Eternal Blue Sky, smog in its capital, Ulaanbaatar, threatens that reputation. While democracy has taken root, government corruption challenges core individual freedoms. A switch to a market economy has created new wealth but has also placed a sizeable portion of the population in dire poverty. Women in Mongolia comprise most of the urban professionals as well as most of the students in higher education, yet they increasingly face difficulties at home. Still, the obstacles are not insurmountable.

Because Mongolian history or culture or anything about Mongolia is rarely mentioned in American schools at any level, it is not surprising that few people know much about the country. I first became interested in Mongolia in the fifth grade—perhaps an unusual experience. This idea lay dormant until my college years, when I finally had the opportunity to study the culture of Mongolia. The College of William and Mary did not offer any courses on Mongolia; however, my anthropology advisor, Vinson Sutlive Jr., encouraged my pursuit of all things Mongolian. From there I ventured to one of the few schools that offered courses on Mongolia—Indiana University. There I had the good fortune to immerse myself in the scholarship of Mongolia. Yet one cannot truly appreciate Mongolia, or any country, until one visits it. Having been in Mongolia during the heat of the summer and also having felt the biting wind of winter, I greatly appreciate this country of contrasts, not only for the stunning and indescribable beauty of the countryside, but also for the bustling growth of Ulaanbaatar, a city like no other.

While this book should be viewed as an introduction to Mongolia, it is by no means complete. The nuances of any single chapter could be a book unto itself. Nonetheless, I hope that those who read it will find it of benefit and also gain an appreciation of the wonderfully complex and fascinating culture of Mongolia.

Acknowledgments

I AM INDEBTED to a number of people for their assistance in writing this book. First, although his contributions occurred years ago, Vinson Sutlive Jr. first developed my interest in shamanism, anthropology, and the study and appreciation of other cultures. I am, of course, indebted to a number of people at my university. I have also benefited greatly from my Mongolian friends and colleagues: L. Munkh-Erdene for photographs and discussions on a number of aspects of Mongolian culture and Saruul-Erdene and Gerelbadrakh for clarifying several points.

Shawn Tonner and the rest of the librarians at North Georgia College and State University, kind folks in the interlibrary loan department, made my research much easier through their tireless efforts. The past and present heads of the Department of History and Philosophy at North Georgia College and State University, Drs. Christopher Jespersen and Georgia Mann, are to be thanked not only for putting up with my endless chatter about Mongolia, but also for providing encouragement and financial support for my trips to Mongolia as well as making it possible for me to write this volume. I also thank my colleagues Richard Byers, Tam Spike, Jennifer Smith, and Eugene Van Sickle for advice on photos for the book. Kaitlin Ciarmiello, my editor at Greenwood Press, deserves special thanks for seemingly endless patience and advice. Finally, I thank my wife, Michaeline, for not only putting up with my interest in Mongolia, but for her encouragement and for showing our children where Mongolia is on the globe when I was away.

Note on Transliteration

THERE IS NO officially accepted method for transliterating the Mongolian language. Most of the transliterations in this volume have been adopted from other works and seem to have become informally standardized. I have omitted umlauts so as not to alienate the general reader, and specialists will recognize the words with or without the marks.

Chronology

35,000–12,000 BCE	Paleolithic period; human habitation of Mongolia begins.
12,000–8000 BCE	Mesolithic period; bow and arrow first appear in petroglyphs.
8000–4000 BCE	Neolithic period; larger human settlements scattered across Mongolia. Khoit Tsenker monochrome cave paintings made.
300 BCE–155 CE	Xiongnu confederation dominates Mongolia.
ca. 546–744	Kok Turk tribal confederation dominates Mongolia and the steppes to the Caspian Sea. Establishment of a few towns in the Orkhon Valley.
573–581	Reign of Qaghan T'o-Po, ruler of the Kok Turks and devout Buddhist. He helped establish several shrines in Mongolia.
744–840	Uighur tribal confederation rules Mongolia and also becomes influential in the Tang Empire of China. Converted to Manichaeism and Buddhism and ruled from the city of Kara Balasghun in the Orkhon river valley.
840	The Kirghiz rebel against the Uighurs and drive them from Mongolia. Society breaks down to a tribal level.
960–1125	The Khitans rule approximately half of Mongolia as the Liao dynasty. They also establish several fortified towns and garrisons in Mongolia.
1125–1206	Period of tribal warfare.

1165	Birth of Temujin.
1203	Defeat of Toghril Ong-Khan.
1206	Formation of the Khamag Mongol Ulus; Temujin takes the title of Chinggis Khan.
1209	Mongols invade Xixia, which will be the first sedentary state to submit to Chinggis Khan. Uighurs of the Tarim Basin also submit to the Mongols.
1211	Chinggis Khan invades the Jin Empire of northern China.
1211–1234	Mongol Empire wars with the Jin Empire.
1218	Mongol-sponsored caravan massacred at Otrar. War with the Khwarazmian Empire begins.
1221	Chinggis Khan defeats Jalal al-Din Khwarazmshah at the Indus River.
1223	Khwarazm War ends.
1227	Chinggis Khan dies while quelling a rebellion in Xixia.
1230	Ogodei, the third son of Chinggis Khan, ascends the throne of the Mongol Empire. The Mongol General Chormaqan invades the Middle East.
1234	The Jin Empire falls to the Mongols.
1236–1239	Mongols invade and conquer the western steppes and the Russian principalities.
1240	Mongols invade and devastate Hungary and Poland.
1241	Ogodei dies; Mongols withdraw from Hungary.
1241–1246	Regency of Ogodei's queen, Toregene.
1246–1248	Guyuk, son of Ogodei, rules as khan of the Mongol Empire.
1248–1250	Regency of Oghul-Qaimish, wife of Guyuk Khan.
1250	Toluid coup; Mongke, son of Tolui, seizes power from Oghul-Qaimish.
1256	Hulegu destroys the Ismailis of northern Iran.
1258	Hulegu sacks Baghdad and executes the Abbasid Caliph.
1259	Death of Mongke in war against the Song Empire in southern China.

1260	Conquest of Syria completed, followed by the loss of Syria after the Mongol defeat at Ayn Jalut.
1260–1265	Civil war between Kublai and Ariq Boke for the throne; the rest of empire begins to separate and attend to their own affairs and quarrels.
1265	The Mongol Empire divides into four separate khanates, with only token recognition to Kublai Khan as the primary ruler. Also, establishment of the Yuan dynasty.
1294–1295	Death of Kublai Khan.
1368	Mongols driven out of China. Rise of the Ming dynasty in China. Although the Yuan dynasty remains in Mongolia, many Mongolian princes resist Yuan rule.
1368–1633	Endemic warfare throughout Mongolia.
1479	Rise of Dayan Khan and unification of the Khalkha Mongols.
1578	Altan Khan converts to Buddhism. The Second Conversion begins.
1585	Altan Khan begins the building of the monastery of Erdene Zuu on the site of Karakorum, the former capital of the Mongol Empire.
1630s	Wars between Ligdan Khan and the Manchus.
1634	Ligdan Khan dies of smallpox.
1635	The first Jebtsundamba Khutukhtu appears in Mongolia.
1636	Present-day Inner Mongolia submits to the Qing Empire.
1670s	Galdan, an Oirat leader, establishes an empire in central Asia and threatens all of Mongolia.
1688	Galdan attempts to conquer the Khalkha Mongols.
1689	Treaty of Nerchinsk defines the border between Mongolia and the Russian Empire.
1690	The Qing Empire defeats Galdan Khan at the battle of Ulanbudang.
1691	Mongolia submits to the Qing Empire for protection from the Zungars with the treaty of Dolonnor.
1697	Galdan Khan dies, ending the Zungar threat to Mongolia. The final defeat of the Zungars occurred in 1757.

1727	Treaty of Kiakhta between the Qing Empire and the Russian Empire finalizes the northern border of Mongolia.
1740	The Qing government determines that the new incarnation of the Jebtsundamba Khutukhtu can no longer be found in Mongolia, but only in Tibet.
1757	End of the Zungars. The wars with the Zungars added Mongolia, Xinjiang, and Tibet to the Qing Empire.
1800s	Mongolia, known as Outer Mongolia in the Qing administration, becomes a neglected province of the Qing Empire.
1904–1905	The Russo-Japanese War. Russia's defeat forces it to concede Manchuria and Korea to Japan's sphere of influence in the Qing Empire. Russia then concentrates on Mongolia, increasing its influence there.
1908	Inner Mongolia officially opened to Han immigration. Unofficially, the Han immigrated to Inner Mongolia for decades prior to this decree.
1911	Mongolian lamas and nobility plot an independence movement at Naadam.
	The Qing dynasty ends.
1912	Mongolia declares its independence from the Qing Empire and Chinese control. Mongolian forces fight with Chinese Nationalist troops. The Jebtsundamba Khutukhtu ascends the throne of Mongolia as Bogd Khan to become the ruler.
1913	Russo-Sino conference convened. Chinese forced to recognize Mongolian autonomy in a secret treaty.
1914	World War I. Mongolia is neutral in the war.
1915	Tripartite Treaty between Russia, Mongolia, and China gives international recognition to Mongolian autonomy.
1919	The Chinese warlord Little Xu occupies Urga and declares the end of Mongolian autonomy.
1920	The White Russian leader Baron Ungern von Sternberg flees Bolshevik forces by fleeing into Mongolia. He lays siege to Urga in October. Sukhebaatar and Choibalsan form the Mongolian People's Revolution Party (MPRP).
1921	Urga falls to von Sternberg in February, and he establishes his rule in Mongolia. The Jebtsundamba Khutukhtu retains his position. The Bolsheviks, along with Mongolian

revolutionaries, invade in July. Von Sternberg is captured and executed.

In October, the MPRP creates a revolutionary government in Urga and becomes the second Communist state in the world.

1924	Sukhebaatar and the Jebtsundamba Khutukhtu die. Urga is renamed Ulaanbaatar (Red Hero) after Sukhebaatar.
1930s	Purge of the Buddhist *sangha*, or "community," and forced collectivization of the herds.
1939	Battle of Khalklin Gol, or Nomunkhan, between Soviet and Mongolian forces on one side and the Japanese. With the defeat of the Japanese, Mongolia remains outside World War II militarily until 1945.
1940	Mongolia, the Soviet Union, and Japan sign a neutrality pact.
1941	Mongolia abandons the vertical script adopted by Chinggis Khan and adopts a modified Cyrillic alphabet.
1944	U.S. Vice President Henry Wallace tours Mongolia. At the Yalta Conference, Stalin convinces President Franklin Roosevelt and British Prime Minister Winston Churchill to recognize Mongolia's independence. Stalin also annexes Tannu Tuva, historically part of Mongolia.
1945	Mongolian troops join Soviet invasion of Manchuria.
1950s	Mongolia navigates between Soviet and Communist Chinese policies while trying to benefit from a relation with both.
1953	Choibalsan dies. Tsendenbal becomes the leader of Mongolia.
1962	Mongolia recognizes Chinggis Khan's eight hundredth anniversary.
1964	The United States gives Mongolia diplomatic recognition.
1965	Sino-Soviet split occurs. Mongolia is firmly in the Soviet camp.
1987	Mongolian-U.S. diplomatic relations begin.
1989	In December, pro-democracy protests occur in Ulaanbaatar.
1990	Democratic elections are held in July. The MPRP is removed from power.
1992	A new constitution is adopted. MPRP voted back into power.
1995	President Ochirbat meets with U.S. President Bill Clinton.

1996	Owing to the worsening economic situation, the MPRP is voted back out of office.
2003	Mongolia joins the U.S.-backed Coalition of the Willing. Mongolian troops will serve in Iraq and Baghdad. Asashoryu becomes the first Mongolian *yokozuna*.
2006	The eight hundredth anniversary of the Mongolian Empire.
2007	Hakuho becomes the sixty-ninth *yokozuna*. Asashoryu is suspended by the Japanese Sumo Association.

1

Land and History

GEOGRAPHY AND ENVIRONMENT

MONGOLIA OFTEN APPEARS to be a country of contrasts, ranging from a world-dominating empire to a pawn between superpowers, and from a devout Buddhist theocracy to an atheist state. A contrast also appears in the country's climate and geography.

The climate is harsh; its little precipitation averages thirteen inches per year, with the Gobi Desert in the south averaging three inches per year, but with annual precipitation of up to twenty-four inches in some areas of the north. Most of the precipitation comes during the summer months in the form of rain, but great icestorms and snowstorms, known as *zhud*, can occur in the winter (October to March), with devastating effects. The capital, Ulaanbaatar, is the coldest capital in the world, and the country itself experiences temperature ranges with lows from −40 to −61 degrees Fahrenheit in January to highs from 82 to 109 degrees Fahrenheit in the Gobi in July. Even so, the temperature can drop thirty degrees at night.

With a total land area of 1,564,116 square kilometers, or 971,896.62 miles, Mongolia is approximately the size of the United States east of the Mississippi River, excluding Maine. The population, however, is considerably smaller, with approximately 3 million people (2,951,786) in 2007. With its vast size, it is not surprising that Mongolia has a diverse geography. Although the steppes of Mongolia are known from their history, the mountains of Mongolia define much of the geography on the eastern and western sides of the country. River basins and the steppes dominate the central portions of the country, with the Gobi Desert comprising much of the southern region of Mongolia. Indeed, true steppe terrain comprises only 20 percent of Mongolia's territory. The rest consists of 35 percent forest-steppe and 40 percent *gobi*, which is a gravelly, semidesert region with scarce vegetation. The remainder consists of scattered true forests and sandy desert. Most of the forests and forest-steppes are located in the northern parts of Mongolia.

Eastern Mongolia

Eastern Mongolia consists of the region between the Khentiy Mountains and runs east to the border with China—more specifically, Manchuria. In general, the region is mountainous and then gradually transforms from hills into steppe and, finally, into the gravelly desert known as the Gobi in the south. The Khentiy Mountains serve as a watershed, with the Onon and Kherlen rivers flowing north and, eventually, into the Pacific. Both rivers flow through mountainous and forested terrain. This region has traditionally been quite abundant in the "five snouts," or major domesticated animals—horses, camels, cattle, sheep, and goats—although the *zhuds* in the late 1990s devastated many herds and, along with them, the livelihood of many people.

Central Mongolia

Central Mongolia consists of the territory between the Khangay and Khentiy Mountains. Ulaanbaatar, the capital and largest city, is located in the northern section of central Mongolia. The Khangay and Khentiy mountains dominate much of central Mongolia, while also serving as watersheds. North of the Khangay are the Selenge and Orkhon Rivers, which flow into Lake Baikal in Russia, whereas the Tuul River flows from the Khentiy into Lake Baikal. The Zavhan River then flows in a southerly and westerly direction into the salt lakes in western Mongolia from the Khangay Mountains. The Kherlen and Onon Rivers flow east of the Khentiy Mountains and, ultimately, into the Pacific Ocean.

As with all of Mongolia, the northern section tends to have more forested land, which blends into true steppeland. This area also possesses soil that is viable for commercial agriculture. However, there is a reason that agriculture never became a major livelihood in Mongolia: Wind erosion, low precipitation, and a short growing season make sustainable farming difficult. The southern portion consists of steppes that then turn into the Gobi Desert. The Khangay Mountains serve as the demarcation between the northern and southern terrain types.

Western Mongolia

Situated between the Khangay and Altai Mountains, western Mongolia contains terrain ranging from flat steppes to high mountains. The Altai Mountains in the west rise more than 4,000 meters (13,000 feet) and stretch for almost 400 miles. The highest peak in the Mongolian Altai Mountains is Altai Tavan Bogd Mountain, which reaches 14,350 feet and, like many of the other highest peaks, possesses glaciers. The Altai Mountains also form the barrier border between Mongolia and Kazakhstan, Russia, and part of China. To the northwest, there is the Tannu Ola, or Tannu Mountains, which border the Tannu Tuva Republic of Russia. The Sayan mountain range also borders Russia around Irkutsk and the Buryat Republic. The area wedged between these mountains is known as the Great Lakes Depression, consisting of the Uvs, Khar, Khar Us, and Khovsgol Lakes, with Khovsgol being the largest body of freshwater in Mongolia. It is also the world's second deepest lake (238 meters, or 780 feet, deep), with only Lake Baikal to the north being deeper. Whereas the northern section is hilly and gradually becomes mountainous in the east and north, the southern part of western Mongolia is flat, excluding the Altai Mountains.

HISTORY

Early Mongolia

Humans have inhabited Mongolia since the Paleolithic period (35,000–12,000 BCE). During the Mesolithic period (12,000–8000 BCE), the iconic weapon of Mongolia, the bow and arrow, was first manufactured. The Neolithic period (8000–4000 BCE) saw settlements of varying sizes scattered across Mongolia. These early humans left considerable evidence regarding the conditions of Mongolia. The best examples come from the Khoit Tsenkher Cave in Khovd Aimag. There, monochrome paintings provide evidence that the wildlife of Mongolia has changed considerably. Included in the drawings are images of not only what appear to be *Ovis ammon*, or Argali bighorn sheep, which still exist in Mongolia, and early camels, but also ostriches and elephants, indicating that at one point, the climate of Mongolia was much warmer.

The early recorded history of Mongolia is one of pastoral nomadic confederations. These confederations were usually known by the dominant tribe of the confederation. The most important one during the ancient period was the Xiongnu, known more popularly in the West as the Huns. The Xiongnu were active from the third century BCE to roughly 155 CE. During this period, they were a perennial antagonist to China's Qin (221–207 BCE) and Han (207 BCE–220 CE). Defensive walls, early predecessors to the Great Wall, were built in an effort to keep the nomads out and also to claim or reclaim territory that the nomads had vacated. The walls, however, were not extremely effective. Economic policies and marriage alliances proved to be a greater deterrence to Xiongnu attacks. Han gifts of luxury goods, such as gold, silver, and silks, as well as other goods that the nomads could not produce helped forestall raids. In addition, to sweeten the deal, occasionally the Han emperor sent a princess as a wife to Xiongnu leaders.

Nonetheless, the Xiongnu still raided China. Part of the standing of a leader of a steppe confederation was based on his ability to provide goods for his subordinates. While tribute helped, the leader, known as the *shanyu*, also had to prove his martial valor, and thus raiding was a necessity. Raiding China kept the nomadic warriors occupied and less likely to become involved in tribal warfare. Although the Han attempted several punitive invasions, few were successful, as the nomads simply drifted deeper into the steppe, waiting until the Chinese overextended their supply lines. They then attacked, and usually destroyed, the imperial armies. Gradually, the Chinese developed strategies to promote tribal warfare.

Their strategies eventually worked. Plagued with internal feuds, the Xiongnu split after internecine warfare into northern and southern confederations in 54 BCE and then later in 91 CE. Eventually, many of the Xiongnu left Mongolia altogether and migrated west out of Mongolia. Their descendents are thought to be the Huns who attacked the Roman Empire.

A new confederation emerged from southern Mongolia, now known as the Inner Mongolian Autonomous Region of China. The Xianbei, probably with Chinese encouragement, brought the Xiongnu to heel in 155 CE. Chinese enthusiasm waned quickly as the Xianbei also raided China. The Xiongnu still existed but remained a greatly reduced power. Some Xiongnu clans were part of the Xianbei, whereas others were allied with China. Ultimately, the Xiongnu disappeared as an entity by 349 CE.

The Xianbei's dominance eventually declined as well. Increased contact with China led to the acculturation of many of the elite. Indeed, members of the Toba clan of the Xianbei established the Northern Wei dynasty (386–528) and encouraged full contact with China. Their dominance over Mongolia eroded under attacks from what appear to have been a Mongolian people known as the Jujuan, based in the Orkhon river valley. What is known of Jujuan history from Chinese history consists of little more than stories of raids across the Gobi Desert into China. It was with the Jujuan, however, that rulers first used the title of khan, which became the standard title for steppe rulers.

The Jujuan's true importance in the larger picture of history is not their own history, but that of one of their subordinate tribes, the Turks, known in Chinese history as the T'u-chueh. In 546 the Turks, aided by the Toba, rebelled against the Jujuan and defeated them. While some undoubtedly remained in Mongolia, the majority fled west from Mongolia. On the western steppes, they dominated other tribes and were known in Europe as the Avars, a dominant force in eastern Europe until their defeat by Charlemagne in 790 and their final defeat in 800 by the new Bulgarian state.

Turkic tribal confederations dominated Mongolia from the mid-sixth century until about 840. While these remained pastoral and nomadic to a large degree, they also successfully created imperial states that extended beyond Mongolia. Indeed, the Kok Turks (552–744) possessed an empire that extended to the Caspian Sea, whereas the Uighurs (744–840) extended southwest into central Asia and intervened, on occasion, in the affairs of the Tang dynasty of China. In addition, both states developed imperial cities, albeit quite small in scale compared with those of their Chinese neighbors. Nonetheless, an increasing level of political and economic complexity marked the period of Turkic domination of Mongolia. In addition to imperial designs, both Uighur and Turks experimented with religion. Both Turks and Uighurs dabbled in Buddhism, whereas the Uighur leadership eventually converted to Manichaeism.

The adoption of an imperial culture and religious influences did have a cost, though. The imperial elite began to separate themselves from their fellow nomads. By having a capital, they tended to spend more time there and became increasingly sedentary. In addition, to maintain imperial appearances, especially to foreign powers such as various Chinese states, the rulers invested greatly in luxury goods, which widened the gulf between them and their subjects. In many ways, the innovations that occurred in the Turkic periods left them vulnerable to attack by other nomads.[1]

Indeed, the Kirghiz, a marginal Turkic group, eventually drove the Uighurs from their capital, Kara Balasghun, located in the Orkhon river basin. Kara Balasghun was destroyed and the Uighurs driven from Mongolia.

The Kirghiz did not replicate the imperial pretensions of the Uighurs, and Mongolia lapsed into a period of disorganization until the late twelfth century. No tribe dominated the region, as violence was rife. Tribes ascended and descended from power frequently. Only in the tenth century did a serious power emerge in the Khitans, a proto-Mongolian people who founded the Liao dynasty in northern China (960–1125). They maintained a presence in Mongolia with a number of small, fortified towns, which included support facilities such as blacksmiths and others. It is uncertain, however, how much control the Khitans actually asserted over the tribes.

Mongol Empire

The formation of the Mongol Empire was a slow and arduous process, beginning with the unification of the Mongol and Turkic tribes that dwelt on the Mongolian steppes. Temujin (1165–1227) emerged on the steppes as a charismatic leader, slowly gaining a following before becoming a *nokhor* (companion or vassal) to Toghril (d. ca. 1203–1204), khan of the Kereits, the dominant tribe in central Mongolia. While in the service of Toghril, Temujin's talents allowed him to become a major leader among the Mongol tribes. Eventually, Temujin's increase in power and the jealousy it invoked among others of Toghril's supporters caused Temujin and Toghril to part ways and, ultimately, to clash in battle. Their quarrel came to a head in 1203, with Temujin emerging as the victor.

Temujin unified the tribes of Mongolia by 1206 into a single supratribe known as the Khamag Mongol Ulus, or All Mongol State. In doing so, Temujin reorganized social structure by dissolving old tribal lines and regrouping them into an army based on a decimal system (units of ten, one hundred, and one thousand). Furthermore, he instilled a strong sense of discipline into the army. Although he had defeated all of his rivals by 1204, it was not until 1206 that Temujin's followers recognized him as the sole authority in Mongolia by granting him the title of Chinggis Khan (Genghis Khan), meaning "Firm, Fierce, or Resolute Ruler."[2]

Mongol power quickly extended beyond Mongolia, as the Mongols conquered the Tangut kingdom Xixia (modern Ningxia and Gansu provinces of China) by 1209.[3] In 1211 Chinggis Khan invaded the Jin Empire (1125–1234) of northern China. Although these campaigns began as raids, as their successes increased, the Mongols began to retain the territory they plundered after resistance ceased. Although the Mongols won stunning victories and conquered most of the Jin Empire by 1216, Jin opposition to the Mongols continued until 1234, seven years after the death of Chinggis Khan.[4]

Mongol expansion into central Asia began in 1209, as the Mongols pursued tribal leaders who opposed Chinggis Khan's rise to power in Mongolia and thus constituted a threat to his authority. With their victories, the Mongols gained new territory. Several smaller polities, such as the Uighurs of the Tarim Basin, also sought the protection of Chinggis Khan as vassals. Ultimately, the Mongols found themselves with a large empire, now bordering not only the Chinese states but also the Islamic world in central Asia, including the Khwarazmian Empire, which spanned portions of central Asia, Afghanistan, Iran, and modern-day Iraq.[5]

Initially, Chinggis Khan sought a peaceful commercial relationship with the Khwarazmian state. This abruptly came to an end with the massacre of a Mongol-sponsored caravan by the governor of Otrar, a Khwarazmian border town. After diplomatic means failed to resolve the issue, Chinggis Khan left a token force in northern China and marched against the Khwarazmians in 1218.[6]

After capturing Otrar, Chinggis Khan divided his army and struck the Khwarazmian Empire at several points. With his more numerous army spread across the empire in an attempt to defend its cities, Muhammad Khwarazmshah II could not compete with the more mobile Mongol army in the field. For the Muslim population, their defeat went beyond simple military conquest: It appeared that God had forsaken them. Indeed, the Mongols cultivated this idea. After capturing Bukhara, Chinggis Khan ascended the pulpit in the Friday mosque and announced,

O people, know that you have committed great sins, and that the great ones among you have committed these sins. If you ask me what proof I have for these words, I say it is because I am the punishment of God. If you had not committed great sins, God would not have sent a punishment like me upon you.[7]

Meanwhile, Muhammad II watched his cities fall one by one, until he fled with a Mongol force in pursuit. He successfully eluded them and escaped to an island in the Caspian Sea, where he died shortly thereafter from dysentery. Although his son Jalal al-Din (d. 1230) attempted to rally the empire in Afghanistan, Chinggis Khan defeated him near the Indus River in 1221, forcing Jalal al-Din to flee to India.

The Khwarazmian Empire was then ripe for annexation, but Chinggis Khan kept only the territory north of the Amu Darya, thus not overextending his army. He then returned to Mongolia to deal with a rebellion in Xixia by the Tangut, the dominant ethnicity, which broke out while the Mongol leader was in central Asia.[8] After resting his army, he invaded Xixia in 1227 and besieged the capital of Zhongxing. During the course of the siege, Chinggis Khan died from injuries sustained from a fall from his horse while hunting, but he ordered his sons and army to continue the war against Xixia. Indeed, even as he lay ill in his bed, Chinggis Khan instructed them, "While I take my meals you must talk about the killing and the destruction of the Tang'ut and say, 'Maimed and tamed, they are no more.'"[9]

The army that Chinggis Khan organized was the key to Mongol expansion. It fought and operated in a fashion that other medieval armies did not or could not replicate.[10] In essence, it operated very much as a modern army does, over multiple fronts and in several corps, but in a coordinated effort. Also, the Mongols fought in the manner of total war. The only result that mattered was the defeat of enemies by any means necessary, including the use of ruses and trickery. The famous traveler Marco Polo observed,

In truth they are stout and valiant soldiers, and inured to war. And you perceive that it is just when the enemy sees them run, and imagines that he gained the battle, that he has in reality lost it, for the [Mongols] wheel round in a moment when they judge the right time has come. And after this fashion they have won many a fight.[11]

Ogodei (d. ca. 1240–1241), Chinggis Khan's second son, ascended the throne in 1230 and quickly resumed operations against the Jin Empire, successfully conquering it in 1234. Although Chinggis Khan had announced previously that he had been sent as the scourge of God, Ogodei promoted the idea that Heaven (Tengri, the sky god) declared that the Mongols were destined to rule the world. Before invading a region, Mongol envoys delivered correspondence indicating that as Heaven had decreed that the Mongols were to rule the earth, a prince should come to the Mongol court and offer his submission. Any refusal of this request was seen as an act of rebellion not only against the Mongols, but also against the will of Heaven. This process was aided by a multiethnic bureaucracy staffed not only by some Mongols, but also largely by the educated elite of the sedentary conquered populations such as the Chinese, Persians, and Uighurs. Thus the letters were translated and delivered in triplicate—each one being in another language so that there was a high probability that someone at the other court could read the letter.

Ogodei backed his intentions of world domination by sending armies out to multiple fronts. While Ogodei led his army against the Jin, another army conquered Iran, Armenia, and Georgia under the command of Chormaqan (d. 1240). Meanwhile, a massive force under the leadership of Prince Batu (fl. 1227–1255) and Subedei (1176–1248), the renowned Mongol general, marched west in 1236 and proceeded to conquer the Russian principalities and the Pontic and Caspian steppes before invading Hungary and Poland. While they did not seek to control Hungary and Poland, the Mongols left both areas devastated before departing after Ogodei's death in 1241.

Ogodei's son Guyuk came to the throne in 1246, only after a lengthy debate over who would succeed Ogodei. In the interim, Guyuk's mother, Toregene, served as regent. Once in power, Guyuk accomplished little in terms of conquest, as he died in 1248. His wife, Oghul-Qaimish, served as regent but did little to assist in choosing a new khan. Her inattention led to a coup, in which Mongke b. Tolui seized power with the backing of most of the Chinggisid princes in 1250. Under his reign, the Mongol armies were once again on the march. In 1256 he and his brother Kublai (d. 1295) led armies into the territory of China's Southern Song (1126–1279), south of the Yangtze River, while Hulegu (d. 1265), another brother, led an army into the Middle East.

Hulegu's forces successfully destroyed the Ismailis, a Shia group also known as the Assassins, in 1256 in northern Iran. The Persian chronicler Juvaini, who also worked in the Mongol bureaucracy, reveled in the destruction of the much feared Ismailis, who used assassination to intimidate and extend their influence in parts of the Middle East. Juvaini wrote, "So was the world cleansed which had been polluted by their evil. Wayfarers now ply to and fro

without fear or dread or the inconvenience of paying a toll and pray for the
fortune of the happy King who uprooted their foundations and left no trace
of anyone of them."[12]

Hulegu then moved against the Abbasid Caliphate in Baghdad. The caliph,
nominally the titular leader of Sunni Islam, refused to capitulate but did little
to defend the city. The Mongols sacked Baghdad and executed the caliph, ending the position of caliph among the Sunnis in 1258. Hulegu's armies invaded
Syria, successfully capturing Aleppo and Damascus. Hulegu, however, with-
drew the bulk of his army in 1259–1260, after receiving news that Mongke
had died during the war against the Song. Meanwhile, the Mamluk Sultanate
of Egypt struck the Mongol garrisons in Syria, defeating them at Ayn Jalut in
1260. As the Mongol Empire spiraled into civil war after the death of Mongke,
Hulegu never recovered the Syrian conquests. Instead, civil war with the Mongols on the Pontic and Caspian steppes (the so-called Golden Horde) and with
those in central Asia occupied much of his attention.

Owing to the lack of a clear principle of succession, other than being descended from Chinggis Khan, warfare between rival claimants was frequent.
Civil war erupted after Mongke's death as two of his brothers vied for the
throne. Kublai eventually defeated Ariq Boke in 1265, but the damage to the
territorial integrity of the empire was great. While the other princes nominally
accepted Kublai as the khan of the empire, his influence dwindled outside
Mongolia and China. Kublai and his successors, known as the Yuan dynasty
(1279–1368), found their closest allies in Hulegu and his successors. Hulegu's
kingdom, known as the Il-khanate of Persia, dominated Iran, Iraq, modern-
day Turkey, Armenia, Azerbaijan, and Georgia. Central Asia was ruled by the
Chaghatayids, the descendents of Chaghatay, Chinggis Khan's third son, although often, they were the puppets of Qaidu, a descendent of Ogodei and
a rival of Kublai Khan. Meanwhile, in Russia and on the Pontic and Caspian
steppes, descendents of Jochi, Chinggis Khan's first son, held power. Their
state was often referred to as the Golden Horde in later periods.

Postempire

The history of Mongolia after the dissolution of the Mongol Empire is really the history of the Yuan dynasty. Ariq Boke's unsuccessful challenge and
claim to the throne of the Mongol Empire in 1260 was the death knell for
Mongolia. Ariq Boke represented the interests of the old steppe elite, whereas
Kublai represented a new vision of empire, focused more on the sedentary
lands. With Kublai's ascension to the throne, the capital of the Mongol Empire moved from Karakorum in the Orkhon river valley to northern China,
near modern-day Beijing. He named it "Shangdu" (Upper Capital), which
eventually appeared as "Xanadu" in Samuel Coleridge's poem "Kubla Khan."

Moving the capital from Mongolia had a deleterious effect on the country. Quite simply, without the capital, Mongolia became a backwater. Kublai and his successors did attempt to maintain support there simply because it remained an important troop reservoir—the importance of Mongol cavalry did not diminish. Indeed, there was concern that control of Mongolia, as it did during the civil wars between Kublai and Ariq Boke, and then those with Qaidu, could gravitate to the Mongol lords of central Asia. The Yuan dynasty, however, successfully prevented that from happening. As the civil wars dwindled after Kublai's death circa 1294–1295, that fear also diminished, and less emphasis was placed on maintaining important ties to Mongolia.

As time passed, the ruling dynasty increasingly assimilated aspects of Chinese culture as well as Buddhist influences, consequently appearing very un-Mongol to the Mongols in Mongolia. Ever since the move of the capital, an increasing dissatisfaction with the rulers existed in Mongolia. In addition, the Yuan emperor Toghon Temur (r. 1333–1368) was unable to deal with the myriad of problems he inherited. These included rebellions in southern China; wars on the frontier, which were not dynasty threatening but still a drain on resources; widespread corruption within the government and the royal family; and then a series of natural disasters, including major flooding on the Huanghe River. Thus, when the Yuan dynasty was overthrown by rebellion and the nascent Ming dynasty (1368–1644) in 1368, the Yuan emperor Toghon Temur fled from China to Mongolia. According to legend, only six of the reported forty *tumens*, or "ten-thousands," were able to escape. The rest were cut off and eventually surrendered. Even with the Ming's hatred of the Mongols, Mongol warriors were simply too important to massacre. If this legend is true, it also indicates a rather large demographic loss for Mongolia as well.[13]

Most of the people whom Toghon Temur led back to Mongolia were soldiers, so he had a sizeable force of forty to sixty thousand men. Once in Mongolia, he still viewed himself as the ruler, just without territory south of the modern-day Great Wall of China, which was constructed by the Ming dynasty. He then headed toward the Onon-Kerulan river basin, the ancestral homeland of the Mongols, to assert his authority. At the same time, a Ming army pursued him to ensure that the Mongols did not launch a counterattack.

Despite the loss of a vast amount of territory and his presence in Mongolia, Toghon Temur found very little support for his claims as ruler in Mongolia. The decades of antipathy toward the royal family manifested primarily in the descendents of Ariq Boke, who were the dominant element in Mongolia. In addition to the still simmering feud between Ariq Boke and Kublai, the Mongols of Mongolia simply viewed Toghon Temur and the returning Mongols as outsiders—essentially as Chinese, and not Mongol. Thus war erupted between the two parties.

A third element also entered the fray in the form of the Oirats, or western Mongols, who were located around the Altai Mountains. They had been a marginal group for much of the history of the Mongol Empire, with little connection to the royal family, as the lineage of the Oirats was of non-Chinggisid descent, and thus their own claims to the khanship and dominance over other Mongols was viewed as anathema.

Warfare became endemic for much of the fourteenth and fifteenth centuries. The Ming emperors invaded Mongolia on several occasions, but with mixed results. Although they might have defeated the Mongols, the Ming armies suffered constant attacks as they departed Mongolia. Complicating the matter was the fact that the Ming could not sustain their presence on the steppe for the long term. In addition, the Ming attempted to play various Mongolian factions off each other, a time-honored tradition in Chinese foreign policy on the steppe, and granted titles to rulers to legitimize them. The principal idea was that the Ming state attempted to weaken the Mongols through the policy of divide and rule. To them, it did not matter who they worked with—Chinggisids or Oirat leaders. Yet, at the same time, there was the risk that one leader could coalesce sufficient power to attack China. Such attacks were not a large enough threat to topple the Ming dynasty, but nonetheless, they were a danger. One such example was the particularly dangerous Oirat leader, Esen (r. 1439–1455), who created a nomadic empire that stretched from Lake Balkash to the borders of China.

After Esen's death, Mongolia again erupted in internecine warfare, particularly between eastern Mongols (Khalkhas) and the Oirats. It was not until the rise of Dayan Khan as the twenty-eighth successor to Chinggis Khan in 1479 that stability returned to Mongolia. Dayan, benefiting from his father, Mandaghol's (r. 1473–1479), unification of the Khalkha Mongols, defeated the Oirats and drove them out of what is now Mongolia.

The unity did not last for long. Dayan's nine sons soon squabbled over the empire. Clear division arose from this. One of Dayan's actions divided his realm into two parts, consisting of six *tumens*, with three in each part. These *tumens*, the Chahar, Urianghai, Khalkha, Ordos, Tumed, and Yungsiyebu, became the tribes of Mongolia. The head of the Chahar was recognized with the title of khan, but it was more of a first-among-equals title, as his brothers named themselves as his peers. Soon they all used the title of khan, thus relegating the title of khan to simply the title of one who led the Chahar (or any other) *tumen*. As all were descendents of Chinggis Khan, they all technically had claims to the title and ascendancy over all.

Civil war between the various Chinggisids and with the Oirats continued into the 1600s. Very little changed in Mongolia between the death of Dayan and the eventual dominance of the Manchus over Mongolia, with the exception of the introduction of Buddhism into Mongolia. This is often called the

"Second Conversion," as Kublai's conversion is considered the first. Altan, the khan of the Tumed Mongols, in what is now Inner Mongolia, invited the leader of the Gelukpa sect of Tibetan Buddhism (also known as the Yellow sect) to meet with him near Koke-Nur. There the two exchanged titles and the revelation that the Yellow sect was the reincarnation of "Phags-Pa," the Buddhist advisor to Kublai Khan, and that Altan was the reincarnation of Kublai. They also exchanged titles in 1573. The Yellow leader, bSod-nams rGya-mtsho, gave legitimacy to Altan's use of the title of khan, thus theoretically raising him above his fellow khans. Meanwhile, Altan bestowed a title unto the Yellow leader to reflect the monk's wisdom and piety, which was as boundless as the sea—hence Dalai Lama (Oceanic Priest). This will be discussed further in chapter 3, which is concerned with religion.

The true implication of this was the linking of Tibetan-style Buddhism with political power. As all of the political leaders, excluding the Oirats, were descended from Chinggis Khan, other than by pure military supremacy, there was no way to assert political dominance in Mongolia. The use of Buddhism was a way to gain additional legitimacy, not necessarily replacing ties to Chinggis Khan, but adding an additional qualifier.

In China, the conversion to Buddhism was seen as a positive action, as the Ming had high hopes that Buddhism would tame the Mongols. While this would later be used as an explanation for the demise of Mongol independence, it certainly did not prevent the Mongols from fighting among themselves or from raiding China. Indeed, the Mongol conversion to the Yellow variant of Buddhism was pivotal to the rise of the Dalai Lama in Tibet, where there were several different sects. Altan Khan's troops assisted in convincing the other sects of the paramountcy of the Yellow sect, often in a not-so-subtle fashion. Indeed, the Mongols, particularly the Oirats, were crucial to the Dalai Lama's challenge of religious and temporal authority in Tibet. In 1640 the Oirats, under Gushi Khan, ended all Tibetan secular authority in Tibet; however, it was not until Gushi's death in 1654 that the Dalai Lama actually wielded temporal power.

Nonetheless, despite the influence of Buddhism and the capability of talented leaders such as Altan Khan, the Mongols could not find any method with which to unify themselves. Whereas Chinggis Khan was the cause and creator of the Mongol state, he was also an obstacle for maintaining unity, as any Chinggisid prince had a claim to authority.

Qing Empire

While the Mongol princes fought among themselves, farther to the east, a new power emerged from the forests and steppes of Manchuria. The Manchus, a Tungus tribe, became the dominant force in the region, expanding into

China. Curiously, several Mongol princes in the far eastern part of Mongolia joined the Manchus. Their decision was partly due to the stability that the Manchus offered over the endless wars among the Mongol princes. Also, there was the fear of Ligdan Khan.

Ligdan, the ruler of the Chahar Mongols, was the last great Chinggisid khan. Although he had aspirations of carrying the mantle of Chinggis Khan, he did not control all of Mongolia. The basis of his power existed south of Gobi, in what is now Inner Mongolia. Nonetheless, as the Chahars inherited the title of khan from Dayan Khan, Ligdan maintained that he was the legitimate ruler of all Mongols. Naturally, the other Mongol princes did not agree, but Ligdan's growing military might was persuasive, particularly to those near him. Ligdan also realized that the Manchus could be a threat not only to China, but to his own rule, as he tried to revitalize Mongolian imperial aspirations. As he attempted to assert his rule over the other Mongols, many resisted. Those bordering the Manchus found in them an entity that could assist them in maintaining their independence from Ligdan.

When warfare finally broke out between the Manchus and Ligdan Khan, the Manchus emerged victorious. Although Ligdan attempted to withstand them, he had squandered any chance of alliance through his heavy-handed attempts to assert his authority over all Mongols. Forced to flee westward, Ligdan died in 1634 from smallpox. By 1636 Ligdan's territory and virtually all of the lands between the Great Wall and the Gobi fell to the Manchus. This territory then became known as Inner Mongolia, which was a Manchu administrative division. In addition, the Manchus acquired the jade seal of Chinggis Khan, previously in the possession of Ligdan Khan and which had buttressed his claim to paramountcy.

With the jade seal, the Manchus could then claim the mantle of Chinggis Khan legitimately in the eyes of many Mongols. This, however, did not mean that all Mongols joined the Manchus. Neither the Khalkhas in Mongolia nor the Oirats recognized the Manchus as their overlords. Nonetheless, after the defeat of Ligdan Khan, the Khalkha Mongols maintained peaceful relations with the Manchus.

The Manchus, of course, went on to conquer the Ming Empire, completing the task in 1644, and thus had little interest in embarking on a conquest of Mongolia. Meanwhile, the Mongols under their control were an important element in the Qing (the dynastic name of the Manchus) government. Not only did they comprise a significant number of troops in the Qing military, but the Manchus often intermarried with them and adopted the Mongol vertical script as their own, with a few changes.

Meanwhile, Buddhism as a political force increased in Mongolia. In 1635 the first Jebtsundamba Khutukhtu, an incarnate lama, was born to the

Tushetu khan, Gombo-dorji. After studying under the Dalai Lama, the Jebt-sundamba Khutukhtu returned to Mongolia. As his religious and political prestige increased, he became empowered to dispense titles in 1659, not only among the Khalkha Mongols, but also among the Oirats. Owing to his lineage, his influence was greater among the Khalkha Mongols than among the Oirats.

In the meantime, the Khalkha Mongols had separated into three distinct khanates and periodically gave tribute to their powerful Manchu neighbor. Although the Qing did not rule Mongolia, they could and did exert influence on it. The Mongol khans married Manchu princesses, thus tying them at least indirectly to the court. The three khanates were derived from the territory of Geresenje, the son of Dayan Khan, who controlled the Khalkhas. On his death, his sons then subdivided the territory, and titles were given by the Dalai Lama. The Tushetu Khanate formed in central Mongolia, whereas the Setsen Khanate formed in the Kerulen River basin. Meanwhile, the Zasagtu Khanate formed in western Mongolia. A fourth khanate, the Sain Noyon Khanate, formed in west central Mongolia in 1725 from the western portion of the Tushetu Khanate.

With the absence of a coherent inheritance plan and incessant Qing meddling, the Mongols weakened themselves as they carved out small hereditary appanages from the khanates. This ultimately left them as pawns in a game of empire between the Zungars, as the Oirats were known in the seventeenth and eighteenth centuries, and the Qing Empire.

In the 1670s, Galdan, the khan of the Zungars, built an empire around Koknur and expanded into Kashgaria and Kazazkhstan. In 1685 he received the title of Bosghugtu Khan, signifying that he was the equal of any Chinggisid prince. In 1688 he moved eastward to bring his Khalkha brethren into the fold, one way or another. Khalkha resistance was futile, and, ultimately, they fled before the advancing Zungars.

Meanwhile, the Qing Empire became increasingly concerned about the growing might of Galdan. With the flight of the Khalkhas, the Qing sent an army into Mongolia and defeated Galdan in 1690 at Ulanbudang. This was only a temporary reprieve, though. Emperor Kangxi (1662–1722) then brought the Khalkhas under Manchu domination. The Khalkhas met at Dolonnor (the Seven Lakes) and pledged their loyalty to Kangxi and the Qing Empire. In truth, they had little choice other than to join Galdan Khan, which to them was not an option, as it was evident that the Khalkha Mongols were too disorganized to present a unified front against Galdan.

The war between Galdan and Kangxi boiled down to two factors: Buddhism and dominance among the Mongols. Kangxi was a patron of Buddhism, and the Qing emperor was often referred to as Bogd Khan, or the

"Holy Emperor," by the Mongols. With the rising influence of Buddhism among the Mongols, the Chinggisid factor could be overridden by a legitimate Buddhist ruler. Kangxi fit this model, as did Galdan. As a youth, he spent considerable time in Tibet and was given his title of khan by the Dalai Lama.

To whom would the Mongols look for support? If the Mongols became disgruntled with the Qing, they could turn to the Zungars. Although the Khalkhas were afraid of Galdan, the Mongols in Inner Mongolia could easily switch loyalties. As Buddhists, the Inner Mongols viewed the Dalai Lama's support of Galdan as very appealing. Indeed, the key factor that offset the Dalai Lama's influence among the Khalkhas was the presence of the Jebtsundamba Khutukhtu. Although not a challenger for the Dalai Lama's prestige, within the Khalkha world, he was paramount among the commoners. Furthermore, as the Jebtsundamba Khutukhtu was from the Khalkha aristocracy, his influence was considerable among them as well. Nonetheless, the threat of the Inner Mongols joining the Zungars was a major concern, as the Qing army had a sizeable force of Mongols in it. Such a switch would have been disastrous.

Diplomatic efforts between Kangxi and Galdan did not resolve the issue. At one point, Galdan demanded that the Jebtsundamba Khutukhtu be executed. The Treaty of Dolonnor in 1691 sealed the fate of Mongolia. The Khalkha princes became the subjects of the Qing Empire. Kangxi awarded titles to the nobles, and their territory became a military base for expeditions against Galdan and the Zungars.

The war had a grave impact for Mongolia, as resources, including manpower and herds of animals, were directed toward the war. The animals were not only used for food, but also, horses were used for cavalry and camels for draft animals and artillery. The camels did not pull cannon on a cart, but rather, the cannon sat on a saddle, from which they could be fired. Both sides used these, although the Qing had the edge in artillery. For several years, it was uncertain if the Khalkha had chosen the right side, as Galdan overran much of Khalkha territory in 1695, even to the Kerulen River. Ultimately, the Qing emerged victorious.

Although Galdan was defeated and died in 1697 from suicide, poison, or illness,[14] the Zungar threat was not completely removed. Ultimately, the Zungar were finally crushed in 1757, but during this process, the Qing gained Tibet and what is now known as Xinjiang. Mongolia, however, was secure from the Zungar threat after 1697. Furthermore, the Qing took immediate steps to prevent Mongolia from ever presenting a unified front.

To control Mongolia, the Qing instituted a control system that divided the former khanates into thirty-four smaller territories known as banners. This broke the power of the Mongolian khans and reduced them to the status of lesser aristocrats. This balkanization of territory continued over the next century so that the banners numbered over a hundred. The most potent aspect of the system was the introduction of political and military boundaries. Although the Qing did not end pastoral nomadism, they did impede it. The new banner boundaries cut across many nomadic migration routes. Although it was impossible to keep the nomads from moving across borders, the new policies did hamper the nomadic lifestyle and prevented the herds of the nobility from increasing tremendously. This, in turn, impacted the wealth or acquisition of wealth of the nobility. Essentially, if the nomads crossed into another banner, the lord of the banner had the right to collect rent from them for use of the pasture.

In addition, the Qing garrisoned the border with Russia with watch posts to curtail Russian trade and contact as much as possible. Nonetheless, some contact occurred. While trade with Russia was beneficial for the Mongols, the Russians also brought diseases against which the Mongols had little defense, such as tuberculosis, syphilis, and smallpox.

While there were negative aspects of Qing policy, the Qing attempted to prevent economic exploitation of Mongolia, particularly by the Russians, but also, they prevented ethnic Han Chinese colonization. Although most of the Manchu armies were withdrawn from Mongolia by 1761, Mongolian troops were maintained to police the region. A series of treaties gradually formed the border with Russia: Nerchinsk in 1689 and Kiakhta in 1727. Meanwhile, the Qing ruled Mongolia from Urga, now Ulaanbaatar, and other locations through governors known as *ambans*. The Mongolian nobles continued to be closely tied to the Qing and supported the dynasty loyally. Several Mongol princes even served as *ambans*. As long at the Mongols did not disrupt state control, the Qing left them to their own devices as a frontier province known as Outer Mongolia. They had subverted the princes and organized them in a table of ranks and given stipends. If they rebelled, they were destroyed, and thus the Qing bought and bound them as a fifth column in their own country.

In general, the Qing viewed Mongolia as a troop reservoir. Indeed, Mongol troops served throughout the Qing Empire until its end. After the end of the Zungar threat in 1757, the Qing relaxed its attitude toward Chinese penetration of Mongolia. Although large numbers of Chinese settlers did not arrive, Chinese traders and merchants did. It is rather astonishing how quickly the nobility and the commoners succumbed to the temptation of buying goods, often at high cost. Indeed, much of what was bought was done so on credit with high interest rates. By the twentieth century, most of Mongolia was in debt and mortgaged to Chinese merchants. Occasional revolts broke out, less against Qing control and more against the Chinese merchants. In many cases, the Mongolian nobility backed the revolts behind the scenes in the hope of gaining independence, although the majority of the participants were simply attacking exploitative merchants.

In addition, the Qing controlled the Buddhist religion in Mongolia. The Qing court saw it, as did the Ming dynasty, as a pacifying force among the Mongols. Buddhism did little to diminish the martial valor of the Mongolians, but it did have an impact on the economy and control of Mongolia. All of the major monasteries in Mongolia contained an incarnate lama, known as a *khutukhtu* in Mongolian, one who had reached enlightenment and had chosen to stay on earth to assist others on the path to enlightenment. The highest-ranking incarnate lama was the Jebtsundamba Khutukhtu. In 1740 the Qing court made a monumental decision and mandated that the Jebtsundamba Khutukhtu could not be found in Mongolia anymore, but in Tibet. In the same mandate, it was also ruled that the Dalai Lama could not be found in Tibet, but among the Mongols in western China. The idea was to break any ties to the religious figure, as he would no longer be a native of the region and thus could not easily become a rallying point against the Qing.

To a certain extent, it worked. In addition to the *khutukhtus* at the major monasteries, the Qing also created a new position of Da Lama, or "Great Lama." This was a political position and oversaw what occurred at a monastery. In most cases, the Da Lama was a Manchu and not a Mongol. He reported directly to the government and tracked the wealth of the monastery.

Meanwhile, the vast majority of the population consisted of commoners, known as *arat*. These were the herdsmen who served the nobles. In addition, the monasteries and *ambans* also had commoners attached to their properties, who became, essentially, serfs, without many rights and impoverished. In the monasteries, they were known as *shabinar*, and they maintained the herds of the monasteries as well as performed other jobs. By the twentieth century, the population of Mongolia was roughly 1 million, possibly less, with roughly 10 percent of the population enserfed and all of Mongolia stricken with poverty, illiteracy, disease, and little potential to change the situation from within Mongolia; outside Mongolia, the Qing court saw little reason to waste time or effort on the country.

Independence

By 1900 the Qing administration of Mongolia was ineffective. Mongolia became a neglected backwater province; however, another country took some interest in the region: Russia. In the nineteenth century, Russian influence crept steadily into Mongolia through merchants and diplomats. In the late nineteenth century, as the Qing Empire opened up to Western influences and spheres of influence were created by the Western powers (including the United States), Russia's sphere included Mongolia. Russian interest in Mongolia increased after 1905 with Japan's victory over the Russians in the Russo-Japanese War. Now excluded from Manchuria, in which the Russian Empire had originally been most interested, the tsar's government focused its attention on Mongolia.

At the same time, many Mongolians began to view the Russians as a counterweight to the Qing government and increasing Chinese influence. Although the Qing prevented massive Chinese immigration to Mongolia, it still occurred in smaller numbers. As the Qing government weakened, ideas of independence arose in Mongolia. The Russians did nothing to discourage the idea. Russia, however, chose not to become directly involved in an independence movement out of fear of becoming embroiled in a war with China: the idea of another war on the fringes of the sparsely populated Siberian frontier did not sit well with the tsarist government.

A revolution brewed within Mongolia, yet on the surface, there was little reason to think that independence was possible from either the Russian or Chinese perspective. The ruling class was broken into a series of ranks that performed the civil and clerical duties of the region. The nobility were scattered throughout the countryside in a variety of civil jurisdictions. Mongolia had been organized into six provinces, or *aimags*, four of which were the pre-Qing conquest khanates, and two of which were in western Mongolia, carved out of the defeat of the Zungars and administered from the town of Khovd. A khan ruled each *aimag*, but his position existed only by appointment by the Qing emperor. The *aimags* were broken into subdistricts, where the other nobility ruled, who again were appointed and received a salary. These again were subdivided and ruled by lower-ranking nobility, who again were appointed and paid by the Qing emperor.

At the highest level, there existed a congress of nobility known as the National Khural that was empowered to meet every three years, but it rarely did. In addition, Qing observers strictly controlled it. Thus the Mongolian administration had a structure, but it did not truly function. All of the nobles were tied to the Qing state, and none of them, even at the level of khan, had a tremendous amount of authority to be viewed as a national leader.

A parallel level of government existed in the Buddhist monasteries, which the Qing also tightly controlled. The thirteen *khutukhtus* possessed territories that were independent of the *aimag* system. In addition, there were more than one hundred lesser incarnations, known as *khubilgans*, who also possessed their own territories. Most of the incarnate lamas came from the nobility. As with the secular administration, the Qing government approved their appointments. All of the *khutukhtu* monasteries possessed a Qing official, known as the Da Lama, who reported back to the government. No meeting could be held in his absence, and often, he was not a monk. The Da Lama also kept a staff of clerks and accountants, who focused on the wealth of the monastery, which could be immense.

Each of the incarnate lamas (*khutukhtu* and *khubilgan*) had a treasury known as a *shang*, which was separate from the monastery's treasury. It included portable wealth and was passed to the next incarnation of the lama. Many of the incarnations were very careful with the wealth they accumulated through the years, and it grew to an immense amount. Meanwhile, the general treasury was known as the *zhos* and was separate from the *shang*. It included fixed and moveable assets, including herds of animals.

In short, the monasteries held the wealth of most of Mongolia. The secular government was bankrupt, even with subsidies from the Qing government, and the nobility was too far in debt. In addition to a heavy debt with Chinese merchants, the nobility had other forms of impoverishing themselves. Indeed, the Qing government planned it. The Qing required the nobility to live in Beijing for a portion of the year. Thus at any given time, roughly one-third of the Mongolian nobility could be found there. This not only prevented them from effectively administering their territories, but it also meant that they had to spend an excessive amount of money to maintain a second home and live according to their rank.

Thus high-ranking officials traveled with a retinue, which included a military detachment, servants, officials, concubines, and others. They also needed to dress accordingly and bring presents for the emperor. The salary received from the Qing was insufficient for this, and the Mongol nobility often mortgaged their herds and property to Chinese money lenders. By 1911 their debt was insurmountable and the source of growing resentment between the Mongols, the government, and the Chinese in Mongolia. Indeed, this issue would carry over even after the Qing Empire collapsed.

Thus no Mongol had the capability of unifying the Mongolians to rise against the Qing. With the lack of a common political ideology and a national literature, there was no national figure. No one among the Mongolian aristocracy had the ability or the wealth to finance such an action; however, there was one figure who could transcend these difficulties: the Jebtsundamba Khutukhtu. Nonetheless, by this time, the Jebtsundamba Khutukhtu was a Tibetan, not a Mongol, and was generally not politically motivated.

An impetus for independence was building with influence from Mongolians external to the Qing state. Buryat Mongols, who dwelled around Lake Baikal and thus were part of the Russian Empire, began to envision a pan-Mongol state. Drawing on ideas gained from Russian intellectuals exiled to Siberia, these Buryats viewed a so-called Greater Mongolia. The driving idealist was Peter Badmaev (1851–1919), a Buryat who also became a friend to

Rasputin. He may have even influenced Rasputin's reputation as a miracle worker, as Peter Badmaev was also a shaman and may have taught Rasputin a few trade secrets. Considering that most of the Buryat intellectuals gained their education from radicals and anarchists sentenced to Siberia, it is not surprising that they became radicals as well.

The Buryats did face a problem, though, as did many minority groups in the Russian Empire: how to express their ideas in a state that did not tolerate any talk of independence or autonomy. Thus the focus of the Buryat intellectuals moved to Mongolia. With the increase of Russian influence in Mongolia, the Buryats could now move there more freely.

At the same time, many Inner Mongolian princes were gravitating toward Mongolia. They shared many of the same problems as the princes of Mongolia: poverty due to duties in Beijing, Chinese money lenders, excessive spending. Yet they also faced the realization that Chinese immigration increased greatly with the advent of railroads to Inner Mongolia, and the Qing government did little, if anything, to prevent it. By 1908 Inner Mongolia was officially opened by the government to immigration. Aspirations of independence ended quickly, as more ethnic Chinese soldiers were stationed in Inner Mongolia to protect the immigrants and stop so-called banditry—which included actual bandits, clashes between Mongol nomads and Chinese farmers vying for the same land, and full-fledged rebellions.

Urga, the city of the Jebtsundamba Khutukhtu, became the epicenter of discontent for all Mongols. Urga, in the early twentieth century, consisted mostly of Mongols but was largely a monastery city surrounded by the *gers*, or yurts, of those attached to the monastery or providing services to it. In addition, non-Mongols, such as Russian diplomats along with a few French and British representatives on Consul Hill, lived nearby as well as in the Chinese trading quarter, where the Inner Mongols also settled, as they found Urga to be less appealing.

Urga had a population of roughly thirty thousand, perhaps forty thousand if one included the Chinese trading town. Most of the population, with the exception of the foreigners and roughly one thousand monks, was illiterate. The arrival of the Buryats changed this. Driven by the hope of a Greater Mongolia, they tried to find unifying elements. Buryat scholars, such as Rinchino (not to be confused with his contemporary, Rinchen) and Zhamtsarano, began intensive studies of folklore, oral history, epic poetry, and other aspects of culture. Zhamtsarano's efforts, in particular, led to the foundation of modern Mongolian literature. Through this, the Buryats created a mixed school— one that combined elements of the traditional religious education provided in the monasteries with Western education. Although many of the Buryats were not Buddhists, they valued Buddhism as a unifying element for a Greater Mongolia.

Thus, by 1911, diverse elements existed in Mongolia, with different views but a common goal of independence. They congregated in July 1911 to discuss the future of Mongolia. In July of every year was Naadam, a festival of traditional sports such as wrestling, archery, and horsemanship (all of which are discussed in chapter 8). As Mongols came from everywhere for this event, it became the perfect cover under which the discontented could discuss the failure of the Qing government, the position of Mongols in the world, and the burden of their financial debt to the Chinese.

Some government officials attended, but they were Mongols and sympathetic to the cause. All of the attendees were either nobles or lamas—none of the radical Buryats were in attendance. All agreed that the Qing government was on its last legs and only propped up by Western powers. In the end, they concluded on three items: (1) declare independence, (2) declare an end to Qing sovereignty, and (3) find outside aid to implement these goals. Despite their own dreams of independence, the conspirators were realistic enough to know that they needed outside help. The obvious contenders were the Russians and the Japanese. Some thought of the Qing government, but only if they abandoned China and ruled Mongolia independently. A few considered the United States and European powers.

They then sent messages out to the world powers. Most of them were ignored—the message to the U.S. Department of State was not even translated. Of course, it is very probable that no one affiliated with the U.S. government could have translated it at the time. Gradually, the greatest interest came from Russia. There the Buryats also lobbied the Russian government for support. As a result, they received aid, both financial and military, in the form of weapons and trainers, but only about one-third of what they had hoped.

Thus, in January 1912, the Autonomous Government of Mongolia was formed. Urga became the capital. The timing of the independence movement was perfect, as the Qing dynasty fell at the end of 1911 to nationalist movements in China. With the rise of the Chinese Republic, the Mongols felt that they were fully independent. The Chinese government disagreed but could do little about it at the time.

Unfortunately, the aims of the Mongolian independence movement were too large for their resources. Swept away by the idea of a Greater Mongolia, they tried to include Mongolian regions in Manchuria, Inner Mongolia, Xinjiang, and even Buryatia. Naturally, the Japanese, now the dominant influence in Manchuria, had no interest in losing any part of it. The Russians quickly but diplomatically ended this, not only for their own possessions in

Buryatia, but also out of fear of war with the Japanese. The Russians also had plans for Xinjiang, as they planned to extend their railroad to the region and, by extension, their own influence. Thus the Russians cut off military aid, which stopped the Mongolian armies. Indeed, at the time, the Mongolian armies had not only liberated all of Mongolia, but had driven into Inner Mongolia and enjoyed considerable success.

The issue was resolved at the Russo-Sino conference in 1913, where the Russians forced the new Chinese government to recognize Mongolian autonomy. Theoretically, five Chinese governors were present. Rather than a Greater Mongolia, only the former Qing region of Outer Mongolia was independent. The Tripartite Treaty between Russia, Mongolia, and China began as a secret treaty but received international recognition in 1915, when the international community accepted Mongolia's quasi-independent status.

The Jebtsundamba Khutukhtu became the first leader of Mongolia, despite his advanced age and deteriorating health. Other figures who led armies in the war for independence garnered consideration, but the Jebtsundamba Khutukhtu was the only person with sufficient status inside and outside Mongolia to garner enough respect. He had been officially placed in charge in 1912 and given two titles. The first was Bogd Gegen, which was a religious title meaning "Elevated by All." The second was the political title of Bogd Khan, or "Holy King." Thus Mongolia became a theocracy, and the Jebtsundamba Khutukhtu ruled with authority given through secular and spiritual means.

Although the Mongolians formed a quasi-representative government, with a legislative body consisting of upper and lower houses, the houses consisted of higher- and lower-ranking nobles and lamas. In addition, they lacked any real authority because the Jebtsundamba Khutukhtu could dismiss the government at will; furthermore, the government did not really function beyond Urga.

Despite autonomy, Mongolia's status did not improve. Russia's influence declined after 1915, largely due to World War I. The Tripartite Treaty of 1915 was made partially so that Russia could focus its attentions on matters in the West yet keep some stability in Mongolia. Meanwhile, the government consisted largely of monks. Yet new forms of education began to appear, through Buryat and Russian influence, including members of the Communist movement.

Meanwhile, in 1918, there was a change of status for Mongolia. With the fall of imperial Russia to the Bolsheviks, the Chinese felt confident enough to change the status of Mongolia. They sought to force the Jebtsundamba Khutukhtu to renounce the Tripartite Treaty, dissolve the government, and become part of China. The Jebtsundamba Khutukhtu resisted as best as he could, stalling while he tried to find aid from the Russians or Japanese. In the meantime, the Chinese warlord known as Little Xu marched into Mongolia and declared an end to the autonomous government in January 1919. There was little significant resistance. Many of the government actually welcomed it, as the Jebtsundamba Khutukhtu was ill and an ineffective ruler.

Chinese rule was brief, as the Bolshevik Revolution entered Mongolia in 1921. Before the Red Army entered Mongolia, the White Russian troops appeared under the command of Baron Ungern von Sternberg, a cavalry commander under Semenov, one of the leading White Russian commanders. With the defeat of Semenov by Trotsky's Red Army, von Sternberg entered Mongolia. The siege of Urga began in October 1920, and the city fell before the Whites in February 1921. Von Sternberg massacred the Chinese garrison and drove the Chinese out.

Although Mongolia was now liberated from the Chinese, unfortunately, Baron Ungern von Sternberg, a Lithuanian by birth, was insane, as was his rule. He saw himself as the reincarnation of Chinggis Khan and sought to restore his rule over Mongolia. His armies spread out from Urga and massacred Chinese merchants, who had returned under Little Xu's protection, in Khovd and Uliasustai in the west. He then began a pogrom of individuals whom he thought were connected to the Russian Bolsheviks. Many of his victims were innocent; however, there was a budding Communist movement among the Mongolians. As his insanity grew, so did his paranoia. Soon he purged his own command staff.

Thus, when the Red Army arrived, it was not surprising that the population, although thankful that the Chinese were gone, was also relieved to see the end of von Sternberg. By July 1921, the Bolsheviks captured Urga, and von Sternberg fled south to the Gobi. He was captured in August 1921 and executed. With the death of von Sternberg, Mongolia entered its Communist phase.

Communist Era

While Little Xu occupied Mongolia, he also purged the Bolshevik and Communist agents in Mongolia. This ended the Russian community in Urga. Many Mongolians grew disillusioned with the theocracy, feared the permanent Chinese presence, and looked toward the dynamism of the Communist movement in Russia. In 1920 the Mongolian People's Revolution Party (MPRP) formed under the leadership of Sukhebaatar and Choibalsan. In Irkutsk, they established a provisional government.

The Red Army invaded Mongolia to destroy Baron Ungern von Sternberg at the request of the Mongolian Provisional Government, and in November

1921, the Mongolian Provisional Government arrived in Urga. For the next seventy years, Mongolia would be little more than an unannexed appendage of the Soviet Union.

This government faced the same problem that had haunted Mongolia when it first gained its independence in 1921: the only person of national repute was the Jebtsundamba Khutukhtu. The Soviet advisors quickly recognized the importance of keeping him as a figurehead to gain support, despite the fact that they did not trust him and were concerned about his power, although he was extremely ill. Nonetheless, he remained the head of state but lacked any real power. Meanwhile, the Mongolian Provisional Government adopted a constitution that was a virtual copy of the Soviet one.

The year 1924 was momentous for Mongolia and marked a major transition. The Jebtsundamba Khutukhtu died, and the Soviets did not allow another to be found. In addition, Sukhebaatar, who had been the minister of war and commander in chief of the armed forces, died. Officially, he died from natural causes at an early age, but some suspected poison.

The position of Sukhebaatar in Mongolia was an odd one. He is attributed with inviting the Soviets in and thus saving Mongolia from Chinese occupation or worse. Indeed, he led the Mongol forces that ousted von Sternberg, although their role and numbers remain a matter of debate. Nonetheless, his role has been magnified greatly, and Sukhebaatar became the embodiment of the revolution. Urga was renamed for him in 1924—Ulaanbaatar means "Red Hero." Indeed, the Mongolian equivalent to Red Square is Sukhebaatar Square, where a statue resides along with his tomb, meant to be the equivalent of Lenin's tomb, who died in the same year, in Moscow.

The next shift in Mongolia occurred in the 1930s with the rise of Marshal Choibalsan. At this point, while some initiative occurred in Ulaanbaatar, government actions mirrored actions in the Soviet Union under Stalin. Indeed, Choibalsan was the Mongolian equivalent of Stalin. One of Choibalsan's major programs was the destruction of Buddhism in Mongolia. With the death of Jebtsundamba Khutukhtu, the religion was leaderless.

The state taxed and purged the lamas out of existence while confiscating property under socialist concepts of property ownership. This included the confiscation not only of land, but also of herds, artwork, and material wealth from the monasteries. Even the killing of monks was permitted. The fact that the monks and others rebelled, thus forcing the state to call in tanks and armored vehicles, only aided the process. By the time the government was finished, only a few thousand lamas and a handful of monasteries remained. Prior to Choibalsan's actions, over one hundred thousand monks had existed. Most were simply forced to leave the religion. It was a risky move, but the corruption of the Buddhist institution in Mongolia diminished its influence among the population. In general, despite the number of monks, both lay and actual clergy, the population largely did not take part in the resistance to its destruction.

Unfortunately, religion was not the only target of Choibalsan. Just as political purges began in Moscow, a similar one occurred in Mongolia. The purges started slowly, before 1930, when several leading figures in the MPRP were removed. This, however, was only a warm-up for the massive purges that took place between the 1930s and the 1950s. A conservative figure places the victims at thirty thousand dead, or roughly 3 percent of the population. Other estimates place the number of victims at over one hundred thousand. Like the victims in the Soviet Union, the victims in Mongolia were accused of being antiparty, having ties to the Japanese, or a variety of other offences that placed them outside the needs of the government. Everyone feared the arrival of the so-called Green Hats, the Mongolian equivalent of the Komitet Gosudarstvennoi Bezopasnosti, better known as the KGB, at his or her home. Usually, if a family saw a loved one arrested by the Green Hats, they did not see the family member again.

In addition to political and religious purges came a third program that mirrored events in the Soviet Union. As Stalin forced the collectivization of agriculture and the livestock of nomads, Choibalsan forced the collectivization of the herds of the Mongolian nomads, or *arats*. The herdsmen resisted and preferred to kill many of their animals rather than see them become part of the collective. As a result, the government ceased its collectivization program for the time being. Between the massive slaughter of animals and the violence between the herdsmen and government troops, the policy was not deemed worthwhile. After all, what good would collectivization be without any animals?

Collectivization, however, was not forgotten. In the 1950s, the government attempted the program again, with better results. Again, herdsmen killed large numbers of animals, but the government also confiscated them through more subtle means such as taxes in kind. Thus, by the late 1950s, most of the herds had joined collectives.

Although the purges were, of course, detrimental to Mongolia, not all of the end results were negative. With the rise of the socialist state, the Mongolians also saw many benefits. Prior to the rise of socialism, medical care came from traditional and Buddhist methods, although in Urga, there were a number of Jewish Russian doctors. These, however, were killed or driven out by Little Xu and then, of the remaining, by von Sternberg. In addition, education was compulsory not only for the urban children, but also for those of the herdsmen. The government constructed boarding schools to deal with the problem of a population dispersed across the steppe.

Once the collectives came into being, the herders remained in a position to take care of the animals, while also receiving medical care, pensions, and other benefits. The government did not intervene with how they took care of the animals, instead relying on their traditional knowledge born out of centuries of practice. Under socialist theory, private ownership of land did not exist, which actually aligned with nomadic custom. In the past, the nomads owned animals, but not land.

The purpose of collectivization was, of course, to break up potential sources of wealth and assert the government's control. In addition, it would ideally increase the size of the animal herds. Unfortunately, this did not happen. One reason is that the loss of animals by the herders' resistance was severe. In addition, spells of bad weather undermined it, especially when a *zhud* occurred. The *zhud* was an ice storm of such severity that it could decimate the animal population. As the nomads traditionally did not use barns or other shelters, during the winter, the animals huddled together for warmth. In a *zhud*, the entire mass of animals could be iced over and killed. Furthermore, there was no incentive for the herders to increase the size of their herds. As the animals were not their property, they saw no increased benefit if they produced more animals.

Another reason for the interruption of the collectivization policy was the outbreak of World War II. Mongolia's role was limited, yet significant. The battle of Khalkhin Gol, or Nomunkhan, located on the border of Mongolia and Manchuria, took place in 1939. The Soviets were convinced that the Japanese planned to invade Mongolia as part of their campaign in Inner Mongolia and China. From there, they would then move into Siberia. There were also fears that they might coordinate an attack with the Nazis. Indeed, this was one motivating factor for the signing of the Molotov-Ribbentrop Pact in 1939, which was a nonaggression treaty between the Germans and the Soviets.

Indeed, when an army numbering eighty thousand men invaded Mongolia, this seemed a reality. The Soviets, led by General Zhukov, were outnumbered but successfully thwarted the Japanese attack. Ironically, it was Zhukov's use of classic maneuvers from the era of Chinggis Khan that won the day in September 1939. After a monthlong battle, the Japanese faced defeat and the real possibility of a Soviet invasion of Manchuria. Thus, in early 1940, the Union of Soviet Socialist Republics (USSR) and Japan signed a neutrality pact. Mongolia also signed it and became officially neutral for the war, although it contributed troops to the battle. Inner Mongolians were on the side of Japan. Local accounts mention that the Mongolians on both sides shared intelligence so that they could let the Japanese and Soviets shoot each other without the loss of Mongolian life. The battle was momentous, as the loss hurt the prestige of the Japanese army. Thus the Japanese navy gained new influence in directing Japanese expansion into the Pacific Ocean, ultimately leading to Pearl Harbor.

From 1939 to 1945, Mongolia was free from the war, but it still suffered. The Soviets extracted animals for the war effort. In addition, Mongolian coal and gold resources supported the Soviet effort, without compensation. Choibalsan reputedly offered Stalin ten thousand Mongolian cavalrymen, but Stalin refused, preferring Mongolia's resources.

Mongolia entered the war again in 1944, but in a diplomatic quandary. With the end of the war in sight, U.S. Vice President Henry Wallace toured Siberia and Mongolia as part of a fact-finding tour for the Yalta Conference. Stalin, Winston Churchill, and Franklin Roosevelt primarily discussed Europe, but matters eventually turned to Asia. Part of the discussion concerned the request that the Soviets end their neutrality against the Japanese. As part of the negotiations, the shape of the postwar world came to light. Stalin insisted on Mongolian independence and that the Chinese government (the Nationalists) renounce their claims. Furthermore, Tannu Tuva would become part of the Soviet Union. Historically, Tannu Tuva, ethnically a Turkic region, but culturally Mongolian, had been part of Mongolia for hundreds of years. No one knows why Stalin desired Tannu Tuva, but Churchill and Roosevelt conceded to that demand and to Mongolia's independence. Chang-kai Shek, the Nationalist Chinese leader, did not recognize Mongolia's independence, but with Soviet protection, there was little he could do.

After World War II, Mongolia continued as a satellite of the Soviet Union. Much like the collectivization process, the economy was mismanaged. Mongolia received subsidies from the Soviets and Eastern European states. Most of its industry was light industry and focused on animal products such as cashmere, leather, and meat; however, by the 1970s, mineral exploitation began on a large scale. One result was the creation of a new city, Erdenet, which was the center of the copper industry—and still thrives.

Not surprisingly, the bulk of Mongolia's trade was with the Soviet Union and the Warsaw Pact states. Mongolian students studied in the USSR and beyond. Other factors also kept Mongolia closely tied to the Soviet Union. Despite this, Mongolia could not ignore its neighbor to the south.

With the victory of Communism in China, the entire context of relations between Mongolia and China changed. Mao's attitude toward Mongolia was ambivalent. Although China still claimed Mongolia, Mao also made overtures to it. Most of the construction that took place in Mongolia from 1950 to 1965 was through Chinese labor. In addition to access to Chinese labor and technical expertise, which the Mongolians sorely lacked, China eventually recognized Mongolia's independence. Ultimately, Chinese interest in Mongolia also increased Russian attention, as they vied for influence. Mongolia learned to navigate between the two, which became increasingly difficult with the Sino-Soviet split in 1965.

Into this scenario came Tsendenbal, who governed Mongolia after the death of Choibalsan in 1953—the same year as Stalin's death. By this time, although the MPRP ran the state, it was truly a one-man rule. Choibalsan did this in emulation of Stalin's cult of personality. Like Stalin in the Soviet Union, statues of Choibalsan were omnipresent, and an industrial city was even named after him. The Mongolian leaders truly became tied to Moscow, particularly in light of Chinese interest in Mongolia. Tsendenbal toed the line that came from Moscow. It was even thought by some that his Russian wife was there to ensure that he remained loyal to Soviet interests. This, of course, meant more Soviet investment and subsidies. It also meant, however, the expulsion of Chinese workers.

As a result, the economy of Mongolia was tied to that of the Soviet Union and gave the Soviets increasing leverage. Many projects that were undertaken were advised or managed by Soviet advisors, usually in the realm of heavy industry. Also, many of the projects were meant to better connect Mongolia to the USSR. Thus the infrastructure throughout Mongolia was ignored, except what was essential for trade between the two nations. The connection was cemented after the Sino-Soviet split, when several Soviet divisions were stationed in Mongolia, ostensibly to protect it from China. Also, the educational system was oriented toward the Soviet Union. In 1941 the Mongols switched to a Cyrillic script, abandoning the Uighur vertical script introduced by Chinggis Khan. This was a common tactic used by Stalin to cut off nationalities from their heritage, thus making it easier to reorient them to new ideals.

The switch to Cyrillic foreshadowed increasing exchanges with the Soviet Union. Most of the students who left Mongolia to study went to universities in the Soviet Union and then to Eastern Bloc countries. The Mongolian Academy of Sciences became a mirror of the Soviet one. In addition, Mongolians also received advanced technical training in engineering and medicine from the Soviets. Furthermore, with strong ties and subsidies from the Soviet Union, the Mongolian government provided a wide range of benefits to all of its citizens, ranging from medical care to educational and welfare benefits. Steadily, the Mongolian population grew.

Of course, the dissolution of the Soviet Union had a huge impact on Mongolia. With the advent of glasnost and perestroika, the Soviet Union underwent several minor and major upheavals. The tremors from these policies also reached Mongolia. Beginning in 1987, Mongolia began to act with increasing independence. Although the United States did not recognize Mongolia until 1964, Mongolia initiated diplomatic relations with the United States in 1987. In addition, it renewed contact with China. A clear sign that the

Soviet Union had experienced a major shift was the withdrawal of army units from Mongolia. This gave the government increasing confidence, allowing officials to publicly denounce many of the activities of Choibalsan and Tsendenbal, particularly their roles in the purges and suppression of the people. Yet the officials also accused them of having caused Mongolia's economic problems.

Starting at government levels, the spirit of revolution and protest trickled down to the masses. In December 1989, protests erupted in Ulaanbaatar among students and others, who espoused the end of one-party rule and the creation of a democratic government along with economic reforms. The MPRP wisely understood the way the winds of change were blowing and supported the protesters. As a result, democratic elections were held in July 1990. The Ikh Khural, the legislative body, was elected, and P. Ochirbat became the first president of Mongolia, with D. Byambasuren as prime minister.

Post-Communism

The leaders of the student protests included many who had studied in Eastern Europe when the Berlin Wall fell. At the forefront was Sanjaasurengiyn Zorig. For the rest of his life, he would continually be at the forefront of democratic reforms and movements. After learning of the banning of the Soviet Communist Party after its failed coup to remove Mikhail Gorbachev from power in Russia, Zorig pushed for a similar ban against the MPRP. President Ochirbat followed through with a ban on MPRP members holding positions in the upper levels of the government, military, and judiciary.

In addition to governmental changes, Mongolia underwent fundamental changes in its economy. The herding collectives were abolished, and livestock became private property. Whereas the total herd numbers during the Communist era saw only modest gains throughout the period, after the 1990 revolution, the herds increased substantially. Unfortunately, the market for animals and goods from animals shrank through privatization. State farms were also dissolved, and food production decreased. In addition, the debt to Russia had to be settled in 1991 U.S. dollars. This burden, combined with speculative dealing on international exchange markets, drained Mongolia of most of its hard currency reserves. The year 1991, however, ended on a good note, as a new constitution (Mongolia's fourth) was drafted, and then adopted in 1992, guaranteeing an elected parliament and president.

Despite the changes, the first elections to the parliament in 1992 brought the MPRP seventy-one of seventy-six seats. Nonetheless, this did not mean that the MPRP was the same party. It recast itself as a liberal democratic party committed to the unity of the new Mongolia. In reaction to the success and dominance of the MPRP, the five other political parties that ran against the

MPRP formed a new party, the Mongolian National Democratic Party. Other parties soon followed.

In the meantime, the economy was still stagnant and burdened by Mongolia's debt to Russia, which amounted, in 1995, to 10 billion rubles. Negotiations on this failed to produce any results, even in determining the true amount of the debt. With inflation rising faster than salaries, discontent among the populace was rife. Thus, in 1996, the MPRP was voted out of office, and the Democratic Alliance (National and Social Democrats) took charge.

Unfortunately, the economy did not change. A drop in copper prices hurt Mongolia, and the togrog, Mongolia's currency, dropped in value. Mongolia quickly learned that the fortunes of political parties can be determined by the economy. In the May 1997 presidential elections, the incumbent President Ochirbat of the Democratic Alliance was ousted in favor of the MPRP candidate Bagabandi.

Mongolia also dealt with other setbacks. Although in 1999 the animal herd reached 33,568,900 animals, in 2000 Mongolia suffered from droughts in the fall and then from a severe winter that included *zhuds*. As a result, almost 3 million animals died, which crippled the livelihood of many herders. Indeed, several herders did not recover from the winter. Severe winters followed during the next couple of years.

In the meantime, Mongolia continued to inject itself into the world community. Part of this process was finding other trading, cultural, and educational partners beyond Russia and China. Contact with Kazakhstan, Taiwan, Japan, and Korea occurred in 1991. Contact with Kazakhstan was significant, as Kazakhs comprise approximately 10 percent of the population in Mongolia. In addition, the Dalai Lama visited Mongolia over the protestations of China. More significant international contact occurred in 1995, when President Ochirbat visited Europe and then the United States, where he met with President Bill Clinton. Annual visits with foreign dignitaries continued. One of the primary initiatives of all these visits was the prospect of establishing a so-called third neighbor, as Mongolia is surrounded by China and Russia.

Ties with the United States, Japan, and especially Korea grew. Korean fashions have become the standard for most of Ulaanbaatar's young generation. All three states receive Mongolian students, send aid, and maintain strong diplomatic ties. Turkey has also actively engaged with Mongolia, particularly in the realm of historical culture, as the Turks originated from Mongolia. As a result, archaeological projects and museums particularly have benefited.

In 2003, with the U.S. invasion of Iraq, Mongolia's military options rose to new levels as it became a member of the Coalition of the Willing. While it is easy to explain this as simply Mongolia looking for military leverage against Russia and China as well as for economic incentives, Mongolia also benefited from having its small armed forces engaged in peacekeeping and potential military engagement. Indeed, in 2006, Mongolia hosted Khan-quest, a series of multinational peacekeeping exercises that involved Mongolian, Tongan, American, and Indian troops, along with Russian and Chinese observers.

Although Mongolia is still struggling after the end of seventy years of Soviet dominance, it remains committed to democracy and a symbol of the successful transition from a one-party system to a democratic government. Whereas most of the former Soviet republics have democracy in name only, Mongolia achieved it early and continues to grow. With a growing interest in Mongolia's mineral and tourism resources, one can only hope that its economy will blossom.

NOTES

1. Larry Moses and Stephen A. Halkovic Jr., *Introduction to Mongolian History and Culture,* Uralic and Altaic Series 149 (Bloomington: Indiana University Press, 1985), 23.

2. Igor de Rachewiltz, "The Title Cinggis Chan/Chaghan Re-examined," in *Gedanke und Wirkung: Festschrift zum 90. Geburtstag von Nicholaus Poppe*, ed. W. Heissig and K. Sagaster (Wiesbaden, Germany: Harrassowitz, 1989), 281–98. Previously, it was assumed that Chinggis Khan meant "Oceanic Ruler," based on early-twentieth-century attempts to link it to the Turkic word *tenggis*, which translates as "sea" or "ocean."

3. Xixia was a state dominated by the Tangut, a Tibetan people, although the population of the state consisted of Turkic nomads as well as ethnic Han Chinese.

4. The Jin Empire was founded in 1125, when the Manchurian Jurchen tribes invaded and conquered the Liao dynasty (916–1125). The Jurchen, a seminomadic people, took the dynastic name of Jin (or "Golden") and ruled northern China until the Mongols conquered the empire in 1234.

5. The Khwarazmian Empire came into existence in the twelfth century. After the Seljuk Empire, which had dominated much of the Middle East in the eleventh and twelfth centuries, collapsed, the governors of Khwarazm, located south of the Aral Sea, around the modern-day city of Khiva, became independent. Sultan Muhammad II (1200–1220) expanded the empire to its greatest extent. The dynasty was Turkic in origin and had strong marital ties to the Qangli Turks in central Asia.

6. V. V. Bartold, *Turkestan down to the Mongol Invasion* (New Delhi: Munshi-ram Manoharlal, 1992), 400–401; Henry Schwarz, "Otrâr," *Central Asian Survey* 17 (1998): 5–10; Thomas Allsen, "Mongolian Princes and Their Merchant Partners, 1200–1260," *Asia Major* 2 (1989): 83–126; Minhâj Sirâj Jûzjânî, *Tabaqât-i-Nasirî*,

vol. 2, ed. Abd al-Habîbî (Kabul: Anjuman-i Târîkh-i Afghanistan, 1964–1965), 650–51; Minhâj Sirâj Jûzjânî, *Tabakât-i-Nasirî: A General History of the Muhammadan Dynasties of Asia*, vol. 2, trans. from the Persian by H. G. Raverty (New Delhi: Oriental Books, 1970), 966.

7. Ata Malik Juvaini, *Genghis Khan: The History of the World Conqueror*, trans. J. A. Boyle (Seattle: University of Washington Press, 1997), 105.

8. Ibid., 139.

9. Igor de Rachewiltz, ed., *The Secret History of the Mongols*, Brill's Inner Asian Library 7 (Leiden, Netherlands: Brill, 2004), 196–200.

10. For a more thorough discussion of the Mongol army, see Timothy May, *The Mongol Art of War* (Yardley, PA: Westholme, 2007).

11. Marco Polo, *The Travels of Marco Polo,* trans. Henry Yule (New York: Dover, 1993), 263.

12. Juvaini, *Genghis Khan*, 725.

13. Paul D. Buell, *Historical Dictionary of the Mongol World Empire* (Lanham, MD: Scarecrow Press, 2003), 66.

14. Peter Perdue, *China Marches West: The Qing Conquest of Central Eurasia* (Cambridge, MA: Harvard University Press, 2005), 203.

2

Pastoral Nomadism

ALTHOUGH ONLY ABOUT half of the population of Mongolia may be considered pastoral nomads today, pastoral nomadism remains a central part of the Mongolian identity. Even today, urban Mongolians who were not raised in the countryside try to spend time there with relatives for at least a few weeks during the year. Pastoral nomadism in Mongolia stretches back for centuries. Indeed, nomadic influences appear not only in Mongolia's long history of tribal confederations and empires, but also in its literature and art. Two figures are most apparent throughout Mongolian culture: one is Chinggis Khan, and the other is the horse, the animal that makes pastoral nomadism possible.

The very geography of Mongolia probably led to pastoral nomadism, as agrarian farming suffered from a lack of sufficient precipitation in most areas. Furthermore, the abundance of pasture made it easy to feed the animals. There was no need to cut and store fodder. Even today, and after seventy years of socialist economic management, barns and other shelters—for better or worse—are infrequent.

Nomadism is often thought of as simply wandering about in search of grass and water, yet this is not at all accurate; rather, pastoral nomadism consists of moving from one pasture to another in a planned migration so as not to exhaust the pasture. In the summer, the nomads migrate to the highlands, where it is cooler. In the winter, they migrate to the lowlands and into valleys. Of course, in the ancient and medieval periods of Mongolian history, population increases among either animals or people and drought could lead to competition for pasture and eventual war between tribes.

Nonetheless, even today, the rotation of pastureland is necessary. Animals eat grass in different fashions: goats and sheep tend to nibble the grass close to the ground, while horses and cows do not. Careful management allows the herders to use the pasture without exhausting it. If the land is overgrazed, the sharp hooves of the animals inadvertently cause wind erosion by cutting into the soil, thus allowing the wind to blow away the exposed soil. Also, if the animals linger too long in an area, their dung—which also fertilizes—and urine saturate the soil and kill the grass. Thus seasonal migration not only prevents overgrazing, but also allows pastures to recover.

FIVE SNOUTS

The dominant economic mode and way of life, until the modern era, on the Central Eurasian steppe, which stretches from Mongolia to Hungary, was pastoral nomadism. Although nomadism varied across the globe, on the Mongolian steppe, pastoral nomadism was dependent on the "five snouts," all of which were used not only as food sources, but also for their by-products such as wool, hair, and leather. The five snouts comprised horses, sheep, goats, cattle (including beef cows, yaks, and/or oxen), and camels. This generally remains true today. The exact composition of the nomad's herd, however, varies with the geography. These animals are more than just farm animals; rather, they need to be viewed as capital. When the herder sells them, they produce profit, and until then, they provide the necessities of life.

Although it does occur, most Mongolian herders do not perform selective breeding. As a result, most of the animals tend to produce smaller quantities of meat, milk, and wool than their Western equivalents. In general, the climate is the best determiner of strengthening the herd. The cold, scarce water resources and primarily being pasture-fed leave little room for weakness among the animals. Mongolian breeds have adapted to the climate, whereas some efforts to introduce Western breeds have not succeeded, as these breeds tend to require more water and cannot handle the winters as well.

The primary animal is the horse. Without the horse, pastoral nomadism simply will not work. Owing to this, the horse holds an honored status not only an animal, but also as a symbol. Naturally, the horse was essential for herding all the other animals, but it was also important for hunting and warfare. While wealth was based on the number of animals one owned, the condition of one's horses was often indicative of one's social and economic status. In literature, mention of a horse with little hair on its tail indicated dire poverty. Or one might state that one has no whip, except for one's horse's tail. In Mongolia, spurs have never been used. To prod the horse, a baton or whip was used.

Sheep are the secondary animal of importance and are a necessity not only for their wool, but also for their meat. Indeed, mutton is the major source of protein for all of Mongolia. Goats supplement this, particularly in areas where there is less pasture, such as in the mountains or near the Gobi Desert. Of course, goats are also important for cashmere, made from their soft undercoats. The cashmere industry is becoming an increasing source of revenue for nomads. As a consequence, the numbers of goats in nomadic herds have increased dramatically.

Cows and yaks are the fourth most important animals, with their importance varying depending on the altitude. Fewer are kept compared with other animals. Still, they do provide dairy products, although the amount of beef and milk produced by Mongolian cattle tends to be lower than in Western countries. Nonetheless, they are well suited to climatic conditions characterized by high altitude and scarce water. Yaks are particularly used by herders who live in the mountains and highlands at altitudes over 2,500 meters (8,200 feet). Another animal in use is the *khainag*, a yak-cow crossbreed that is quite suited for altitudes between 1,600 meters (5,250 feet) and 2,500 meters, as even Mongolian cattle can find these altitudes trying. These animals also serve as draft animals for pulling carts; however, pickup trucks are steadily replacing them in that function. Nonetheless, they are important, but the incorporation of cattle into the herds of the nomad requires management, as cattle and sheep do not graze in the same fashion. Cattle tend to eat grass higher up on the blade, while sheep nibble almost to the ground.

Camels of the two-humped Bactrian variety are the fifth animal, although not all herders possess camels. They are valued not only for their fat-rich milk, but also for their wool, which is used to make warm blankets and other clothing such as sweaters for Mongolia's burgeoning fashion industry. A camel produces about ten pounds of hair a year, and thus a few camels can provide a sufficient supply of wool for this purpose. In addition, the camels can be used as beasts of burden, capable of carrying, on average, 400 pounds, or of pulling loaded carts of up to almost 950 pounds. They tend to be more common in the desert regions, although in all areas their numbers have declined, primarily due to the increased use of automobiles to transport loads. Nonetheless, their numbers fluctuate, and in periods of high fuel prices or shortages, the camel as a beast of burden becomes important once more.

While not technically one of the five snouts, a nomad's encampment would be incomplete without a dog. Dogs tend to be very large and of mixed breeding. They are not used as herding dogs, but rather as guard animals, capable of fending off wolves and people. Indeed, a long-held custom is that strangers do not approach the camp until the dog is restrained. Indeed, the phrase *nokhoi khorio*, or "please restrain the dog," has become a casual way of saying hello. For valid reasons, even Chinggis Khan feared dogs as a child.

All of the animals provide the services or products that make pastoral nomadism possible. Among the most important by-products is felt, which is made by taking the wool of the sheep and pounding and crushing it together. As wool has microscopic scales, when it is pounded, the scales interlock and form a compact layer. In addition to clothing, felt is used as material for the nomad's shelter, known as a yurt, or *ger* in Mongolian. These round shelters are made with a wooden latticework covered by felt. In cold weather, more layers of felt are added. When moving, the *gers* are easily disassembled and loaded onto camels, trucks, or carts and transported to the next site. In the past, the *gers* were sometimes kept assembled and placed on platforms drawn by oxen, making them easily transportable.

Leather, of course, is made from all the animals' skins as well as from animals gained from hunting and is used in a wide variety of applications. Mongolia has become well known for its leatherwork. In addition to felt and leather, the nomads use other animal by-products for clothing production. As mentioned before, goat and camel hair are used in the production of cashmere and other garments.

In terms of diet, the nomads subsist primarily on dairy products. Although mutton dominates meals, meat from the other animals is used, although camel meat tends to be eaten only in emergencies or if an animal dies. The reluctance to eat camels is due to their considerable value. Milk from all of the animals produces a variety of foodstuffs such as cheese, yogurt, and cheese curds. The cheese tends to be harder than forms to which Americans and Europeans are accustomed. Some have described it as rock hard, and one person who spent considerable time in Mongolia stated that it was impossible to find a Mongolian cheese that would melt sufficiently on a pizza. This will be discussed further in chapter 6.

During the era of the Mongol Empire, the Mongols were known for producing a powdered milk or paste to which they added water in a container. They tied the container to their saddles, and the bouncing motion of the horse while riding served to blend the mixture into a suitable consistency. Today, this is not commonly made.

A key item made from mare's milk is *airag*, an alcoholic drink made from churning the milk in a large leather bag (*koumiss* is the Turkic word for it). Through the churning action, the milk eventually ferments into a drink with a low alcohol content. It is possible, however, to make a more potent form and even to distill it into hard liquor. Owing to the fact that milk is usually only available during the foaling season of spring and early summer, it is difficult to acquire it after early autumn. Nonetheless, even urban Mongolians tend to desire it, and it is not unusual for them to acquire it from relatives in the countryside or to visit nomads to purchase it. For Westerners, however, it is an acquired taste and should be only be consumed gradually, as it can wreak havoc on one's gastrointestinal system until the body acclimates to it.

Although the variety of animals used in pastoral nomadism supplies most of the materials needed to survive, self-sufficiency is nearly impossible. Thus nomads have a symbiotic relationship with more sedentary cultures. In the past, it was with China, but now it is with the cities. In the premodern era, the nomads traded or raided for goods they could not produce, such as silk, grains, tea, and other luxuries, from the sedentary agrarian communities. Although there were a few blacksmiths on the steppe, the nomads usually acquired metal weapons and tools from their sedentary neighbors. In the modern world, herders can now produce materials for industry. Rather than trading animals and animal products for goods, they can be sold for cash. Indeed, during the socialist phase of Mongolia, rather than attempting heavy industry, the government focused on light industry and took advantage of the extant animal resources. Thus food-processing plants, hide-processing plants, shoe factories, and other related factories were established. The nomads can simply take their animals to the plants on the hoof. Thus it is possible for the nomads to acquire generators of various sorts, televisions, motorcycles, and so on. In this manner, the nomads are not a throwback to a bygone age, but rather have adapted to modernization.

FAMILY LIFE

Although in the premodern era large numbers of nomads congregated for war and tribal meetings, nomads have typically lived miles from anyone else due to the need for sufficient pastureland for their animals. A family could consist of a few *gers* in a camp, known as an *ail*. In the medieval period, there was one *ger* for each wife, but now there are one or more, depending on if the grandparents also live with the family. Extended families might dwell in the same vicinity as well, to share resources. Indeed, the number of animals in use dictates the number of people needed to properly handle them and also what other kinds of animal are needed.

Determining this is not an exact science, as factors such as altitude, type of pasture, and the mix of animals vary considerably. Nonetheless, certain general standards can be determined. At bare minimum, a family needs about twenty sheep and one horse. A second horse and herder will be needed once fifty sheep are in the flock, and then a third horse and rider after about two hundred sheep. Yet the number of animals will fluctuate, as the sheep can be replaced by other animals. For instance, a camel is usually worth six sheep in terms of resources used, a horse is worth six, a cow is worth five, and a goat is worth slightly less than a sheep.

The task of caring for the animals is shared by men and women. Men handle the animals unless they are hunting or away from the family for military (in the past) or other reasons. Their job duties include lassoing and breaking the horses. They also take the animals out to pasture—this could be several miles from the camp. A key tool in this process is the *uurga*, which is a long pole with a lasso on it. Rather than the lariat used in the American West, Mongolian herders use the pole to lasso their horses or other animals. The advantage of this tool is that it allows the herders to guide the animals, or they can use it as a prod or goad when moving the animals from the *ail* to the pasture and back. The men and older boys also castrate animals, kill and butcher animals for food, hunt, and skin the animals. Men also construct and repair the *gers*, any animal enclosures, and wagons, although this often becomes a task for the entire family. When it is time to move, the men load the wagons. A traditional task for the men is also to milk the mares and then churn the *koumiss* as well as to turn hides into leather for saddles, riding equipment, and other uses.

While the men take the animals out to pasture, women remain near the *ail* and perform most of the household duties such as cooking, making butter and other dairy products, processing the meat into products such as blood sausage, dressing animal skins, and making felt. Although clothes may be purchased, many women make clothing for their family as well as repair and wash them. During the migration periods, the women also drive the carts and wagons. When their husbands or sons are away, the women take care of the animals. While this division of labor existed and still exists, it is not unusual for either sex to do the traditional work of the other. Indeed, many jobs are shared simply because of the need for many hands when shearing the sheep, penning and counting animals at night, and combing the fur of the goats for cashmere.

Even though motorcycles have entered the steppe and are a fairly common possession, one still needs good horsemanship. Today, it is still true that, at times, the children raised in a nomadic family learn to ride before they learn to walk. The children also are involved in daily tasks from a young age. Children assist in the care of the animals but also procure fuel for the fire, which is another job women do near the *ail*. As wood is scarce on the steppe and is needed for the construction of other things, such as the latticework of a *ger*, it is not considered a fuel for fire. Instead, the children gather dried animal dung, which, if properly dried, burns with little odor. Cattle, sheep, and goat dung are preferred, in that order. Horse dung does not burn as clean or as well and tends to be avoided, except in cases of necessity.

Owing to the often precarious nature of nomadic life, which depends on men and women often performing the same duties to ensure the survival of the family, pastoral nomads tend to have a strong egalitarian streak in their social and political institutions. This is not to say that there is no differentiation in social classes or in politics, but much less so than in the overwhelmingly patriarchal agrarian societies that bordered the steppe. Nonetheless, the life of the nomad is not a romantic one, but one that has endured change and transformation and also provides Mongolia with much of its national character.

THREATS TO NOMADISM

The egalitarian nature of family life also carries over to views on property. Traditionally, nomadic societies have rarely viewed land as something one owns. One owns animals, but not land. Pastureland could become somewhat owned through tradition, but it was not something that one bought and sold. This view carried over during the Communist era, with Communism's view on property. Now that Mongolia is in a market economy, views on land ownership are changing. This is most apparent in the cities, where buildings have been erected in a seemingly haphazard plan. Western-style zoning is still a novel concept to a society that, until recently, never considered land as property. Currently this is not a problem on the steppe, but one cannot rule out that it might become a problem in the future.

A real land threat to nomadism is the desertification of the steppe. Overgrazing can potentially turn pasture into desert as the grass is stripped away and the soil is blown away by the wind. This is a real issue, as many of the nomads are fairly new to the process. Although nomadism has been part of Mongolia's culture for thousands of years, the Soviet era drastically changed the tending of livestock through collectivization. While many nomads preferred to slaughter their animals than turn them over to the government, collectivization still occurred. At its peak, 310 of these collectives, or *negdels*, existed. Fifty of these included intensive crop cultivation. Although some locations in Mongolia are ideal for crop cultivation, it initially involved a trial-and-error process that often led to at least temporary soil erosion.

During the socialist period, there would be a central settlement, with pastoral households surrounding it and maintaining the animals from the *negdel*. This process could be tightly controlled with quotas, and the nomads organized into work brigades and were often told which pastures to use to maximize efficiency (although the end result was not always realized).

With the fall of socialism, economic reforms began, including the Mongolian government's efforts at privatizing the collective herds. Thus the animals and much of the equipment, including tractors and other machinery, became private property. The redistribution of property was completed by 1993. Although many nomads were now independent, some cooperatives existed as members pooled their resources. Many of these attempted to operate as the old *negdel* did, but now, most of them are bankrupt.[1] Their goal was to serve as a common marketplace, particularly for raising vegetables, or as a distribution center for other pastoral families. In the end, most pastoral families have become independent.

The threat to the nomads' way of life is partially due to lack of experience, although after almost two decades, this is getting better. Nonetheless, many herders have abandoned the pastoral life because of the change in the economy. Although they are now independent herdsmen, the price for goods and services has increased dramatically, often far ahead of what the nomads earn from selling their animals or animal products. One of the boons of the socialist era was free and accessible medical care and education, but with the weak economy, not only have these become beyond the economic means of many nomads, but they are also hard to get in remote areas—and this includes veterinary care.

The changed economy has also affected the nomads in other ways. While many nomads gained tractors and trucks from the decollectivization of the *negdel* system, much of the machinery is now useless due to the increase in oil prices and the expense and difficulty of obtaining spare parts. Thus it has become more difficult to get goods to the markets. During the socialist era, there was also a move toward feeding the animals fodder during the winter months. Prior to this, the herds ate only through grazing. With the move to fodder, ideally to prevent the loss of animals due to malnutrition during the winter months, it was necessary to grow and cut hay. The tractors of the *negdel* greatly facilitated this; however, with the breakdown of machinery, it is now more common to cut hay by hand with scythes. Furthermore, moving to different pastures has also become more difficult without the use of machinery, especially in the *negdel* fashion, which involved seasonal moves four times a year.

Another consequence of the breakup of the collectives was that many "city slickers" attempted to move back to the country. Most commonly, these were government employees who sought to take advantage of the privatization of the herds and who also had a genuine interest in returning to their roots. Unfortunately, many of them had little understanding of how to be a nomad. Thus they tended to reside near the city and mainly raised goats, hoping to tap into the lucrative cashmere market. Furthermore, they only moved their animals after the animals overgrazed the land, stripping it bare. Even shrubbery was destroyed, but usually for its use as fuel, as they did not keep the larger animals, whose dung could be used as fuel. Not surprisingly, many of these new nomads have ceased to be nomads or to be involved with livestock.

Yet, at the same time, this process is forcing the nomads to relearn many traditional skills such as constructing and using yak, camel, and oxen as modes of transportation and to move their animals completely on foot (or, rather, hooves). Now, rather than four seasonal moves, the nomads have reverted to the presocialist moves of summer and winter migration. In addition, families have relearned how to make felt and other products by hand, rather than relying on machinery. Nonetheless, much like American family farms, many Mongolian nomads are finding that their children do not always want to live the lifestyle of their parents. Having been exposed to alternative opportunities through education and exposure to urban life, many seek to leave the steppe.

Another threat to nomadism has become more prevalent recently, although it has always existed—the *zhud*. *Zhud* means a disaster caused by starvation. The actual cause of the *zhud* is climatic shifts that prevent grazing. There are several types of *zhud*; while they are all similar in the aspect that pasture is scarce or unavailable, they differ in their causes. *Gan zhud* is where the pastures dry up from drought. *Khar zhud* occurs when there is a lack of snow in the winter, and thus the pastures are insufficient in waterless areas. The *khurray zhud*, or arid *zhud*, is due to extreme heat, which dries up the pastures. There is also a hoof *zhud*, or *tuurayn zhud*, caused by too many animals in an area—their hooves tear up or trample the pasture to such an extent that it becomes unusable. Finally, there is also the *tsagaan zhud*, or white *zhud*, which occurs when snow becomes too deep for animals to reach the grass beneath. This *zhud* has been particularly devastating in the new millennium—in addition to the snow, freezing temperatures and ice can cause havoc, as the animals may huddle together for warmth, and ice can coat all the animals together, thus causing a tremendous loss of life among a herder's animals. For instance, in 1999, the average herd size per family was 177 animals, but this decreased to 144 and 89 in 2000 and 2001, respectively, due to the *tsagaan zhud* in those years. Two years of consecutive *zhuds* have led to the loss of 8.3 million animals.[2] In some cases, the *tsagaan zhud* is so overwhelming that an entire herd can be wiped out in one season. Indeed, in 2000 alone, 2,400 families lost all of their livestock. The following year, the *zhud* was more severe, and an additional 7,400 families lost all of their animals, while another 13,300 families lost more than 50 percent of their herds. The *zhud* continued to wreak havoc on the animals after it passed. Owing to malnutrition, numerous animals miscarried during pregnancy, further damaging the herd's recovery.[3] With such devastation, the psychological and economic impact for the family is too great to continue a pastoral lifestyle.

Despite the difficulties, the nomads have reacquired many skills and are doing well, as the herd sizes of Mongolia have increased. Indeed, in the four-year span from the collapse of the socialist state in 1990 to complete privatization in 1994, the herd increased from 26 million animals to 27 million.[4] Today, estimates vary greatly, from 30 million to almost 50 million. More important, it continues to shape the character and identity of the country, as approximately 40 percent of the population remains pastoral nomads.

NOTES

1. David Sneath, "Mobility, Technology, and Decollectivization of Pastoralism in Mongolia," in *Mongolia in the Twentieth Century: Landlocked Cosmopolitan*, ed. Stephen Kotkin and Bruce A. Elleman (Armonk, NY: M. E. Sharpe, 1999), 226.

2. Enkhbayar Shagdar, "The Mongolian Livestock Sector: Vital for the Economy and People, but Vulnerable to Natural Phenomena," http://www.erina.or.jp/en/Research/db/pdf2002/02160e.pdf.

3. Ibid.

4. Sneath, "Mobility," 231.

3

Religion

RELIGION HAS PLAYED a curious role in Mongolian history and culture. Mongolia is one of the few places that has gone from a traditional religion, to being one of the most religiously tolerant places in history, to virtually 100 percent inclusion in one religion, to being officially atheistic, and, finally, to experiencing a new religious awakening. The oldest religious tradition in Mongolia is shamanism, and although it has declined over the centuries, shamanic practices have been incorporated into the other religions that entered Mongolia. Furthermore, shamans still exist.

SHAMANISM

Derived from the Tungus word *saman* (he who knows), a shaman was a central figure in most central Eurasian societies of the premodern world. While the term has become synonymous with *medicine man*, *witch doctor*, and a wide variety of other religious terms, shamanism better describes the religious traditions of the nomadic and hunter-gatherer peoples of Siberia and the Eurasian steppes. In Mongolia, the shaman is known as the *boo* or (in the past) *boge*.

Shamanism is not quite a religion in the Western sense of the word. The afterlife is not transcendental, meaning that it is not better than the present life. There is no salvation from sin or a holy text. Indeed, in many ways, the shaman is more comparable to a psychiatrist than a priest. Unlike in other religions, shamans do not have a standardized practice of rites and rituals. While they may perform regular rites during certain seasons, shamans perform these as needed, and there exists great variation in their roles and how they carry out their functions.

The shaman is not a priest, but rather an intermediary between the mundane world and the spirit world. While gods exist in the shamanic world, the focus is on the ancestor spirits and other more baleful spirits that might interact with the mundane world and cause harm. By entering an ecstatic state, often marked by trembling and a trance, the shaman uses a variety of methods to cure and alleviate distress. As many illnesses are associated with the theft of one's soul by an offended spirit, the shaman is essential to providing comfort and a cure. In his or her ecstatic trance, the shaman's soul enters the spirit world and retrieves the lost soul. The shaman also assists with the ascension of an individual's soul into the spirit world at the individual's death.

In addition to handling matters of life and death, shamans communicate with the spirit world. Using the information gathered from the spirits, the shaman can predict the future. This usually takes the form of scalpumancy, or the reading of cracks in burned bones, or allowing a spirit to possess the shaman's body, thus allowing the spirit to communicate directly with the physical world.

In the past and in the present, the shaman not only protects people from spirits, but in a sense, the shaman enters into a relationship with the spirit world. Thus the shaman is able to control spirits so that they assist him or her. At the same time, the spirits use the shaman to express their needs to the mundane world. As many of the local spirits are also ancestral spirits, this is a crucial role of the shaman. Without the shaman, society is exposed to psychic threats from the spiritual world and is thus vulnerable to a number of maladies. Only the shaman can deal with the spirit world and understand its needs.

As in any other religious profession, the shaman undergoes rites of initiation and instruction by other shamans. Nonetheless, the position of shaman is often hereditary, which may not be surprising should the psychological or physical manifestation of shamanic ability be genetic. While most shamans tend to be male, female shamans are not uncommon, as the importance of ability is greater than gender considerations.

One does not become a shaman by choice, but rather, a person is imbued with the ability at an early age. A shaman often possesses what might be termed psychological problems and may suffer from a variety of seizures or hallucinations. In modern societies, the shaman would probably be a person who, owing to these issues, is marginalized by society or is viewed as having epilepsy or any number of other nervous or mental afflictions. In shamanic societies, however, the person is viewed as having an affinity with the spirit world. Sometimes one acquires the abilities after a traumatic and unusual experience such as being struck by lightning or recovering from a near-death experience.

The shaman possesses several tools, many of which have not changed through the centuries. A key item is the *ongghot*, which is a doll made from felt, although other materials are not uncommon. The *ongghot* represents a protective spirit. The shaman, during a ceremony, wears a traditional ceremonial dress covered with a number of metal plates or mirrors. Long strips hang from it. The shaman also wears a hat or cowl covered with feathers, silk, or horns. The costume of the shaman is distinct and separate from the dress of everyone else. The mirrors affixed to the costume are of importance, as they house the spirit helpers such as the horse on which the shaman rides on his spirit journeys to retrieve lost souls. In addition, the mirrors can be used as weapons against evil spirits, as they are frightened of them. They also shield the shaman from the attacks of evil spirits.

The most important instrument is the drum and its accompanying drumstick. The drum tends to be large, but small enough to be carried by one person. The drum also houses the spirit helpers of the shaman. The drumming assists the shaman in entering a trance, while the sound frightens off evil spirits. The drumstick will often have a carved horse head, again tying the shaman to the nomadic culture of the steppe. The stick also allows the shaman to fly into the spirit world by serving as the shaman's mount. As the great scholar of Mongolian religion, Walther Heissig, demonstrated, this is analogous to the idea of a witch flying on a broomstick in the Western world.[1]

Shamanism declined after the arrival of Buddhism in Mongolia, but it did not disappear. Indeed, Buddhism adopted many characteristics of shamanism, and vice versa. The ubiquitous *oboos* (also transliterated as *owoo* and *ovoo*) of the steppe are one such example. An *oboo* appears to the untrained eye to simply be a pile of rocks. Indeed it is, but the stones are placed there as offerings to the spirits of that locale. Someone making an offering or prayer places a rock on the pile. These usually appear on heights (being closer to the sky and spirit world) and at crossroads—places that are considered to be nexus points between the mundane and spirit worlds. Now the *oboo* has become part of Mongolian Buddhist practice, as blue strips of silk, often with prayers written on them, are placed as flags. As the wind blows, the prayer is carried up to heaven.

In addition, it is not uncommon to see people driving through the countryside, shamanic, Buddhist, both, or neither, giving offerings of vodka to the spirits. Some will insert their finger into a bottle of vodka and flick the liquid in a myriad of directions to ensure that a local spirit will receive part of the offering. Indeed, although many will turn to shamans in their times of need or for certain requests, most Mongolians today tend to lean toward Buddhism.

Shamanism's decline began in 1575 with the arrival of Gelukpa, or Yellow Buddhism. A wave of persecution and repression gradually removed shamans and shamanic practices from the daily life of Mongolia. The *ongghot*, or felt images, were burned in fires. Prior to this, Buddhism and shamanism had coexisted since the period of the Mongol Empire. Shamanism also had difficulty dealing with the persecutions, as shamanism is not a religion with a hierarchy, per se, beyond the clan level. Buddhism also offered great political legitimization for the tribal leaders. Buddhism soon dominated most of Mongolia, while shamanism thrived on the fringes of Mongolia and beyond, such as among the Buryats, who reside primarily in Russia and the far eastern regions of Mongolia.

Gradually, the gods and spirits of the shamans were incorporated into the Buddhist pantheon beginning in the eighteenth century. These included the White Old Man, an earth spirit; the ancestral genius of Chinggis Khan; and, of course, other local spirits, along with the use of the *oboo*. By the nineteenth century, most of the shamanic sacred sites had become Buddhist, although the spirits that inhabited the sites were the same as the ones used by the shamans.

During the 1930s, with Communist repression of all religions, but particularly Buddhism, some common cause was made between Buddhists and shamans. In general, however, lay and clergy lamas, or monks, had little to do with shamans. Since 1991 and the advent of democracy, there has been a revival of shamanism. Its appeal is that it has an air of authenticity or "Mongolness"—it is the practice of the ancestors. This is an idea that carries a lot of weight for an essentially new state searching for its identity after seventy years of an outside identity being forced on it. *Oboos* are common once again, and respect for the Koke Mongke Tengri, or "Eternal Blue Sky," manifests itself in blessings and prayers. Shamanic rites are also appearing once again in community rites, both in the cities and the countryside. Thus shamanism endures in Mongolia.

BUDDHISM

The history and role of Buddhism in Mongolia is one of sudden starts and stops. From the introduction of Buddhism to the nomads of Mongolia to the present, there have been years and even centuries during which its influence was virtually nonexistent. Yet there were also periods in which it was either the state religion or played an important role in almost every aspect of daily life. Thus, much like the Buddhist belief that history is cyclical, so is the history of Buddhism in Mongolia.

Buddhism first arrived in Mongolia in the first century BCE with the Xiongnu tribes. The religion, however, did not become widespread. Indeed, after the decline of the Xiongnu, Buddhism was not prevalent, if at all present. The post-Xiongnu era began in the first period during which the influence of Buddhism was negligible. With the ascension of the Jujuan in the early sixth century CE, Buddhism experienced a revival, although monasteries were not built. Essentially, lamas were able to travel through Mongolia and proselytize, but they did not carry much influence.

The status of Buddhism improved greatly with the rise of the Turks. It particularly flourished during the reign of the Qaghan T'o-Po (573–581 CE), who was a devout Buddhist. T'o-Po even commissioned shrines to be built within Mongolia. Eventually, however, Buddhism went into another decline. The precise reasons for this are uncertain. One reason may have been that the Turkic warrior aristocracy became wary of it, as it did not promote a warrior spirit. Another key reason was the defeat of the ruling royal family in 617, which may have been viewed in conjunction with the previous reason. Or the Turks may have concluded that if the royal family, who had converted to Buddhism, had been defeated, then Buddhism had little to offer in terms of spiritual power. A final reason that has been offered suggests that Buddhism declined due to perpetual wars with the Uighurs. Although the Uighurs were initially Buddhists, they eventually converted to Manichaeism in 744 in an effort to prevent acculturation with the Chinese due to the growing influence of the Buddhist Tang dynasty.

Mongolia did not experience another Buddhist revival until the tenth century, although Buddhism increasingly influenced northern China. During the Khitan era (970–1125), Buddhism once again flourished in Mongolia. The Khitans, a Mongol people who conquered part of Mongolia and northern China, established cities in Mongolia that became centers of Buddhism. The cities, particularly those on the Kerulen and Orkhon rivers, were important. Buddhism for the Khitans became a state religion and acted as a counter to Chinese Confucianism, which often permeated the courts and bureaucracies of the foreign powers that conquered China. It also served as a method to help bond the people to the new rulers, as it gave them a common tie. Although Buddhism flourished in the cities that were built in Mongolia, Buddhism it-self did not win many converts among the nomads, and thus few monasteries were actually established outside the cities.

After the fall of the Khitans and their defeat by the Jurchen, Tungus tribes from Manchuria, Buddhism was eclipsed again. Not until the establishment of the Mongol Empire did Buddhism once again surface as a force in Mongolia. Even then, its hold was tenuous at best and dependent on court favor. The Mongols as a whole were shamanistic, although there was a sizeable number of Nestorian Christians within Mongolia. Buddhism as well as Islam only had an impact later. No one is sure which of the Mongol princes invited lamas from Tibet to Mongolia. Some credit Chinggis Khan, but it is more likely that either his son Ogodei or Chinggis Khan's grandson Koten, who ruled the area around Koke Nur in western China, established Buddhism once more in Mongolia. Owing to the Mongol habit of supporting all of the religions they encountered, Buddhism did not gain many adherents until the reign of Kublai Khan.

In 1550 Mongolia was in complete chaos. Twelve princes struggled for mastery over the Mongols, yet none of them had sufficient power to dominate the others. In the northern part of Mongolia, Tumet Khan dominated with support from Russian Cossacks. In central Mongolia, Abatai, khan of the Khalkha Mongols, slowly emerged as the principal figure. In the south, in what is now Inner Mongolia, Altan Khan appeared as the major player. In addition, the Oirat Mongols, whose rulers were not descended from Chinggis Khan, also competed for power.

Altan (1508–1582), despite being a very competent general, could not secure enough support to rise above anyone else. He realized that he needed something to cancel the Chinggisid factor of the other khans, something to which the other Mongols could rally. During the civil wars with other Mongols, and also during renewed attacks against the Ming dynasty of China, a number of Buddhists joined Altan's court. Beginning in 1551, after Altan's success against the Ming armies, many Buddhists viewed him as a potential savior against the Confucian persecution of Buddhists. In his wars, they served as guides into China but also helped smuggle goods to him from China.

Altan Khan's career continued and his influence spread. One of his nephews entered Tibet after campaigning against the Oirats. There he gained the submission of some regions of Tibet, and in the process of doing so, he encountered members of the Gelukpa, or Yellow sect. From them, Altan Khan's nephew learned that there were numerous sects in Tibet, also struggling for control of the country and of Buddhism. The Yellow sect, in the course of this, emerged as the dominant power. The nephew returned to Altan Khan and reported this intelligence, which began a long series of contacts between the Yellow sect and the Mongols.

Between the years 1567 and 1576, Altan Khan invited many lamas to his court in Hohhot (the Blue City), now located in Inner Mongolia. In 1571 Altan Khan and his wife, Noyanchu Junggen (1551–1612), who was also his granddaughter, received instruction in Buddhism from a Tibetan lama. Altan then proceeded to build a magnificent Buddhist temple known as Maidari Zuu. Finally, in 1578, he invited the chief Yellow sect lama, Sonam Gyatso, to instruct him personally in Buddhism. Although Altan's was probably a sincere conversion, there was also a political aspect to it.

During their meeting in the summer of 1578, Sonam Gyatso recognized Altan Khan not only as the khan of the Tumed Mongols, but also as the universal khan of all Mongols. Furthermore, he was also the reincarnation of Kublai Khan, the grandson of Chinggis Khan. This carried great ramifications, as Altan Khan did seek to be the supreme power on the steppe. The problem was that any descendent of Chinggis Khan could claim some power, but obviously, the incarnation of Kublai Khan was certainly a good omen of power and destiny. Sonam Gyatso and Altan Khan agreed that Mongolia should be Buddhist and that Altan Khan would support the conversion. Meanwhile, Altan Khan would lend support to Sonam Gyatso in Tibet. They finalized the treaty through an exchange of gifts and titles. Altan Khan was confirmed in his title but recognized as a much more powerful entity than before. Altan Khan then bestowed a title on Sonam Gyatso, recognizing the boundless depths of his wisdom and piety with the title of Dalai Lama, or "Oceanic Priest." He was actually recognized as the third Dalai Lama, as he was the third incarnation of the previous leaders of the Yellow sect. Those two individuals gained posthumous titles. In addition, the Dalai Lama had another incarnate lama, Manjushri Khutukhtu, return to Hohhot with Altan Khan to further the khan's Buddhist education.

It is difficult to say just how extensive Buddhism was in Altan Khan's realm. The meeting with monks and exchange of titles was all well and fine for the court, but the event that really triggered the switch from traditional beliefs to Buddhism occurred in 1580. Stricken with gout, Altan Khan sought to cure the ailment through a traditional, yet grisly, procedure of having his feet bathed in the chest of a slave. Manjushri Khutugtu intervened, probably to the relief of the slave, and healed Altan. This demonstration of healing and power convinced Altan Khan of the greatness of Buddhism and rededicated him to the religion. Others soon followed. Later in the year, he banned the use of *ongghots* and shamans. This practice continued after his death in 1582.

From southern Mongolia, presently the Inner Mongolia Autonomous Region of China, Buddhism spread into northern Mongolia through Abatai Khan (1554–1588). His conversion may have been for political purposes: to gain the support of the Buddhists after the death of Altan. Nonetheless, he was instrumental in the spread of Buddhism, as he assisted in the building of a monastery, Erdene Zuu, from the ruins of the old Mongol capital of Karakorum in 1585. Gradually, the common people also began to convert. Before long, other Mongol princes also converted to Buddhism. The Dalai Lama encouraged the conversion of the Khalkha Mongols by sending relics and even consecrating Erdene Zuu in 1586.

Between Altan Khan's conversion in 1578 and 1640, Mongolia was transformed slowly through waves of conversion and a Buddhist renaissance. The religion extended from Tibet into northern and southern Mongolia and eventually reached the Oirats in western Mongolia. Buddhism then reached the Buryat Mongols around Lake Baikal, but only those on the eastern shore of

Lake Baikal actually converted, while those on the western shore remained shamanists.

This period of the Second Conversion, as mentioned in chapter 1, also sought to eliminate shamanism. With the support of the major Mongol khans, the destruction of *ongghots* and other shamanic paraphernalia was successful. Harsh penalties were applied to those who associated with shamanism in any form, although many of these were lessened in the 1640 law code. In addition, other forms of Buddhism (such as the Red and Black sects—named for the color of the monks' garments) suffered persecution. The fifth Dalai Lama (1617–1682) ardently advocated the prohibition of any other forms of Buddhist teachings, and, gradually, the Yellow sect dominated Mongolia. This persecution also won the Yellow sect champions to defend its interests in Tibet, particularly among the Oirats.

The Mongols practiced the Tibetan form of Buddhism, often referred to as Lamaism or monastic Buddhism, which is very complicated but consists of five basic characteristics:

1. Lamas were sheltered in monasteries from most of the population.
2. Lamas were mendicants. They were not to beg but were still dependent on the population to support them.
3. Rebirth was an essential belief.
4. Only males were permitted in the religious orders.
5. Celibacy was practiced.

Over time, the number of lamas increased dramatically. Often, a son from each herdsman family entered the clergy. Even the sons of the nobility joined them. This was a practice that Altan Khan initiated and others followed. By the twentieth century, 40 percent of all Mongolian males were lamas; however, the severity of the vows also declined. It should be noted that many of the lamas were also lay figures and did not spend all their time in the monastery.

For the people, the religious practices of the lamas could be esoteric, both then and now. For the average person, the tenets of Vajrayana Buddhism, or the "Diamond Vehicle," as it is often called, can be summarized in a few points. The key principle is to obtain enlightenment and end the cycle of birth and rebirth. In Vajrayana Buddhism, enlightenment may be gained through learning, primarily through the education of a lama. Owing to this emulation of education, simply copying scripture is deemed an act of merit. The emphasis for laypeople, however, is on self-improvement and doing no harm to others to achieve internal peace: one should focus on helping others until altruistic action is second nature and done without thinking. The layperson should also meditate, say prayers, and make offerings to the gods and ancestors.

The spread of Buddhism in Mongolia had the unintended effect of promoting urbanism. The monasteries became urban centers, with nomadic families clustered around them. It became an almost feudal arrangement. In return for shelter in times of war, welfare in times of need, or medical and spiritual care, the nomads provided alms and donations of goods. The monasteries also served as banks and commercial centers. Furthermore, the monasteries benefited Mongolia by providing educational services.

Almost eight hundred monasteries arose in Mongolia, often at crossroads. Fewer than two hundred supported one hundred lamas or more. Of these, two dozen monasteries had five hundred to one thousand lamas. These large monasteries were headed by a figure called a *khubilgan*, or an incarnation of a previous lama. Eventually, the number of *khubilgans* rose to one hundred thirty. Each of the *khubilgans* possessed a monastery and territory. Above these, there existed fourteen *khutukhtus* or *bodhisattvas*, or those who had reached enlightenment but had chosen to stay on earth to help others instead of ascending to Nirvana.

The *khutukhtus* resided in the thirteen largest monasteries, which were also centers of political power. One of the monasteries possessed two *khutukhtus*, one of whom was the Jebtsundamba Khutukhtu, who emerged as the primary lama in Mongolia. Furthermore, he was ranked third in all of Tibetan Buddhism, behind the Dalai Lama and the Panchen Lama. The first few Jebtsundamba Khutukhtus were Mongols, but after the Manchu Empire brought Mongolia under its control, they realized the religious and political importance of the Jebtsundamba Khutukhtu. In 1740 the Manchus, or Qing dynasty, mandated that the Jebtsundamba Khutukhtu's incarnation could only be found in Tibet. The Dalai Lama, by the same mandate, was selected from among the Mongols of western China.

The monasteries of the *khutukhtus* were also transformed into major trade centers that accumulated vast amounts of wealth. The wealth that the *khutukhtu* amassed was then inherited by his successor. By the twentieth century, the treasuries of the *khutukhtus* stored almost one-quarter of Mongolia's wealth, while more than one-third of Mongolia's male population served as lamas or were connected to the monasteries in some form. Most of these were essentially serfs, known as *shabi* (singular) or *shabinar* (plural), who were permanently attached to the monastery. The *shabinar* maintained the herds of the monasteries and also did work from which the lamas were prohibited: slaughtering animals, tanning, and gathering dung for fuel.

During the period when Mongolia was part of the Manchu, or Qing, Empire, another lama existed within the monasteries of the *khutukhtus*. This individual was the Da Lama. The Da Lama was an administrative figure placed in the monasteries by the Manchus. The Da Lama did not possess any religious function. He simply oversaw what happened in the monastery. Meetings could not be held without his presence. In almost all cases, the Da Lama was not a Mongol, but a Manchu. Often, the Da Lama had not received any training as a lama and possessed a separate staff of bookkeepers and accountants. In this fashion, the Manchus maintained control over the wealth of the monasteries and ensured that the monasteries did not become staging grounds for revolt.

One widely held misconception is that the Qing and Ming dynasties encouraged the spread of Buddhism in Mongolia, as they believed it would pacify the Mongols and lessen the threat of raids. Although these dynasties certainly held that desire, there is little evidence to substantiate the claim that Buddhism lessened Mongolian valor. The Qing did not conquer the Khalkha or eastern Mongols. Instead, the Khalkha sought the Manchus' protection against the Oirat, or western Mongols, who were also Buddhists. The Oirats' martial prowess was so great that they were not subdued until the mid-eighteenth century. In addition, the Kalmyks (a portion of the Oirats who migrated west) of the Volga River in Russia actively served in the armies of Peter the Great and also raided the Muslim tribes of the steppe until the late eighteenth century, when the majority of them returned to the Qing Empire. Curiously, this idea of Buddhism making the Mongols docile still rears its head today in Mongolia. A few Christian converts justify their religious switch with the idea that before Buddhism, Mongolia ruled other countries, but then Buddhism came and made it weak. Through this explanation, the converts as well as many evangelical missionaries infer that Christianity will make Mongolia powerful again, perhaps emulating Western Christian countries. Apparently, some of the teachings of Jesus have not been stressed.

Between the mass conversions of the Mongols in the sixteenth and seventeenth centuries and the twentieth century, Buddhism became an integral part of daily life. Lamas were frequently consulted regarding medical, spiritual, and even herding problems. The Mongols consulted a lama before undertaking any major endeavor during this time.

When the twentieth century began, Mongolia and much of the Manchu Empire were in a state of foment. When the empire collapsed in 1911 and 1912, Mongolia won its independence, although the treaty of 1915 between imperial Russia, China, and Mongolia relegated it to an autonomous part of China. The Mongols established a theocracy, with the Jebtsundamba Khutukhtu as head of state. Although he was not Mongolian, the Jebtsundamba Khutukhtu remained the single figure in all of Mongolia who served as a unifier. Although many of the commoners and nobility of Mongolia saw the lamas as less than holy, the Buddhist faith was still revered by and important to them.

In 1921 Chinese suzerainty over Mongolia ended with the invasion of a White Russian army, which attempted to establish a base against the Bolsheviks. Again, the Jebtsundamba Khutukhtu was kept as the nominal head of the government. The Whites were quickly replaced by the Bolsheviks in late 1921. When the Soviets and the Mongolian revolutionaries took over, they quickly realized that there still was no one of national repute except the Jebtsundamba Khutukhtu. Owing to this, they recognized the importance of keeping the Jebtsundamba Khutukhtu as a figurehead to gain popular support. Still, the Mongolian People's Revolutionary Party (MPRP) did not trust him, or any of the lamas, and forced him to relinquish all of his secular powers. In 1924 the problem was removed, as he was either assassinated or died from a stroke. The MPRP and the Soviets also decreed that the eighth Jebtsundamba Khutukhtu was to be the last. Furthermore, they found or forged documents that supported their claims. Thus Mongolian Buddhism lost its titular leader.

The MPRP, following the doctrine of Karl Marx, viewed Buddhism as the "opium of the people"; however, the majority of the Mongols still considered themselves Buddhists, although a considerable portion of the population had become disillusioned with the abuses of the monastic institutions. Even so, Buddhism and the monasteries were too integral to the daily life of Mongolia. Several prominent members of the military and government lost their lives when they disagreed with Stalin that Buddhism needed to be eradicated in Mongolia. It was not until Stalin's puppet Choibalsan ascended to power that action was taken against the monasteries.

At first, force was attempted. Troops were sent against the monasteries to seize their wealth. Not only were the monetary assets of the monasteries seized, but texts were burned, and those who resisted were executed. Naturally, resistance to the MPRP began. The rebellion was sporadic and unorganized, but it also gained some support from the people. The MPRP under Choibalsan labeled such resistance as counterrevolutionary. Although the resistance of the lamas was unsuccessful, the violence against the lamas did considerably weaken the government's stance in the eyes of the populace.

Forced to change its tactics, the MPRP attacked the monasteries through legal means. New taxation laws were passed. Legislation that prohibited the building of new religious buildings and limited the political activity of the lamas came into existence. Thus the wealth of the monasteries was drained, and monasteries that had been destroyed earlier could not be rebuilt. Religious instruction was also prohibited, so new monks could no longer be trained. Furthermore, conspiracies were created in which many lamas were accused of spying for the Japanese, then a very real threat to Mongolia, or other countries. Thus they were arrested, tortured into confession, and then imprisoned or executed. By 1939 the population of the monasteries numbered in the hundreds, as opposed to the thousands of a few years prior.

By the end of the purge, only a few monasteries remained, and none of the incarnate lamas was left. Although the Communists did not totally eradicate Buddhism, as a functioning religion, Buddhism disappeared from Mongolia until the fall of Communism in 1989–1990. During the 1990s, Buddhism once again flourished, albeit on a much more limited level. In 1995 the Dalai Lama revealed the ninth Jebtsundamba Khutukhtu. He was born in Tibet in 1932 and recognized as the ninth Jebtsundamba Khutukhtu in 1936. Out of fear of assassination, his identity was kept a closely guarded secret. His first visit to Mongolia came as a surprise in 1999, partially due to concerns of Russian and Chinese protests. Otherwise, the institution of the incarnate lama has not been revived. Indeed, while many people identify with Buddhism, it appears to be more out of traditional respect than devotion. A massive outpouring of faith has not developed, except when the Dalai Lama visited Mongolia. Although it is unlikely that Buddhism and the monasteries will ever return to the importance they once held, there has been a rebirth of interest in and practice of the Buddhist religion. By 2001, over one hundred monasteries and temples opened or reopened, with three thousand monks attending them.[2] Some of the new monks view this as a way of helping the people of Mongolia, particularly people near their monasteries. Many of the monasteries are built on the grounds of former monasteries or are restored from those abandoned in the 1930s. In some instances, locals served as caretakers and kept the monasteries in reasonable shape during the Communist period. Much of the funding for building projects has come from other Buddhist countries such as Taiwan. Buddhist influences, however, have manifested not so much in devotional practices as in parts of Mongolian daily life.

For example, Buddhist influences can be seen in naming practices: during the pre-twentieth-century period of Mongolian Buddhism, Mongolian names tended to have attributes associated with Buddhism, such as those concerning peace (e.g., Engkhe or Amur). Most names, however, tended to come from Tibetan or Sanskrit, the Indian language that appears in many Buddhist scriptures. Names of deities were popular (Damdin and Jamayang), as were other Buddhist terms such as Dorji (power or thunderbolt) or Rinchen (jewel). Even today, the days of the week are often referred to by their Tibetan names. The use of Tibetan names associated with Buddhism dwindled during the Communist period but did not disappear completely, although purely Mongolian names were more common.

Buddhism continues to play an important role in funerary practices. Even during the Communist period, most funerals maintained Buddhist practice, with lamas presiding over the funeral. This practice continues today. Most bodies are buried or, in the countryside, left exposed, which was legalized in 1990 after being banned by the Communists. Some are cremated.

It is too early to tell just how the Buddhist revival in Mongolia will play out. The Dalai Lama has visited Mongolia, despite Chinese protestations, and has taken a personal interest in reviving the Buddhist faith and reestablishing celibate monastic life. Even before the Dalai Lama visited Mongolia, others had been active in training monks. Kushok Bakula Rinpoche, an incarnate lama from India, founded a new monastic school in Ulaanbaatar. Rinpoche has also served as the Indian ambassador to Mongolia. In addition, nunneries have opened, allowing more women to actively participate in Buddhism—an innovation, as nunneries previously did not exist in Mongolia. Lay groups have also been active, particularly in attempts to modernize the liturgy by using Mongolian rather than Tibetan.

An obstacle that Buddhism must overcome is the perception among many of corruption and unethical behavior in the monasteries, which is precisely what undermined it during the Communist purges in the 1930s. Although there are many devout Buddhists, their views of the lamas are colored by suspicion, as many of the new monasteries charge fees for reciting prayers and other services. Perhaps this is simply a carryover of the capitalist fever of the 1990s or a reflection of the reality that monasteries need money to function. Other criticisms have focused on charges of nepotism and misuse of funds, particularly in acquiring statues and artwork. Some of this is understandable, as many of the monasteries have none of the accoutrements that a monastery typically has. Still, skepticism exists among the public (devout and nonbelievers) as well as among some monks.

Buddhism, however, has received support in its revival from the government. Many members in the government view it as an essential part of Mongolia. Others view it as an important counterweight to other religions, which have the potential to undermine Mongolian tradition and society.

ISLAM

Muslims constitute approximately 5 percent of Mongolia's population and are primarily located in the western part of the country, among the Kazakh population, who comprise roughly 6 percent of the population in the Bayan Olgii Aimag (*aimag* means "province"). Beyond the Kazakh population, there are other Muslims among ethnic Mongols, but these comprise a very small segment of Mongolian Muslims. Islam has existed in western Mongolia since the medieval period, always on the fringes. It grew with Russian expansion into what is now Kazakhstan, as Kazakhs fled into regions once dominated by the Zungar Mongols, or Oirats, who had been crushed by the Qing Empire in the eighteenth century.

As with all religions in Mongolia, Islam was suppressed during the Communist era. It continued to exist, albeit underground. Thus the Mongolian version of Islam is quite different from what one would find in Mecca, Damascus, or even Samarqand.

Sufi influences, which tend to be syncretic, mystical, and much more emotive than normal Sunni or Shia practices, are present. With increased contact between Mongolia and Kazakhstan as well as with the larger Islamic world, Mongolian Islam could change. Already, young Muslims are traveling to Turkey to study Islam and are probably realizing that the religion they know is quite different from what they are studying.

CHRISTIANITY

Although Christianity has made a noticeable comeback in Mongolia, it has been present for centuries. Much like today, however, it has never been a dominant religion. Before and during the period of the Mongol Empire, the dominant form of Christianity was Nestorian Christianity, known more properly as the Assyrian Church of the East.

The Church of the East split from Orthodox Christianity in approximately 431 and was deemed heretical by the Byzantine Empire. Orthodox Christianity states that Jesus Christ possessed two natures in one person: human and divine. The archbishop of Constantinople, Nestorius (d. 451), however, determined that Jesus had two natures but that they were not contained in one person. In other words, in Nestorius's view, Jesus was not a human who was also the son of God, but rather, he was a human who was filled with the divine. This then also brought into question the position of Mary. If Jesus was human, born of Mary, and filled with a holy spirit, then Mary could not be called the mother of God, as Jesus's divinity came from God, but not from her. Nestorius's teachings grew in popularity, but they still represented a split from the main body of belief. At Ephesus, located in modern Turkey, religious leaders met in what was later called the Council of Ephesus to discuss the matter. In the end, the council deemed Nestorius to be a heretic and condemned his teachings. A wave of persecutions followed. As a result, the followers of Nestorius took refuge in the Sasanid Empire of Persia (224–651). From there, the Nestorians spread through central Asia, and some eventually appeared in Mongolia.

There they had some success at converting nomadic tribes, particularly among the Naiman in western Mongolia and the Kereit in central Mongolia. In 1007, supposedly two hundred thousand Kereits converted. The process was made easier by loosening the requirements of the religion; for instance, as bread and grape wine did not exist in the nomads' diet, the Eucharist did not include bread, and *airag*, or koumiss, replaced wine. The Assyrian Church spread among a few other tribes as well by 1200. The religion remained very syncretic, and it is questionable just how devout or how numerous the Christian population was in thirteenth-century Mongolia. Nonetheless, the Assyrian Church of the East did become influential. As Chinggis Khan unified the Mongolian plateau, many of his wives and those of his sons came from the nobility of the Naiman, Onggud, and Kereit—all of whom had adopted Christianity at some level. Thus many Christians served as queens of the Mongol Empire and members of the administration, often favoring Christians in other parts of the empire.

Other varieties of Christianity never really developed in Mongolia. While all religions were tolerated, religious views toward the Mongols varied. Eventually, the Armenian and Georgian Churches saw the Mongols as protectors against Muslim oppression in their regions. The Russian Church always viewed the Mongols as infidels and pagans and thus decreed that anything related to them was un-Christian—including using *airag* in the Eucharist. The Roman Catholic Church, which first viewed the Mongols as a punishment of God, eventually determined that most of the non-Christian population of the world existed in the Mongol Empire and thus was ripe for conversion. Beginning under Pope Innocent IV (1243–1254), missionaries were sent to convert the Mongol khans, as the Roman Catholics believed that if the khan converted, then the rest of the empire would follow.

Unfortunately for the Vatican, Roman Catholicism held little appeal for the Mongols because the Mongols would never accept the pope's authority, especially as they believed that heaven favored their empire, rather than any particular religion. Indeed, religious debates often took place at the court of the Mongols, in which Roman Catholic missionaries took part, and the missionaries often thought that they had won over the Mongol khan—but then so did most of the other participants. For the Mongols, these debates tended to be viewed more as entertainment than as episodes resulting from any real interest in conversion. Other issues were that the conditions of conversion tended to be like they were in Europe—often at odds with the culture of the steppe nomads—and that the reputation of the Mongols preceded them. When Kublai Khan asked for one hundred priests to come to his kingdom, only two were found who were willing to travel with Marco Polo and his family. Although a bishopric was developed in China during the period of the Yuan dynasty, after the collapse of the Mongol Empire there in 1368, it did not survive. The Mongols had developed an interest in Islam and Buddhism, and by the time the Vatican understood the dilemma, it was too late.

Nonetheless, Christian attempts at converting the Mongols did not end, but they were delayed considerably. Not until the nineteenth century did efforts revive, although some Russian Orthodox missionaries may have been active between 1600 and 1800—if they had any impact, though, it was negligible. During the nineteenth century, Protestant groups from Europe and the United States sent missionaries. These tended to be few and not very successful, although they did leave numerous travel accounts such as those by James Gilmour and Hertog Larsen, also known as the Duke of Mongolia. Although their efforts at gaining converts in the nineteenth and early twentieth centuries failed, their travel accounts are still read by scholars and the curious alike. As the 1920s arrived, so did Communism. Just as Buddhism was targeted, Christian missionaries of any sort were deported.

Since the fall of Communism, Mongolia has opened up to a number of religions. As discussed, Buddhism, shamanism, and Islam have all staged a renaissance to a certain degree. Christianity has also made significant inroads into Mongolia. Christian missionaries of various denominations have been very active in Mongolia but enjoy varying levels of success.

At the same time, the introduction of Christianity has been disconcerting for many. Indeed, even as Buddhism is undergoing a revival, some Buddhists welcome the arrival of Christianity for its religious ideas and philosophy, while others condemn it and view it as a threat to national identity. Some have referred to the Christian missionaries as *zagalmaitan*, or "Crusaders," bringing with it the meaning that they aim not only to convert, but also to destroy traditional Mongolian culture and Buddhism. Yet there is some backlash against the missionary presence not only by Mongolians, but also by some Westerners who work in nongovernmental organizations (NGOs).

Many Americans who serve in NGOs,[3] often those who teach English abroad, speak of Christian (particularly Protestant) aid groups with derision. Some Mongolians are developing this sentiment as well, as these groups often hand out goods, money, and aid, but do not offer any discussion of religion until they develop a regular relationship with the community in need, and then they use their aid as an avenue for proselytization. At other times, they advertise themselves as providing English language lessons and then use the Bible and religious materials as the only instructional tools—this latter practice is particularly popular among nondenominational evangelical groups.

Aid groups view this as an abuse—essentially as a bribe or as enticing Mongolians to the organization for ulterior motives. It also angers them as other groups who teach English, such as the Peace Corps, are then viewed in the same manner. Some Buddhists find it disturbing because they do it to convert Mongolians but then never explain the teachings and philosophy of the religion, but rather focus on economic success. They tie in the economic prosperity of the United States with Christianity and lead Mongolians to believe that to become successful and wealthy, one needs to be a Christian. Indeed, some missionaries believe that until they convert, Mongolians lack morals and cannot determine right from wrong.[4] In addition, there are concerns about the attitudes of the new converts.

In any religion, new converts tend to be the most ardent and demonstrative in their faith. In some cases, *oboos* have been demolished and crosses erected in their place. Locals will say that it was a bunch of Europeans (which could also mean Americans) who erected the cross, but even so, Mongolian Christians have also participated in their share of desecration. In Bornuur, part of a stupa was demolished by converts, while others have buried Buddhist icons and other sacred materials in a gesture indicating that Buddhism is dead.[5] Of course, the activities of these Christian extremists are not reflective of all Christian efforts in the country.

Most of the converts are young Mongolians, who also make up the majority of the population. During the Communist regime, Mongolia was officially an atheist state, although a few Buddhist monasteries remained open. By and large, few people had a good understanding of Buddhism, or any religion, for that matter. Thus Mongolia has become an area ripe for missionary work. To their credit, the foreign missionaries have made Christianity a dynamic and appealing religion, but still the number of Christians remains small.

As of 2008, twenty-seven missionary organizations were active in Mongolia. It is difficult to ascertain just how successful they have been. Reports on the numbers of converts range from ten to twenty thousand, or roughly 1 percent of the population. Some polls, however, indicate that roughly 7 percent identify themselves as Christian, but most of these are nonpracticing. Although most of the literature concerning missionary activity in Mongolia focuses on Protestants, Roman Catholics and Mormons are quite active.

Mormons seized the opportunity to come to Mongolia as early as 1992. Indeed, the Church of Latter Day Saints has built a five-story church in Ulaanbaatar and reputedly has more than two thousand converts. Although Ulaanbaatar is a city of roughly 1 million people and has some notable buildings, the church is very impressive. The Mormons have been aided by the traditional missionary activity of going from door to door. In Mongolia, this has also meant going out to the steppe to visit nomad families. By teaching a useful and desirable skill like English, Mormon missionaries have successfully gained footholds in several villages and areas in the countryside. In addition, the young missionaries have a certain sex appeal to female Mongolians in some areas, as many of the eligible young Mongolian men are alcoholics. The Mormons appear clean-cut, courteous, and sober.[6]

Not surprisingly, the Roman Catholic Church has returned to Mongolia and has also enjoyed success with the construction of a very impressive cathedral, the Church of St. Peter and St. Paul, and the creation of a bishopric that now numbers in the hundreds. The church building itself is very Mongolian, with the main building having some similarity to a *ger*. Also, educational centers have arisen, which provide not only religious instruction and the teaching of English and other languages, but also access to Western books on Mongolia as well as practical vocational skills such as automotive repair and carpentry. In addition, the Roman Catholic Church, under the leadership of Archbishop Wenceslao Padilla, CICM, has begun outreach programs to help the poor; to work with street children (orphans and abandoned children), who often live in the city sewers; and, particularly, to provide young girls with alternatives to prostitution. Padilla's success in Mongolia earned him recognition in the Vatican. As a result, he was appointed Mongolia's first Apostolic Nunzio, essentially an ambassador, in 2008.

It is difficult to say exactly what the appeal of Christianity is and why it has surged in popularity. The church's concern for the poor and downtrodden has certainly assisted in its gaining some adherents. Obviously, the missionaries will cite religious reasons, but some points that have played a role in the successful spread of many religions, and may explain exactly why Roman Catholicism failed in Mongolia in the thirteenth century, are worth bearing in mind. Whereas medieval Christianity was somewhat inflexible in terms of accepting aspects of non-European and non-Christian cultures, modern Christianity is not. The missionaries, particularly the Mormons, preach in Mongolian, which achieves them instant access. One of the key criticisms against Buddhism is that too much Tibetan, which few Mongolians understand, is used. This was also a similar criticism of the Roman Catholic Church during the Reformation—the people cannot understand the religion unless it is in the vernacular. Also, most of the missionaries are from Western European countries and the United States, which lends credence to the imagery of economic success being tied to Christianity. Indeed, some evangelical Christians argue that the Mongolians' adherence to Buddhism is to blame for their misery, completely ignoring the Soviet extermination of religion followed by the dismantling of government economic controls in what has amounted, at times, to economic anarchy. This approach is not a new idea; indeed, it was part and parcel of nineteenth-century European imperialism, though one may question whether the missionaries understand this. The key difference is that this time around, that message is successful, as Mongolia has a market economy in which wealth is obtainable, but so is dire poverty.

Finally, most of the converts are young Mongolians in their late teens and early twenties. As stated earlier, the number of Christians varies from ten to twenty thousand. The latter figure was cited in 2007 and 2004, while the former number was also cited in these years. So it is difficult to say if the religion is growing. One factor worth mentioning is that for young Mongolians, their interest in Christianity is often similar to the interest of so-called college Buddhists in the United States. Just as a sizeable number of Americans are drawn to Buddhism and Hinduism due to their exoticism and their being an alternative to traditional American Christianity, there is some indication that young Mongolians feel the same way about Christianity. Nevertheless, it will be interesting to see if the popularity of Christianity among young Mongolians is just a fad or reflective of the beginning of long-lasting change. At the same time, the arrival of Christianity may actually assist the Buddhist revival, as the competition may force Buddhists to embrace new methods and become more involved in the community, rather than just in the monastery.

NOTES

1. Walther Heissig, *The Religions of Mongolia,* trans. Geoffrey Samuel (Berkeley: University of California Press, 1980), 22.

2. Morris Rossabi, *Modern Mongolia: From Khans to Commissars to Capitalists* (Berkeley: University of California Press, 2005), 191.

3. Personal conversations with the author.

4. "Missionaries, Democrats in Fight for Mongolian Souls," *Asian Political News,* July 29, 2002.

5. Abbot Choijamts, "An Interview with His Eminence Abbot Choijamts," interviewed by Andrew Shimunek, *Mongol Survey* 20 (2007): 12.

6. Rossabi, *Modern Mongolia,* 40.

4

Literature

OWING TO THE reputation of Chinggis Khan and the Mongols in the West as bloodthirsty barbarians and the perceived remoteness of Mongolia, many people give a quizzical look when one says "Mongolian" and "literature" in the same sentence. Nonetheless, Mongolia has a rich history, and as with so many things, it begins with Chinggis Khan. Although Chinggis Khan died illiterate, he had the foresight to mandate that his offspring and descendents be educated. The key to this was the introduction of a vertical writing script. Chinggis Khan encountered such a script on defeating the Naiman tribal confederation in western Mongolia.

The Naiman had been introduced to Nestorian Christianity in previous centuries, and many had converted. The Naiman probably encountered it from Uighur merchants from the Tarim Basin, who had flirted with Christianity as well. In addition to their religion, the Nestorians also brought with them the Syriac script, a Semitic script that somewhat resembles Arabic. The Uighurs modified it for their language, and the Naiman adopted it as well but wrote it vertically from left to right, possibly mimicking the Chinese. Having conquered the Naiman, the Mongols then adopted the script as well and soon entered the realm of literature.

THE SECRET HISTORY OF THE MONGOLS

The first known piece of written Mongolian literature is *The Secret History of the Mongols*, which is one of the very few existing documents concerning the

Mongols from the Mongolian point of view. Although the cliché is that victors write history, more often than not, the defeated and conquered populations, such as the Persians, Chinese, Russians, Arabs, Armenians, and Western Europeans, wrote it for the medieval Mongols. The sources were those employed by the Mongols as well as those conquered by or who fled from the Mongols. Thus *The Secret History of the Mongols* remains one of the most important resources for the study of the Mongol Empire. Although it ends with the reign of Ogodei, who died in 1241, the final product was finished in 1252 and probably redacted and edited during the reign of Mongke.

The Secret History of the Mongols serves not only as an important historical source, but also as epic literature, often blending history with myth, particularly concerning the origins of the Mongols. The title of the *Secret History* comes from the idea that it was something meant only for the eyes of the Mongols. While this is true, the book does not simply glorify the Mongol rulers. Instead, it gives an intimate portrayal of the rise of Chinggis Khan from his youth to become the ruler of a vast empire and does not attempt to conceal embarrassing facts or weaknesses. From the *Secret History*, we learn that Chinggis Khan killed his half brother, was afraid of dogs, and fled when his wife was kidnapped during an attack on his camp.

Another characteristic of the *Secret History* that adds to its value as a source is that it provides insight into the Mongol mind. As it was written for Mongols, many things are omitted or just barely referred to, as a Mongol would automatically understand certain statements or comprehend what was being implied. To the modern reader, it can be somewhat difficult to understand, with many deeper meanings overlooked in often simple statements, yet it is a rich source of information, particularly on the early stages of the Mongol Empire.

Other Mongolian sources existed and found their way into Chinese and Persian accounts. These help to fill the gaps and verify information from *The Secret History of the Mongols*. One such source was the *Altan Debter* (Golden Book). This was an official court record that is now lost. Non-Mongols were not allowed to view it, much like the *Secret History*; however, material from it and other sources appeared in Rashid al-Din's (1247–1317) *Jami'at al-Tawarikh* (Compendium of Chronicles). Although he was commissioned to write it by the Mongol court of Persia, he did not have access to the *Altan Debter*. Bolad, a high-ranking Mongol and former advisor to Kublai Khan (1215–1295), provided Rashid al-Din with his information and probably with some unofficial gossip as well.

Similar material also appears in the Chinese chronicle known as the *Shengwu Qinzheng Lu* (Record of the Personal Campaigns of the Sagely Warrior). This covers the campaigns of Chinggis Khan and closely corresponds to the *Secret History*. The idiom is clearly Mongolian and appears to be a translation or adaptation of a Mongolian source, possibly the *Altan Debter*. Other sources may also include elements from either the lost *Altan Debter* or even oral tradition. Unfortunately, scholars may never be able to determine exactly what information came from the Mongols and what was observed by the author of each work.

The Secret History of the Mongols survives today due not so much to the Mongols, but rather to the Ming dynasty of China (1368–1644). As the Mongols remained a major threat to the Ming Empire after the fall of the Yuan dynasty, there was a great need for translators and interpreters of Mongolian. Thus the Ming government used the *Secret History* as a textbook. The translations used today come from the Chinese translations, which have been transcribed into a phonetic pronunciation of Mongolian. An original Mongolian copy of the *Secret History* has not been found, although parts of it resurface in other Mongolian chronicles.

It was not translated into Western languages until the nineteenth century, when parts of it were translated into German, French, and Russian. An English translation did not appear until the late 1960s through the 1980s, when the Russian-Australian scholar Igor de Rachewiltz began to translate parts of it in irregular installments. In 1980, Francis W. Cleaves at Harvard University produced a complete translation; however, it was in King James English. He believed that particular idiom was more similar to what the Mongols would have used. Thus it remained relatively inaccessible for years, but since then, numerous, more comprehensible translations have appeared.

POSTEMPIRE

Mongolian literature after the fall of the Yuan dynasty (the Mongol Empire that existed in east Asia) in 1368 went through several phases. After the collapse of Mongol control in China, the khans returned to the steppes of Mongolia but did not receive a warm welcome. In addition to the civil wars that broke out between various Mongol princes, much of the old literature, such as the *Secret History*, *Altan Debter*, and other pieces, were lost, possibly during the Yuan court's flight from China. Still, some pieces remained and appeared almost randomly in other chronicles. Yet new works also appeared.

A popular motif during the pre-nineteenth-century period concerned legends and the history of Chinggis Khan, as the *Erdeni-Yin Tobchi* (The Precious Summary), written in 1662. This was the work of the Sanghang Sechen, one of the most important members of the early modern Mongolian literati. In addition to the history of Chinggis Khan, it covered the history of numerous khans afterward and an early history of the Qing emperors. Other works focusing on Chinggis Khan also appeared. The rise of the Eight White Yurts as a shrine that reputedly possessed the personal effects of Chinggis Khan contributed to this. Although it is now located in the Inner Mongolian Autonomous Region of China, prior to 1636 and the rise of the Qing Empire, it was part of Mongolia. With increased worship of Chinggis Khan as a demigod and genius spirit of the Mongolian nation, legends and the recordings of these legends grew. Indeed, in the Buddhist work *Sira Tuji*, it is revealed that Chinggis Khan is the son of the god Qormuzda (the Mongolian name for the Hindu god Indra). Also, semihistorical pieces appeared concerning other Mongol leaders such as *Lament of Toghan-Temür*, the last Yuan emperor, and his retreat from China.

The chronicles of the sixteenth century began to develop a common form and style. While the main focus of any chronicle was on Mongolia, the first part usually included the history of an ancient Indian king and his descendents. The chronicle then recorded that some of these descendents moved to Tibet and eventually to Mongolia. These then are traced to the ancestors of Chinggis Khan as listed in the *Secret History*. Generally, the first part of the chronicle provides little of historical value; however, it does demonstrate some of the ideas of the time that linked Mongolia to a larger Buddhist world.

During this time period, the intelligentsia also recorded many of the oral traditions and folktales. Many of these were pre-Chinggisid, while others included influences from India and Tibet through Buddhism. The arrival of Buddhism, in the so-called Second Conversion, greatly accelerated the creation of a written literature. Between 1578 and 1749, Mongolian lamas translated the immense collections of Tibetan Buddhist scriptures and canon, known as the *Kanjur* and *Tanjur*, respectively. Other translations soon followed. In addition to translation, the translators often added their own touches to their work through colophons or postscripts. These included not only devotional verses, but also commentary, and provided a distinct Mongolian touch.

Through the medium of Buddhism, new tales—often with minimal ties to the religion—entered Mongolian literature and included locales and objects, including plants and animals, not found in Mongolia, such as seashores and palm trees.[1] Other stories were modified to fit not only the Mongolian environment, but also the Mongolian idiom, and emerged as completely new and original tales. Several Indian story cycles found their way into Mongolian literature, often gaining considerable popularity. Among the most popular are the *Tales of King Vikramaditya* and the *Tales of the Bewitched Corpse*. Although the stories were in Mongolian translation, the Mongolians altered them so that the original stories became the framework under which other stories were housed and tied.

Buddhism also influenced historical writing, as chroniclers and Mongolian historians adopted Buddhist rhetoric and literary styles for their own work. In 1607, a history of Altan Khan and his conversion appeared under the title *The Jewel Translucent Sutra*. Other works included hagiographies of various Mongolian lamas and Buddhist missionaries, particularly in their spiritual battles with shamans, such as found in the *Chindamani Erikhe* (The Rosary of Wishing Jewels), an account of the Buddhist missionary Neichi Toin (1557–1653) written by Parajana-Sagara in 1739.

Although Buddhist influences could appear, the *uliger*, or oral epic literature, remained uniquely Mongolian and formed the bulk of native literature prior to the nineteenth century. The epics were highly stylized stories, told in verse, about great heroes. Throughout the hero's adventures, he is constantly challenged by a number of monsters or demons, most typically the *manggus,* a many-headed monster. Some of the stories were sung, while others were told in a spoken fashion. In either form, some could take several days to tell. In many ways, the epics recorded between the fourteenth and seventeenth centuries are also a reflection of the internecine wars that dominated Mongolia during that period. A hero could be a reflection of a particular leader, while the *manggus* was a rival.[2] Indeed, tribes developed their own local heroes. In addition, no epic was complete without the hero's horse. Just as no mid-twentieth-century American cowboy matinee idol was complete without his horse, the Mongolian epic hero possessed a horse who was not only a companion, but was, at times, his savior, and who also provided advice to the hero in times of crisis. This also reflected the common idea that if one was horseless on the steppe, one was as good as dead. In many cases, these epics were reworkings of earlier pieces but nonetheless reflected the ideals of the age. Indeed, the popularity of the eighteenth-century revolt of the Oirat leader Amursana against the Qing in present-day Xinjiang and western Mongolia is reflected by the number of tales concerning Amursana.[3]

The most extensive collection of epics concerns the Mongolian hero Geser. Originally a Tibetan epic, as it entered into Mongolia, it took on new life in new versions and contained hundreds of episodes. Although the Geser epic dates back to the eleventh century in Tibet, the earliest known form in Mongolia dates to the early seventeenth century and probably entered with Tibetan Buddhism. In this epic, Geser is a god (often associated with Indra) who becomes an earthly hero to combat increasing chaos and evil. Although the stories tend to have a Buddhist flair, Geser's purpose is clearly to destroy evil and restore order.[4] If he can aid the path to enlightenment, it is only as a secondary goal. Along the way, he marries Rogmo the Fair and fights a variety of *manggus* monsters, including one who steals one of his other wives, along with evil kings and, ultimately, the Lord of Hell. The battles are not just fisticuffs or epic melees of weaponry. In many of them, the contestants take on animal and fantastic forms. Yet in others, Geser simply tricks his opponents. As with epics across the world, Geser is accompanied and aided by others.

Literature grew in different ways in the nineteenth century. Although the translation of Buddhist works continued, new chronicles, hagiographies, and other works also appeared. In addition, didactic poetry thrived. This form of poetry existed in previous centuries, beginning with translations of Tibetan and Sanskrit poetry. The first major Mongolian didactic poem was the *Oyun Tulkhigur* (Turquoise Key), which traditionally had been attributed to Chinggis Khan. Modern scholarship, however, indicates that it probably originated in the seventeenth century. In the nineteenth century, the poetry of Lubsangdonub (1854–1907) became very popular throughout Mongolia.

As the monasteries remained the focal point of education and literacy within nineteenth-century Mongolia, it is not surprising that Buddhist poetry also thrived. Danzin-Rabjai (1803–1856) wrote in a wide variety of genres. One work, written in 1831, would become the basis of Mongolian theater and will be discussed in chapter 5.[5]

With Qing rule and the gradual but growing influence of China creeping onto the steppe, one must expect that Chinese literature influenced Mongolian literature. Perhaps what is most surprising is that this influence did not occur, really, until the nineteenth century. Prior to this, while some Chinese novels were translated, most were read for their Buddhist themes. Nonetheless, Chinese novels became increasingly important, first drawing on Buddhist influences, but then historical and romantic fiction also grew in popularity. Of particular importance were the Chinese novels *Romance of the Three Kingdoms* and the *Dream of the Red Chamber*. One writer, Injannashi, was profoundly influenced by these Chinese works, manifesting in his *Khokhe Sudur* (The Blue Chronicle), which was completed in 1870–1871. Injannashi (1837–1892), who lived in what is now Inner Mongolia, retold the history of Chinggis Khan, but in a romantic style, transforming it into a novel.

In a sense, the *Khokhe Sudur* is the peak of early modern Mongolian literature. In addition to tying the history and lore of Chinggis Khan to Chinese novels, he also drew on traditional Mongolian folklore and epics. Although he expressed a negative attitude toward Buddhism, Buddhist literary styles and influences are present. Injannashi also considered the Mongol identity and how it was viewed in his era. With a lucid anti-Buddhist and anti-Qing character, it is not surprising that his intellectual musings helped define Mongolian nationalistic movements.

With the arrival of the twentieth century, new influences permeated Mongolian literature, but this time, they came from Mongolia's northern neighbor, the Russian Empire. A new movement was afoot among the Mongols, but rather than originating from the lamas or nobility, such as Injannashi, it emanated from outsiders: Buryat Mongols. Buryat activity in Mongolia increased, as did Russian penetration into Mongolia. During the later nineteenth century, Mongolia remained Qing territory but was considered by other imperialistic powers, such as the United States and Great Britain, to be part of Russia's sphere of influence. The Buryats served often as Russian agents but also promoted a pan-Mongolian agenda. This movement spanned the arenas not only of politics, but also literature. At the forefront was Zhamtsarano (1881–1942), the leading Buryat, and perhaps Mongolian intellectual, of the early twentieth century.

In 1913 he created *Shin Toli* (The New Mirror), a literary journal. Although the journal had a short life, it did set the tone for the pre-Communist era. Not only did the journal publish Mongolian writings, but it also exposed its readers to translations of Western stories as well nonfiction works (both of Mongolian and Western origin) such as political editorials and documents. As Zhamtsarano received support from the Russians and also knew Russian, most of the translations were from Russian literature. Through this venue, classic works by Tolstoy, Pushkin, Gorky, Chekhov, and others were dispersed. Other Western authors also appeared, usually translated from Russian into Mongolian.

The influences introduced by Zhamtsarano assisted in creating a new awareness among Mongolians. As Mongolia entered into a new period of independence and autonomy, the new forms of literature also aided the political goals of several factions. Literature was used to rally support for ending the rule of the Qing as well as maintaining independence from the new Nationalist China. Furthermore, literature was used to criticize not only the old political regime, but also Buddhist institutions. Despite his role in redirecting Mongolian literature, Zhamtsarano vacated Mongolia, but returned after the Communist revolution there.

COMMUNIST ERA

With the arrival of Communism, Mongolian literature changed drastically. The eradication of Buddhism as a religion proved to be the most dramatic change to the literary landscape, but it was not the only one. Political influences often dictated not only what one could write, but also who could publish. Yet, at the outset, these changes were not always apparent.

Indeed, immediately after the 1921 revolution, Mongolian literature was heavily based not on traditional genres, but rather on Beijing opera. In a sense, this was not too unusual, as during the Yuan dynasty, the Mongol nobility patronized it and indeed assisted in making it a successful genre in China. Unfortunately, very few of the plays survived. Poetry from the period tends to be patriotic in tone, fitting the idea of regaining Mongolian independence from the domination of Chinese warlords.

There were also developments in prose, with one of the major pieces being written by Dambadorji, a political leader, commemorating the 1921 battle of Tolbo Nuur. Dambadorji (1889–1934) led troops in this battle, which eradicated the White Russian presence in western Mongolia.

More translation work also appeared with the creation of the Philology Institute, the forerunner to the Mongolian Academy of Sciences. Zhamtsarano returned to Mongolia and continued his translation work along with other stars of the Mongolian literati, including Natsagdorj, Tsendiin Damdinsuren, and Byambyn Rinchen. These scholars and others translated numerous works, ranging from short stories to full novels, from various Western languages, including English. Much of the early work in the 1920s and 1930s comprised political tracts and translations of Soviet material, particularly stressing the decadence of the Buddhist clergy and old aristocracy. In addition, the traditional Mongolian folktales, classical Mongolian works, and various classics from all of Asia were translated. Other elements were added to these, and new writings as well as political ideology and dogma became part and parcel of the literary scene. Even the most innocuous writing, such as that concerning the life of a herder, was transformed into a polemical piece by polemical writing. Thus it is with this as a backdrop that Zhamtsarano, Natsagdorj, Damdinsuren, and Rinchen were so important.

All of them, excluding Natsagdorj, were members of the 1929 Writer's Circle, which provided a forum for their work and sparked new creativity—some of which eventually led to state oppression of their literary activities. Even creative writing and scholarly work were not immune to the rise of the Communist government, which infiltrated every aspect of society. Nonetheless, the work of these four men deserves closer attention, as they truly laid the groundwork for contemporary Mongolian literature.

Tsyben Zhamtsaranovich Zhamtsarano was a Buryat but spent more than half his life in Mongolia. Educated at first in his village and then in St. Petersburg and Irkutsk, he received a diverse education, which he continued with his own research on Buryat and Inner Mongolian folklore. Although he spent the period between 1911 and 1917 in Mongolia, with the Bolshevik revolution in Russia in 1917, he returned to Buryatia in Russia and eventually taught at Irkutsk University. Before he returned to Russia, however, he had not only contributed to Mongolian culture with his writing but had also developed a moveable type printing press for the Mongolian vertical script.

In 1920 Zhamtsarano returned to Mongolia and joined the new Mongolian People's Party. As a member, he immediately played a key role in drafting the manifesto of the party. While his party role prevented creative literary output, he still greatly shaped the work of others. As a driving force behind the creation of the Philology Institute, Zhamtsarano greatly influenced the development of the cultural arts. Furthermore, during his tenure as a guiding influence, Buddhist writings continued to be viewed with high regard. Even though he condemned many of the lamas for lack of morality and for corruption, he saw Buddhism, as a religion and philosophy, as quite compatible with Communism.

Unfortunately, his actions did not necessarily mesh well with the views of the guiding influences of the Communist International in the Soviet Union. In 1928, at the Seventh Congress of the Mongolian People's Revolutionary Party, Zhamtsarano lost political influence, as he was seen as a rightist due to his nationalistic views. In 1932 the government officially denounced him and exiled Zhamtsarano to the Soviet Union. There he pursued academic work at the Oriental Institute of Leningrad, where he completed his doctoral work, earning a PhD in 1936 with a dissertation titled "Mongolian Chronicles in the Seventeenth Century." Afterward, he returned to Mongolia, but in 1937, as tensions between the Soviet Union and Japan increased due to Japanese activities in Manchuria and on the border of Mongolia, the Mongolian government arrested him. Despite his denial of involvement in any such activities, he underwent torture and ultimately died in a Soviet labor camp on April 14, 1942.

While Zhamtsarano laid the foundation for modern Mongolian literature, Natsagdorj (1906–1937) may be considered its true founder, and indeed, the Metropolitan Central Library of Ulaanbaatar was named after him. Yet, at the outset, Natsagdorj was something of an outsider due to his aristocratic birth. Although officially a noble, his family, even at his birth, was mired in debt. Thus he spent his youth working primarily as a clerk in the ministry of the army. During the 1921 revolution, he became the secretary for General Sukhebaatar, a position which led to posts in other organizations of the government.

Then, in 1925, Natsagdorj left Mongolia for education abroad. After studying at Leningrad's Military-Political Academy for a year, he departed for Germany. There, he studied journalism at the University of Berlin and then at Leipzig University until 1929 under the tutelage of Erich Haenisch, one of Germany's great Mongolists.

When he returned to Mongolia in 1929, he found himself excluded from many circles due to his aristocratic birth. Nonetheless, he established and preserved a solid reputation for his translation work from German, including the travels of Marco Polo. Still, he often found himself at odds with the government. In 1932 he was briefly imprisoned for celebrating Tsagaan Sar, the Mongolian New Year, which was frowned on as being a nationalistic event.

During this time, his marriage collapsed, but he remarried. Unfortunately, his marriage to Nina Chistikova, a Soviet of German ancestry, was also doomed, as she and their daughter were deported from Mongolia. Meanwhile, he found himself in prison again for rightist tendencies. Natsagdorj, always a heavy drinker, took even more comfort in the bottle until one day, in 1937, he was found in a coma in the streets of Ulaanbaatar. He never awoke from it and died that same year. Oddly enough, his end greatly resembled that of the great American author Edgar Allen Poe, whose work Natsagdorj translated into Mongolian.

Despite his relatively short life, Natsagdorj left an indelible mark on Mongolian literature. Most of his writings from his days in Germany are now lost, but one play, *Son of a Mongolian Proletarian Family*, earned him an award. Unfortunately, the script for the play has also been lost. Most of his work covers the time from his return to Mongolia in 1929 to his death in 1937. Among his most famous works is the patriotic poem "Minii Nutag" (My Homeland; 1932). Other poetry focused on nature, and not surprisingly, during his tenure in prison, his poems, often written on candy wrappers, focused not only on freedom, but also on his love for his first wife. Although the government targeted him, Natsagdorj also wrote poems to aid government programs such as those promoting modern medicine and hygiene.

While "My Homeland" remains one of Mongolia's most revered poems, Natsagdorj is best known for his prose. Stories such as "Young Old-Timer" and "Tears of the Reverend Lama" earned him acclaim. The former depicts the isolation and beauty of the steppe, while the latter deals with a lama's love for a prostitute. Yet his crowning achievement was the opera *Uchirtai Gurwan Tolgoi* (Three Fateful Hills), a tale of young love and the interference of oppressive nobles. While it originally had a tragic ending, after his death, the ending was changed to be more optimistic, allowing for the triumph of revolution over the old regime.

Tsendiin Damdinsuren (1908–1986) began his literary career as the editor of *Unen* (Truth), the Mongolian People's Revolutionary Party's official newspaper, in 1927. Prior to this, he served in the army for two years as a company clerk. After holding various other jobs in the government, in 1933 Damdinsuren began his studies at the Oriental Institute of Leningrad. There he met and married a Russian woman and eventually returned to Mongolia in 1938. Unfortunately, he was arrested during the purge and tortured, but not executed. He was eventually released from prison in 1940.

His rise to fame came with his appointment by Marshal Choibalsan to revise Mongolia's writing system. In line with Soviet policies of the time, Damdinsuren had to devise a Cyrillic script, as Mongolia had abandoned the vertical Uighur script that Chinggis Khan had adopted in 1204. His knowledge of Russian aided him because it was the same script, but Damdinsuren also had to devise new letters to accommodate sounds that do not exist in Russian. In addition, he revised the language so that words were spelled as they were pronounced, rather than using a direct transliteration from the old script. Thus *aghula*, or "mountain," became *uul*.

After completing this monumental task, he found himself the editor in chief of *Unen* once more, from 1942 to 1946. He then was permitted to go to Moscow to study and earned a master's degree after completing his thesis on the Geser epic. On returning to Mongolia, he found a position at the Mongolian State University and also joined the Academy of Sciences, publishing numerous articles and books.

In addition to his academic works, Damdinsuren published several short stories and poems. In 1929 he published a story about a poor family's struggle during the 1921 revolution titled "The Rejected Girl." With this story, Damdinsuren also learned the lesson that literature must also conform to politics in a Communist state, as he faced, and ultimately succumbed to, pressure to rewrite the story with more overt ideology inserted. Other stories followed, and he then ventured into other forms of writing, composing the lyrics to the Mongolian national anthem in 1950, while B. Damdinsuren composed the music. (The two Damdinsurens were not related.) This anthem remains Mongolia's national anthem, although some lyrics concerning Lenin, Stalin, Sukhebaatar, and Choibalsan have been removed since 1990. In the original version, politics made it imperative that they were included.

Damdinsuren, however, focused on scholarship. In 1947 he published a modern Mongolian version of *The Secret History of the Mongols* as well as an anthology titled *One Hundred Best Works of Mongolian Literature* in 1955. This anthology boldly consisted of prerevolutionary literature, much of which found publication for the first time, having previously only existed in manuscript form. Furthermore, it covered all genres, including Buddhist and shamanistic writings, and included notes to the works and commentaries on them. This led to trouble with the government.

In 1963 the government criticized Damdinsuren for printing Buddhist and shamanistic texts as well as promoting them to students. Indeed, he even encouraged his students to study them. While he was not imprisoned, government censure, fines, and other forms of punishment appeared. His Russian-Mongolian dictionary, completed in 1969, was recalled in 1970. Damdinsuren, however, did not face worse punishment, as Russian scholars, who admired his work, exerted some influence in Mongolian academic circles.

Byambyn Rinchen (1905–1979) is the last of the founders of modern Mongolian literature and perhaps the most brilliant, particularly in his defense of Mongolian intellectual achievements throughout time. Never compromising his ideals, he criticized Soviet and Western views of Mongolian culture.

Although he was born in Mongolia into a minor noble family, he grew up along the border of the Buryat territories in Siberia and Mongolia. Educated in Mongolian, Manchu, and Russian in Troitskosavsk, Russia, before studying at the Oriental Institute in Leningrad from 1923 to 1927, Rinchen returned to Mongolia and found a position at the Philological Institute (later the Academy of Sciences). In 1929 he became a member of the Writer's Circle, to which many of his peers also belonged, and gained some acclaim for his poem "For the Yellow Parasites," which criticized the lamas.

His work at the Philological Institute also earned him a reputation as a brilliant scholar; however, he eventually was arrested, as were most nonconformist intellectuals, by Choibalsan on charges of Japanese espionage in 1937. In 1942 Choibalsan personally ordered his release. Afterward, Rinchen became an editor of *Unen* along with Damdinsuren. Despite their common interests, the two had frequent arguments. His stint at the newspaper was short, and in 1944 he became a professor at the State University and held a position at the Academy of Sciences.

His literary output was impressive and had a broad range. He is best known for his novels, which included the trilogy *The Rays of Dawn* (1951–1955), Mongolia's first novel, which was based on the events of the 1921 revolution. In addition, he wrote other novels and short stories, including *Zaan Zaluudai*, a children's novel set in Stone Age Mongolia.

Rinchen's other work included the translation of the *Communist Manifesto* (1947), along with numerous scholarly works on Mongolian literature and language such as his multivolume *Grammar of Written Mongolian*. His premodern and non–government-approved Mongolian pursuits also earned him a reputation as a maverick. He published numerous works concerning shamanism as well as folklore, much of which did not prescribe to the Communist worldview or the politics of the era. On top of this, he published his semi-illicit works in West Germany, a North Atlantic Treaty Organization country.

Throughout his life, Rinchen dealt with numerous critics and threats to his brilliant mind. The first came in 1949. The year before, Rinchen had dared to criticize the work of a Soviet scholar who worked with him at the Mongolian State University. Although no action was taken against him at the time, because his criticism was well grounded, the Soviet Politburo castigated him in 1949 for nationalism. A decade went by without further incident, during which he published *Rays of Dawn* and began publishing his work on shamanism in West Germany. In 1959 Rinchen found himself accused once again for nationalistic tendencies, but this time for his script for the movie *Tsogtu Taiji*, based on the Mongolian historical hero of the same name. His lack of appropriate criticism of prerevolutionary events, culture, and lifestyles disturbed his critics. Almost a decade later, the third volume of *Grammar of Written Mongolian* came under attack, again for expressing nationalism. In 1967, the very year of its publication, it was recalled. Rinchen, however, never bowed to the pressure, but his health began to fail, perhaps from stress, and he died from cancer in 1976.

After the Mongolian revolution ended with the destruction of Mongolian Buddhism, standardized literary attacks on the lamas and aristocracy dwindled. Nonetheless, government influences still abounded and shifted to new issues, whether constraining nationalistic ideas, creating models that society should strive toward, or attacking new enemies, such as anti-Japanese literature during World War II.

From the 1960s to the end of the Communist regime, Mongolian literature remained somewhat fettered by the constraints imposed by the government. Still, new forms emerged independent of the so-called big four. As more people moved to Ulaanbaatar and other towns, writers began to discuss this issue in short stories and editorials. Another theme dealt with was sexism and the new roles that women found in a socialist society. Although in a nomadic society, men and women had more of an egalitarian nature to their relations, boundaries certainly existed. The rise of Communism, with its ideals of gender equality, coupled with the new modes of urbanized economy, did cause some startling changes in Mongolia, including the opening of many new opportunities for women. One such instance is depicted in D. Garma's *A Funny Woman,* which told the story of Buma, a female mechanic, traditionally a male occupation, whose son becomes a nurse, traditionally a female role. On learning of his occupation, the mother becomes distraught, ironically not recognizing her own reversal of stereotypes.

Of equal importance was the rise of new outlets of expression such as *Tsog* (Spark), a literary journal. Most of the major writers of the 1980s contributed a variety of writings to *Tsog*, ranging from poems to short stories. As the government reins of censorship loosened, creativity abounded. And with new forms of media appearing, Mongolian literature grew in new directions.

POST-COMMUNISM

With the collapse of the Communist regime, the floodgates opened for Mongolian literature. Of course, with the enthusiasm that came with new freedoms, new journals, books, and newspapers appeared. Naturally, many of them initially succeeded because of the vibrancy of the period; however, as this passed and the economy soured, many endeavors failed.

Nonetheless, new work abounds. Mongolians embraced the Internet revolution, and many newspapers, including English ones such as the *Mongol*

Messenger, have been online for several years. A few journals and magazines, like *Mongolia Today,* an online magazine founded by two Mongolian journalists, have continued and, via the Internet, have made numerous aspects of Mongolian culture and society accessible to a larger audience.

Scholarship has also blossomed under the new political freedom. Whereas under the Communist regime, Chinggis Khan was viewed as a feudal oppressor, the revival of interest in the life of Chinggis Khan has led to new studies not only on him, but also on all aspects of Mongolian history. Now academic studies in the humanities and social sciences no longer have to conform to a Marxist model of history. With an increase in freedom of what can be written, there has been a corresponding surge in the publication of books in all genres and fields.

Although Mongolian literature remains relatively inaccessible to non-Mongolian audiences, a few works have been translated, and one publisher, Kegan Paul, has recently established a series on translated works of Mongolian literature. Thus far, the initial offerings include contemporary poetry and Buddhist poetry from the Qing period. The Mongolia Society, based at Indiana University, has also published a large selection of translated works, ranging from folktales, including some from the Geser cycle, to Buddhist liturgy and contemporary short stories.

NOTES

1. Larry Moses and Stephen A. Halkovic Jr., *Introduction to Mongolian History and Culture,* Uralic and Altaic Series 149 (Bloomington: Indiana University Press, 1985), 202.

2. Nicholas Poppe, *The Heroic Epic of the Khalkha Mongols,* 2nd ed. (Bloomington, IN: Mongolia Society, 1979), 54.

3. Ibid., 53.

4. Walther Heissig, *A Lost Civilization: The Mongols Rediscovered,* trans. D. J. S. Thomson (New York: Basic Books, 1966), 145–50.

5. Ibid., 222.

A woman dressed as a Mongolian queen. Courtesy of the author.

The statue of Choibalsin, the Mongolian prime minister from 1924 to 1952, in front of the National University of Mongolia. Courtesy of the author.

A statue commemorating Sukhebaatar, the hero of the 1921 Revolution and namesake of Ulaanbaatar. Courtesy of the author.

Amarbayasgalant Monastery, Selenge Aimag. Entrance from the inside. One of the active Buddhist monasteries. Construction began in 1726 and was completed in 1736. Most of the lamas were executed in 1937–1938. It reopened in 1990. Courtesy of L. Munkh-Erdene.

Inside the Amarbayasgalant Monastery compound. Courtesy of L. Munkh-Erdene.

Mongolian horses are smaller than most breeds. On the rear of the one in the foreground is a *tamga*, or brand. This was used to keep track of the animals, as families often would pasture their animals together. These are saddled in the fashion of the Mongolian Empire. Courtesy of the author.

A Bactrian camel. Courtesy of the author.

An *oboo* in the steppe outside of Ulaanbaatar. It is a pile of rocks placed by people offering prayers. The streamers are also prayer flags made from a *khadag*. The prayers are to be carried to heaven by the wind. *Oboo* are of shamanistic origins but have become part of the Buddhist tradition in Mongolia. Courtesy of the author.

A shrine at Daschoilon Monastery, which shows more of the traditional Tibetan style of architecture. Courtesy of L. Munkh-Erdene.

The front of the main temple of Daschoilon Monastery. Courtesy of L. Munkh-Erdene.

A protective lion at Daschoilon Monastery. Courtesy of L. Munkh-Erdene.

A recently rebuilt monastery in Arkhangai Aimag. Courtesy of L. Munkh-Erdene.

The yard and front of a Russian Orthodox cathedral. Few Mongolians have converted to Orthodoxy. Additionally, the Orthodox do not actively proselytize in Mongolia. Courtesy of L. Munkh-Erdene.

Posters advertising Mongol Festival, a Christian revival led by Peter Youngren of Celebrate Ministries. According to Celebrate Ministries International, at the Mongol Festival, a blind woman and a man with cancer in his liver were cured. Courtesy of the author.

The Mormon church in north Ulaanbaatar. Located in Chingeltei District, it is very close to the *ger*/shantytown areas. Courtesy of L. Munkh-Erdene.

Inside the Mormon church next to the Zanabazar Art Museum in Ulaanbaatar. The majority of the attendees are female. Courtesy of L. Munkh-Erdene.

Archbishop and Apostolic Nunzio Padilla. He is the highest-ranking Catholic priest in Mongolia. Courtesy of the author.

St. Peter and Paul Cathedral from the southeast. The main structure resembles a *ger*. Courtesy of L. Munkh-Erdene.

Two *morin khuur* musicians and a *yatga* player. In most ensembles, the *yatga* is played primarily by women and men play the *morin khuur*. Courtesy of the author.

A *tsam* dance. The White Old Man, a carryover from shamanism, is on the far right. Courtesy of the author.

In this wrestling tournament, two matches are going on at once, and one of the wrestlers takes a fall. Courtesy of the author.

The ubiquitous white felt tent, commonly known as a *yurt* in the West. This one was set up in downtown Ulaanbaatar near the university. Although the inhabitants sold artwork, they also slept there. Courtesy of the author.

A scene from Ulaanbaatar. As Chinggis Khan becomes the most popular name in advertising, his name graces not only the third in a chain of bars, but also a beer brand. Courtesy of the author.

A special brigade in the Mongolian Army has been trained to ride and perform as soldiers from the time of the Mongol Empire. They are used in the Naadam celebrations as well as other festivals commemorating Chinggis Khan. Courtesy of the author.

The Chinggis Khan statue that sits in the middle of the new memorial complex in front of the government palace. His statue replaces the tomb of Sukhbaatar, the "Red Hero" from which Ulaanbaatar gets its name. Ulaan = red, Baatar = hero. The statue and building were erected in 2006, the 800th anniversary of the Mongol Empire. Courtesy of the author.

5

Traditional and Contemporary Art

THE STANDARD JOKE about Mongolian art is that unless it has a horse in it, it is not art. In many ways, this is true. Modern Mongolian art typically has a focus on horses, particularly as the horse has become symbolic of Mongolian culture and identity. Still, Mongolian art is much more varied than this, and through the ages, numerous influences, including Buddhist, Russian, and Chinese, have played a role in defining art.

BUDDHIST ART

Not surprisingly, Buddhist influences have greatly shaped Mongolian art in a variety of ways. During Buddhism's heyday in Mongolia (1600–1920), the country was an important center of Buddhist painting, sculpture, and other fine arts.

When considering Buddhist art, or any form of art, for that matter, one must consider its purpose. For Buddhist art, the purpose usually is to aid monks and others in meditation—serving as a reference point for contemplation. In addition, the art can be used in worship as an icon or statue of reverence, particularly for nonclergy who do not engage in meditation. Finally, the art also instructs the observer in the religion. This can be either through obvious visual means or through more subtle forms, such as a painting serving as a metaphor for a lesson of the Buddha.

As such, common themes include the life of the Gautama Siddhartha—the Buddha Shakyamuni and the deeds of gods and heroes as well as incarnate lamas. On the outside walls of many temples, one will find paintings of the samsara, or the six births in the wheel of life. Thus they are visible to both clergy and laypeople. Figures in the art, while drawn with some individualistic style, will possess some standard features; for instance, the bodhisattva Manjushri always appears with a topknot and a religious robe resembling a toga, whereas lamas will appear in monastic robes and hats. The central figure varies and is invariably surrounded by minor personages, demons, gods, and other beings, all drawn with mathematical precision so that no one appears disproportionate.

As with all art forms, there are many expressions of Buddhist art, ranging from statuary made from bronze or silver to papier-mâché and terra-cotta amulets and ornaments. In painting, wood and cotton cloth are common media, with wood being used primarily to achieve a three-dimensional aspect, with details carved into the wood. One of the most spectacular forms is the mandala, or sand art, the creation of which is also a contemplative exercise. Using colored sand, the monks meticulously create art, often a depiction of the samsara. On completion, the mandala will eventually be destroyed. As it is a widespread practice, it is not uncommon for mandalas to be created by monks at art museums in the United States and other countries.

The most common form of Buddhist art appears in the form of scroll paintings known as *thangka*. These scrolls decorate monasteries and are also used as tools for meditation. The *thangka* art form, which originated in Tibet, is distinctive in the materials it uses. Cotton cloth is stretched over a frame and then treated with a combination of chalk, glue, and *arkhi* (distilled, fermented mare's milk). After this dries, the artist then uses mineral-based paints, including some made from the shells or scales of crushed insects. While the paintings mirror Tibetan styles, the Mongolian *thangka* style is notable for its incorporation of livestock in the background. Although the Communists' destruction of the Buddhist monastic movement also led to the diminishment of the *thangka* style in Mongolia, it is notable that the Communists also used it, but with socialist themes.

The best-known artist of the Buddhist style, and also one of Mongolia's most famous painters, was the living Buddha known as Zanabazar (1635–1723), also the first Jebtsundamba Khutukhtu. Among his most famous pieces of work is the statue of the deity of compassion, Tara. His work is still displayed in the Zanabazar Museum of Fine Arts and the Winter Palace of the Bogd Khan. As the first religious leader of Mongolia and also an accomplished artist before being enthroned as an incarnate lama in 1639, he left an indelible mark on Mongolian Buddhist art.

Ulaanbaatar, formerly known as Urga, was known even before that as Khuriye, the seat of the Jebtsundamba Khutukhtu. With Zanabazar's enthronement as the first Jebtsundamba Khutukhtu, the settlement grew and eventually evolved into a city. As such, numerous temples arose, and Zanabazar sculpted many of the city's objects of veneration and possibly assisted in the design of some of the new temples. In addition, he painted self-portraits and influenced the development of individual portrait painting as a separate style for lamas.

Modern Buddhist art has been revived. *Thangka* painting survived the Communist period, as some monks were not purged. With the end of the Communist era and the revival of not only religious freedom, but also artistic freedom, the *thangka* style is blossoming again, but on a much smaller scale. Other forms of Buddhist art have yet to recover, partially due to their expense, and largely remain in the form of items that are created as needed for ceremonial purposes.

The most notable practitioner of the *thangka* style is Purevbat, who is a member of the Gandan Thekchenling Monastery. Purevbat, who studied the art among master artists in Nepal and India, is also the subject of a 2005 German film called *Buddhas Maler* (Buddha's Painter). Under his direction, Gandan Thekchenling Monastery now houses the premier Buddhist art institution in Mongolia, officially known as the Zanabazar Mongolian Institute of Buddhist Art.

Nonetheless, the Buddhist art of Mongolia remains a unique feature of its heritage, and even though it virtually disappeared for much of the twentieth century, it remained influential in the minds of secular artists. It will be interesting to see how it adapts to a new, more secular, yet newly religious Mongolia.

MODERN ART FORMS

Known as Mongol *zurag* (literally, "Mongolian painting"), the modern and secular style of Mongolian painting uses mineral-based paints on a cotton canvas, much like the *thangka* style of Mongolian and Tibetan Buddhist art. The Mongol *zurag* art of the early twentieth century was heavily influenced by Western styles imported through the Soviet Union, with an emphasis on portraits and scenes from daily life. Among the best known are those of Sharab, who may also be considered the father of modern secular art as, he is the individual who transformed the *thangka* style into a nonreligious form. His most famous work, still on display at the Zanabazar Museum of Fine Arts, is *One Fine Day in Mongolia*, which combines landscape work with storytelling and is filled with, as the title implies, scenes from daily life in Mongolia. Unfortunately, like many artists, his genius went unappreciated after his death in the 1930s due to the political climate, and many of his works were lost.

Balduugin Sharab, also known as Busybody, truly transformed Mongolian painting. In his youth, he studied with an artist of Buddhist icons, through whom Sharab learned painting and sculpting in the proper Buddhist styles. In the 1890s, Sharab came to Khuriye, or modern Ulaanbaatar, and when not carousing, he made a living by painting furniture and playing cards. Although it was a lowly beginning, his skills were notable, and he became known for his portrait paintings, which eventually attracted the attention of the Jebt-sundamba Khutukhtu, who commissioned several. Thus Sharab became the court painter. It was the Jebtsundamba Khutukhtu who dubbed Sharab with the sobriquet of "Busybody," as the painter dropped his commissions on several occasions and disappeared for days to go gambling.

Whenever he resumed his artistic work, Sharab's skills continued to improve. He quickly mastered new techniques such as using pencils and ink. Although he continued to paint in traditional styles, he also experimented and ultimately incorporated new forms into his repertoire. He painted portraits using poses and backgrounds that one might see in a photograph. His version of a samsara painting incorporated portraits not only of humans, but also of animals. He pushed his medium into what scholar Christopher Atwood has called "ethnographic realism."[1]

Sharab's career took another turn after the 1921 revolution. His artistic skills led him to a new career as a printer, and he designed the various periodicals as well as the new Mongolian currency. The government also called on his skills to design medals and awards. His talent also appeared in translated books as he became a sought-after illustrator. Of course, his portrait skills never went unnoticed, and he painted the portraits of not only Lenin (from a picture), but also of Sukhebaatar and other luminaries of the revolution. Although he died in 1939, few of his works survived to the twenty-first century, particularly his work completed prior to the revolution. This was simply due to the political climate. Unfortunately, many of the paintings of any artist from the early twentieth century did not survive, often destroyed in the purges for displaying themes considered too nationalistic or religious.

After 1940, more artwork survived, as the socialist-realist style was firmly in place. Yet, even while constrained by government-imposed themes, Mongolian artists such as D. Manibadar injected their own visions. Manibadar received permission to use folklore for patriotic purposes, as evinced in his *Old Hero* (1942).

After 1950, *zurag*-style painting gained new momentum even as standard and approved themes came into being. These themes included life on the collective, the 1921 revolution, historical figures who fit government standards (which often fluctuated), and scenes from daily life, including prerevolutionary Mongolia. Not surprisingly, religious themes were still taboo, although some works appeared, such as M. Khaidaw's *White Old Man* (1961).

While government-approved themes dominated the subjects that appeared, artists still found new modes of expression in the styles of painting they used. Shading techniques appeared in Mongolian art that showed a clear influence of the European realism movement. Artists such as Yadamsuren developed new techniques with colors. Although religious topics were frowned on, Buddhist influences never completely disappeared. In the 1960s, several artists ignored modern conventions entirely and followed the Buddhist formats for painting modern scenes or secular iconographic paintings. This trend continued into the 1990s.

In contemporary art, the Mongolian love of horses is very much alive and has taken new forms. This is most visible in the abstract work of M. Erdenebayar as well as in the landscapes of the award-winning work of L. Ganbold. Yet not all artists focus on the horse. Indeed, since the end of the Communist era, religious themes have reentered Mongol *zurag*, in addition to nationalistic topics particularly devoted to Chinggis Khan and the Mongol Empire, in both sculpture and paintings. One of the most notable artists is S. Saransatsralt, who is known for provocative conceptual paintings of the human body and even clothes. Also, the work of S. Tugs-Oyun is notable for the incorporation of mythology into her paintings. In them, one finds not only contemporary interpretations of the deerstones, petrogylphs of camels, but also of Tugs-Oyun's rendition of Buddhist elements.[2]

With greater artistic and religious freedom, art in Mongolia is open to all directions. Several galleries exist in Ulaanbaatar, as do museums. Indeed, it is not uncommon to see artists or others hawking drawings and paintings with a wide variety of themes and styles on the street. Mongolian art is slowly gaining more recognition, as a few artists have shown their works in galleries in the United States, not only in New York, Chicago, and San Francisco, but even in cities such as Atlanta.

MUSIC

One can still hear traditional Mongolian music whether in the countryside or in the cities. Concert performances still attract large audiences, and it is quite different from other styles of music, although one can see regional similarities. Traditional Mongolian music involves a variety of instruments, but one in particular provides the identity of Mongolian music: the *morin khuur*, or "horsey-fiddle." The songs vary from epics of heroes to simple songs sung by herders as they take care of their animals. Indeed, some of the songs have parts that are derived from vocal signals used by herders to direct their animals.

Considering the horse theme that is found throughout Mongolian culture, it is not surprising that the national instrument is the *morin khuur*.

The instrument's origins come from folklore. There are a variety of legends of its origins, but they all possess the same basic elements of a man and his horse. The man is a heroic herder, and the horse, his faithful steed, has wings. As they ride, taking care of their flocks and herds, the wind blows through the horse's mane and produces music. A witch falls in love with the handsome herder. To separate him from his wife, the witch appears in the form of the jealous wife and cuts the horse's wings so that it falls from the sky and dies. The hero laments the death of his beloved horse, and in tribute not only to their friendship, but also to the music made by the wind in the horse's mane, the herder creates the first *morin khuur* from the steed's body. He constructs a wooden box and covers it with the horse's hide. From the tail and mane, the herder entwines horsehair to produce the two strings for the instrument. They follow a long neck and are connected to a peg box. On top of the peg box is an ornate carving of a horse's head. To play the instrument, the herder made a bow, like the one used with the violin. Not surprisingly, the story has become an epic song, with the singer incorporating horse sounds while he or she plays the *morin khuur*.

Other instruments include a lute made with a carved swan's head, akin to the horse's head on the *morin khuur*, known as a *khun tobskhuur*; the *joochin*, or hammered dulcimer; *khuuchir*; *yatga*; *shudraga*; *kluchir*; and a variety of percussion and wind instruments. The wind instruments range from the *bishguur*, a metal trumpet, to the *tsagaan buree*, or white shell—a shell that resembles a conch shell—with other forms in between. Virtually all of them are used in Buddhist ceremonies, particularly the trumpets, or as accompanying instruments in folk orchestras.

The *khun tobskhuur* is also a two-stringed instrument found most commonly in western Mongolia. The instrument is normally made from cedar wood and covered with leather, usually from a camel or goat. The *khuuchir* is another stringed instrument and may have been a precursor to the *morin khuur*. It is smaller and consists of a cylindrical resonator made from wood or metal and is covered with leather, often snakeskin. The bottom of the cylinder is left open, and it has two to four strings, depending on the size of the instrument. Another instrument made with snakeskin is the *shudraga*. This long-necked lute has an oval frame that is covered on both sides with snakeskin. It has three strings that are fixed to a bar. Unlike the other stringed instruments, the *shudraga* is not played with a bow, but rather is plucked with fingers or a pick made from horn or other materials.

The *yatga* is another stringed instrument, similar to a zither but possessing a movable bridge. It looks like a box with a convex surface, with one end bending downward. To play it, one plucks the strings. Traditionally *yatga* performances were reserved only for monasteries and the court, and playing the instrument was considered a sacrosanct rite. This taboo changed over time as new forms of the *yatga* appeared, ranging from a ten-stringed *yatga* that anyone could play to a *yatga* with twenty-one strings.

The *joochin* is primarily used in an orchestral setting. Whereas most of the instruments have their origins among the herders, the *joochin*, or dulcimer, was known only in towns, probably brought in by Chinese or other merchants. It has thirteen double-wire strings that are played with two wooden sticks or hammers. It can be a beautiful instrument in appearance, as the soundboard is often elaborately ornamented.

Another element in traditional music that stands out is the form of singing known as *khoomii*, or "throat-singing," which is found not only in Mongolia, but also in neighboring Tuva, in Russia. *Khoomii* is best known to Americans from Tuvan performers and the movie *Genghis Blues* (1999), which chronicles the efforts of Paul Pena, a blind blues musician from San Francisco, to learn how to throat-sing.

Throat-singing is an astonishing and perhaps even eerie form of music, as the singer produces multiple notes simultaneously. To do this, the singer must have control over his or her larynx, throat, stomach, and even palate. Two notes are produced when performed properly. One is a low tone, akin to a growl, while the other resembles a whistle. *Khoomii* is performed not only as a separate style, but is also often incorporated into other songs, mixing with normal styles of singing. Within *khoomii* are two variations. *Uyangyn*, or "melodic," has a whistling overtone, whereas *kharkhiraa* is a deeper and more thunderous sound. It also lacks the whistling overtone.

In addition to songs on a variety of topics, ranging from love ballads to traditional stories, traditional Mongolian music also has a unique singing style known as *urtyn duu*, or the "long song." It is aptly named, as the song can last for hours. This is not simply due to the lyrics, although some songs do approach twenty thousand verses. The genre also gets its name from a style of singing that draws out the vocals, which can become very complex. Each syllable of a word is extended for several seconds.

The style is derived from the practice of communicating across the steppe. One may imagine the American stereotype of a farmer's wife going to the back porch and yelling her husband's or child's name—starting low in octave range and then increasing, while extending the syllables. In general, traditional forms of Mongolian singing involve attempts to circumvent the limitations of one's natural voice, whether through the *urtyn duu* or the *khoomii* style. At times, listening to Mongolian traditional music seems like an otherworldly experience, in which one cannot discern if one hears an instrument or if the sound is somehow produced by a voice. Nonetheless, traditional Mongolian music has become more easily accessible with the opening of Mongolia. Indeed, some traditional groups have received international recognition, such as Egschiglen (Beautiful Melody), which combines many of the aforementioned styles.

Modern Mongolian music has adjusted with globalization, particularly with European and Korean influences. Videos of Western music genres are viewed on television, and Mongolian singers and music groups have taken to these newer forms. Although the songs are sung in Mongolian, the music generally could be from an American or European band. As such, the Mongolian music scene often parallels what is happening in the rest of the world in terms of popularity. As with most modern cultures, the music scene is often the home of the avant-garde and the testing of social boundaries. A case in point is Ariunna, labeled by the Mongolian press as "Mongolia's Queen of the Erotic."[3] Considering that her stage clothing often consists of lingerie and suggestive dancing, it is an appropriate sobriquet. She is obviously ready for MTV.

And truly, MTV has made an impact. Along with other music channels, it can be viewed via satellite barely twenty years since independence. Prior to 1990, it is unlikely that Ariunna or many of her fellow artists would have been able to perform under the old regime. Thus Mongolia, for better or for worse, has seen its share of indigenous boy bands; hip-hop artists; long-haired, leather-clad heavy metal bands; and pop divas.

As the boy-band craze swept the United States in the late 1990s, Mongolian groups such as Camerton, founded in 1995, at the same time bands such as *NSYNC and the Backstreet Boys were at their height in America, also appeared. Hip-hop also found its way to Mongolia, with the most popular musicians being Tatar and Lumino. An interesting note about the Mongolian hip-hop genre is that single performers do not appear to be successful; groups dominate the genre and only have grown in popularity since 1994.

Some groups and singers have achieved international recognition, such as the female singer Nominjun, who started her career at the age of fourteen in 2003. Her success may be due not only to her talent, but also to her ability to sing in eight different languages. Other groups with more staying power have also appeared, some of them dating to the end of the Communist period, when music was used as a voice for protests.

One such group is called, not surprisingly, Chinggis Khan, often called the "Eagles of Mongolia." Led by Jargalsaikhan, now the head of the Mongolian Singer's Association, the band Chinggis Khan was tied to the end of Communist power. Unlike in the open and bustling music scene of present-day Mongolia, musicians in the 1970s and 1980s could only perform so-called "safe" songs, such as those derived from folktales or with socialist themes. In addition, few bands could write their own songs, but rather had to work with lyrics provided by the Mongolian Union of Writers.[4] In 1988 Jargalsaikhan's band began performing its own song "Chinggis Khan" at a time when the government (both Mongolian and Soviet) frowned on any support for the Mongol leader. The nationalist sentiment of the song easily could have earned the band a jail sentence. Fortunately, in 1989 and 1990, government sentiments began to change. A birthday party was even held for Chinggis Khan, with the band Chinggis Khan playing alongside politicians and academics making speeches about the Mongol leaders. During their moment on stage, forty thousand people filled Sukhebaatar Square, singing to the song "Chinggis Khan."[5]

Other groups carry on some of the same spirit. Groups such as Haranga (Chime), a hard rock group, and Hurd (Speed), a heavy metal group, have achieved staying power. Haranga has been in existence since the early 1990s and has seen some success in Europe as well as Mongolia.

The heavy metal band Hurd, whose first album, *Black Wind*, appeared in 1997, has branched out from Mongolia into China and South Korea, the latter due to Mongolian migrant workers. Indeed, the band's album sales in Inner Mongolia outstrip its success in Mongolia. Much like many Western heavy metal bands during the 1970s and 1980s, Hurd has also found itself the target of censorship. The Chinese government has banned many of its songs after the government asked the band to translate its lyrics into Chinese, apparently not liking the nationalist themes of songs such as "Born in Mongolia." Indeed, in 2004 they were banned from playing in Hohhot, the former capital of Altan Khan and capital of the Inner Mongolia Autonomous Republic. The reason for being banned in Hohhot was never given to the band.[6]

THEATER AND CINEMA

Music, of course, appeared in the theater, usually in the form of opera. Indeed, Mongolian literature after the 1921 revolution was heavily based not on traditional genres, but rather on Beijing opera. In a sense, this was not too unusual, as during the Yuan dynasty, the Mongol nobility patronized it and indeed assisted in making it a successful genre in China. Even into the revolutionary period, Beijing opera troupes traveled and performed throughout Mongolia. Thus, in some ways, it is only proper to say that opera, in some form, also formed the basis of Mongolia's theatrical arts.

One of the most brilliant Mongolian playwrights was Danzin-Rabjai (1803–1856), an incarnate lama of the Gobi Desert. He manifested a talent for poetry at an early age and then continued to build considerable literary talents as well as a reputation for having a wild side. His travels throughout Mongolia were noted for his escort of consorts and drinking binges. Nonetheless, his poetic talents continued to grow, as did his other skills. In 1831 he composed his opera *Saran Khokogen-u Namtar* (The Tale of the Moon Cuckoo) in the Tibetan style. For this, he composed not only the songs but also much of the music, and he designed the costumes and directed the opera. His energy was such that despite his many duties, the opera, an adaptation of a Tibetan opera with the same name, was first performed in 1833.

The story centers on a good and noble prince and his evil friend, both of whom have mastered transferring their souls into other bodies. The key moment is when they become cuckoos: the evil friend then quickly returns to his body and destroys that of the prince, thus trapping him as a bird. The evil companion then becomes the ruler. Trapped as a cuckoo, the prince accepts his lot and teaches Buddhism to birds. Although the evil friend is ultimately defeated by the prince's wife, the prince, tragically, remains a bird. This opera was most notable for its blending of styles. Although it was a Tibetan-style opera, the performers did not wear masks but used makeup, as in Beijing opera. Also, the opera gained enough popularity that it was performed in the Gobi, until the switch to Communism ended it.

The Western form of opera has been part of the Mongolian theater since the revolution. Introduced by the Soviets, it has continued to thrive. One of the most popular operas since independence has been one about Chinggis Khan. In 1942 the first Mongolian Western-style opera, *Uchirtai Gurwan Tolgoi* (Three Fateful Hills), was performed. Natasagdorj's classic opera tells the story of a young couple's love and the attempts of oppressive nobles to disrupt it for their own selfish gain. Although arranged with revolutionary themes, it remains a classic piece.

As the traditional form of opera arrived with Communism, it is not surprising that with a capitalist economy and a Western democratic government, the cultural elite would also take an interest in forms of theater that were formerly taboo. Hence, in 2006, the eight hundredth anniversary of the crowning of Chinggis Khan and the formation of the Mongol Empire, the world was introduced to *Chinggis Khan, The Rock Opera*. Based on *The Secret History of the Mongols*, the opera told the life of Chinggis Khan and received favorable reviews. Composed by Taraa, the performance consisted of forty dancers, sixty singers, a fifty-piece orchestra, and the Mongolian heavy metal group Khar Chono (The Black Wolves). Furthermore, academics reviewed the script to ensure that it remained true to history. The rock opera was innovative, not only for Mongolia, but also for the genre, as it combined opera singing with not only rock music, but also with traditional Mongolian music, such as throat-singing, and the incorporation of the *morin khuur*.

Dramatic theater in the Western sense has existed in Mongolia since the 1921 revolution. Mongolia's first playwright, Buyannemekhu, like many others of the literati in the first half of the twentieth century, had a career marked with alternating periods of government favor and imprisonment. In 1934 Buyannemekhu rose to acclaim for his play *Kharangkhui Zasag* (A Dark Regime), which depicts various members of Qing-era Mongolian society pitted against the protagonists, a lowborn family—an appropriate topic during the period of the purges.

When speaking of theater, one must also include cinema. The Soviets introduced the Mongolians to the cinema, and thus much of twentieth-century Mongolian cinema is strongly Soviet/Russian influenced. Mobile projection tents went into the countryside to show propaganda films to educate the people shortly after the revolution in the 1920s, and the first Mongolian cinema was built in 1934 in Ulaanbaatar. A year later, a Mongolian production company, Mongol Kino, came into being. Aspiring directors learned their craft in Moscow and became well versed in what is known as socialist realism.

From the Communist period, the best-known film is *Serelt* (Awakening; 1957), directed by S. Genden. This film is considered one of the classics and tells the story of a Russian doctor in Mongolia and her attempts to set up a hospital on the steppe. The message of the story is an anti-Buddhist one, as the doctor and her helpers bring modern science to the steppe, thus "awakening" the rural population to the quackery of Buddhist medicine. Other noteworthy films include *Sukhebaatar* (1942), a biography of the hero of the revolution, and, of course, *Tsogtu Taiji* (1945), written by Rinchen, which later was used as evidence against him of nationalistic tendencies.

The collapse of the Soviet Union almost led to the collapse of Mongolian cinema, as the Soviet Union subsidized Mongol Kino. Indeed, many directors and actors lost their jobs in the early 1990s, but Mongolian films have since rebounded and even gained some international attention. In the early 1990s, Mongolia broadened its international relations and sought new investors, not only in the country, but also in other fields. The cinema was no exception. Not surprisingly, one of the first films produced was *Chinggis Khan* (1992), by a Mongolian and Japanese team. Unfortunately, it received little critical acclaim.

At the forefront of this has been the work of Byambasuren Davaa, whose *The Weeping Camel* (2003) won over nine awards from various film festivals as well as a nomination for best foreign film from the American Academy of Motion Picture Arts and Sciences. The film is in part a documentary of a nomad's efforts to reunite an abandoned white camel with its mother. Her next film, *The Cave of the Yellow Dog* (2005), tells the story of a young nomad girl who adopts a stray dog on the steppe against the wishes of her parents. The film incorporates nomadic culture and Buddhist concepts of rebirth as well as the struggle of maintaining nomadic life despite the lure of the city. Davaa's second film also gained international recognition and garnered five film festival awards. Other films, such as *The State of Dogs* (1998) and *Movement of Sand* (2007), also have been received well and bode well for the future of Mongolian cinema.

DANCE

Mongolian dance has a curious history. Although dances existed and were commented on by travelers during the era of the Mongol Empire, religion squelched dance as a popular means of expression during the rise of Mongolian Buddhism. Indeed, folk dancing seems to have survived only in the peripheral regions of Mongolia and not in the central part. Thus one may draw the conclusion that the farther removed from the center of Buddhist authority one was, the safer it was to dance. Some forms did continue but were largely ceremonial, such as the *tsam* dance and the eagle dance used in wrestling, which will be discussed in chapter 8.

Naturally, dancing in Mongolia has adapted to new influences and new forms of music, particularly with the advent of the discotheque and nightclubs. Yet traditional forms of dance and dances associated with religious practices have not disappeared. As stated previously, traditional dances seem to have disappeared from central Mongolia, but the more remote regions have their particular forms of folk dance that are still performed during festivals and celebrations.

A few stand out. In western Mongolia, the *bielgee* is the traditional dance. In the *bielgee*, most of the movement occurs in the upper body. Performed to the music of traditional instruments, such as the *morin khuur*, the *bielgee* dancers often mimic events in daily life, such as hunting or milking an animal. Whereas it started as a folk dance for entertainment, *bielgee* increasingly became viewed as an art. As a result, it also became more regimented in terms of choreography.

There are also several forms of cup dancing, which may be best known in America due to a segment about Mongolian cup dancing on the children's show *Sesame Street*. Some of the dancers have *airag* (koumiss)-filled cups balanced on their hands or heads. One peculiar form of this dance involves dancing in a sitting position while balancing the cup on the knees.

Among the most interesting dances found in Mongolia is the *tsam* dance. This is a ritual dance once performed by monks for the fierce deities, although now it is often performed by professional dancers. The dance arrived during the Second Conversion. Although it existed in Tibet since the thirteenth century, it was not until the end of the eighteenth century that it appeared in Mongolia, first at the Erdene Zuu monastery and then, in 1811, in Khuriye. The Communist government outlawed it in 1937 as part of its eradication of Buddhism; since 1990, it has returned, but most of the dances are much smaller than in the past.

The dancers wear colorful and imaginative papier-mâché masks called *tsam* masks. The dance itself symbolizes battles between gods and demons. Although it became part of Mongolian and Tibetan Buddhism, it incorporates features of Inner Asian shamanism. This manifests most often in the appearance of the White Old Man, an earth god of fertility who is a bit of a trickster at times and a clown, yet who is often the main feature of the performance. Other characters abound in the *tsam*. The characters symbolize not just gods and fantastic creatures, but also positive and negative attributes.

Tsam dancing has a fairly standard performance. After a service for the deity Yamantaka, the dance begins. Characters in masks enter the dance area in a set sequence and dance by bouncing, twirling, or leaping to and fro while wielding swords in mock battle. Toward the end, the White Old Man makes his appearance, with the conclusion coming as thirty-two monks enter. The dance ends with figurines being destroyed as an exorcism of evil.

While Western dancing thrives in the nightclubs of Mongolia, formal, stylized Western forms of dancing entered Mongolia during the Communist era. In 1931 the State Central Theater opened and gave rise to professional dance troupes, including ballet. Most of the dancers studied their art in the Union of Soviet Socialist Republics before returning to Mongolia. B. Jamyandagva was among these early students. He excelled in ballet and became Mongolia's first ballet master and is considered the father of Mongolian ballet.

During the Communist era, ballet blossomed, particularly with the opening of the State Theater of Opera and Ballet on May 15, 1963. There dancers performed numerous classics such as *Swan Lake* and *The Nutcracker*. Since the fall of the Communist regime, ballet has suffered, largely due to a lack of government financial support.

NOTES

1. Christopher Atwood, *Encyclopedia of Mongolia and the Mongol Empire* (New York: Facts on File, 2004), 498.

2. One can view the artwork of numerous artists at the Web site of the Union of Mongolian Artists (http://www.uma.mn). Also see more artwork at the online Mongolian Art Gallery (http://www.mongolianartgallery.com).

3. Peter Marsh, "Mongolia Sings Its Own Song," http://mongoluls.net/ger/sing.shtml.

4. Ibid.

5. Tim Severin, *In Search of Genghis Khan* (New York: Atheneum, 1992), 78.

6. "The Mongolians Are Coming to China! With Heavy Metal!," *New York Times*, November 26, 2004.

6

Cuisine and Dress

CUISINE

As the Mongolians have historically been nomads, it is not surprising that the cuisine of Mongolia has consisted largely of meat and dairy products. Although historically, fruits and vegetables have been meager, the Communist era did change that through attempts to farm virgin lands and use greenhouses. Nevertheless, wild vegetables, grains, berries, and wild fruits have been part of the Mongolian diet. Farming, however, remains relatively difficult, simply due to the short growing season, soil quality, and wind erosion. Thus the traditional focus on meat and dairy remains prevalent.

Although Mongolian barbecue restaurants are popular in the United States, they are not truly Mongolian. One Mongol immigrant who ate at one with his American wife commented on this and said that it was Chinese food. She then asked him what he could serve in a Mongolian restaurant. His answer? Chinese food.

While an amusing anecdote, there is some truth to his response. It is almost easier to find an American-style cheeseburger (although sometimes made with yak meat) in Ulaanbaatar than traditional Mongolian cuisine. The number of Chinese and Korean, and even German restaurants, gives one the impression that a true Mongolian cuisine does not exist. Indeed, outside of someone's home, it can be difficult to find a restaurant in Ulaanbaatar that serves Mongolian food. While Mongolia may not have its own Julia Child or Gordon Ramsey, it does have its own unique culinary style.

Some food preparation techniques are as old as the steppe. Indeed, animals are still slaughtered in the same way. Of course, modern agribusiness has streamlined the slaughter of animals, and many societies developed particular styles of slaughtering animals. The most well known to Westerners is what one might call "kosher," as Jewish and Muslim butchers kill animals in the same manner—cutting the throat so that the blood quickly drains from the animal.

Historically, the Mongols have always slaughtered the animal in the same way since, if not before, the Mongol Empire. The animal is rolled onto its back and an incision is made into its chest so that the person may reach in and still the heart of the animal or quickly rip the aorta, killing the animal with internal hemorrhaging. Whereas the kosher method is meant to drain the blood, the Mongolian way attempts to keep the blood within the animal. Traditionally, this was done so as not to waste the blood, so that it could be used with sausages and other foods.

As the Mongols expanded their empire, they also came into contact with new foods, which then became incorporated into the culinary practices of the Mongolians. Some faded as the empire receded, while others became firmly implanted. The most common form of food during the Mongol Empire was *shuul,* a thick soup made with meat and whatever else was available. Also in the soup was millet gruel, as millet was one of the few grains that could grow sufficiently on the Mongolian plateau. Roasted meat was usually reserved for special occasions. This remains a traditional meal, known as *shuulte khool,* or "soup with food"—basically a stew of broth, chunks of boiled mutton, noodles, and some potatoes.

The most common form of meat used in all dishes was and remains mutton. It is usually boiled in chunks. When completed, it is all ladled into a container. Thus one may get his or her choice of meat, organs, or even the sheep's head. Indeed, on ceremonial occasions, one should expect to see a whole boiled sheep on a plate, complete with legs, head, and tail—much like one would see a turkey on Thanksgiving. Mutton also forms the basis of *shuul* and can be roasted and made into virtually anything. Yet, occasionally, excess meat remains, or the herder sets about preserving food for the winter or for long journeys. Thus the Mongolians of the empire and today created *borts,* a form of jerky. It is often made the same way today as it was in the past. Meat is cut into strips and then dried by hanging in the sun and the wind. Oddly enough, just as beef jerky seems to be a common item in gas stations and truck stops in the United States, *borts* remains a common food for long-distance drivers. This preservation technique allowed for the meat to be preserved for several seasons. Sausages, made from stuffed intestines, are preserved with a similar technique.

   While Mongolian barbecue restaurants in the United States may not be authentic, although one apparently opened in Mongolia in 2005, one can experience true Mongolian barbecue in two forms. The first is *boodog*, which is cooked inside of the skin of an animal. On the steppe, the herders use a goat, sheep, or marmot. The bones and internal organs of the animal must be removed first, through the neck. Meat that is on the bones is removed and then placed back in the animal, along with spices. While the animal is being cleaned, rocks are heated in a fire. These, too, are placed in the animal, and the neck is tied shut. The herders then use fire, either with a torch or a blowtorch, to remove the hair from the outside of the animal. Most of the cooking, however, is performed by the rocks inside the animal.

   The other method of Mongolian barbecue is *khorkhog*. *Khorkhog* evolved from the *boodog* style. Rather than using the whole animal as the vessel for cooking, the cook used the stomach and then bronze pots. Today on the steppe, large metal containers, such as milk containers, are used, with chopped meat placed in layers with potatoes, vegetables, spices, and hot rocks. The container is then set on top of a fire, cooking the contents from within and without and with pressure, similar to so-called trash can cooking in the United States. Naturally, this style of cooking makes an abundance of food, but restaurants have substituted aluminum foil for the animal carcass or stomach. Yet, in the restaurant, one misses out on the opportunity to play "hot potato" with the hot and inevitably greasy rock that was used to cook the food, which is thought to be beneficial to your health.

   In addition to meat, the other major part of the Mongolian diet consists of dairy products. Yogurt, milk, cream, and cheese, and, of course, *airag*, or fermented mare's milk, dominate summer meals. All of these goods can be prepared from the milk of a number of animals: cow, sheep, goat, mare, or even camel. Even snack food in Mongolia can come from dairy products. One of the most common is *aaruul*, a dried cheese curd that has been described by travelers over the centuries as being as hard as iron. As such, it can be stored for months and travels well. To the outsider, its appeal can be a bit mysterious, but Mongolians love it. The hardness of *aaruul* is due simply to the drying process (in which it is placed on boards on top of a *ger* and left to dry in the sun and wind), but when eaten fresh, it can be soft. Most Mongolians, however, do not bite into a hard *aaruul*, but suck on it, almost like a hard candy. Another variant of *aaruul* is *khorkhoi aaruul*, or "worm" *aaruul*. Rather than being pressed into cheese, the curd is placed in a meat grinder, and thus the cheese is pressed into strands. In this form, the cheese stays softer and is preferred by small children. The flavor of *aaruul* is on the sour side, but one can detect notes of sweetness.

Other cheeses include two derived from sour milk: *byaslag* and *eezgii*. *Byaslag* is usually made from cow's or yak's milk. Sheep's or goat's milk can make a more aromatic cheese, but no matter what milk is used, the flavor of Mongolian cheeses tends to be bland compared with European cheeses. *Eezgii* does not really have a true shape but is a mass or grainy. It, like *aaruul*, tends to be used more for a snack. Unlike *aaruul*, *eezgii* has a slightly sweet flavor but a grainy texture. The sweetness is probably due to the roasting process. After the curd forms, the cheese is roasted until all of the liquid dissipates.

Among the more appealing dairy foods are *aarts* and *orom*, or *uurag*. The first is a soft but slightly fermented cheese. *Orom* is a rich and sweet cream. Although it may be made from any type of milk, *orom* made from yak milk contains the most milk fat and thus makes the sweetest cream.

The cuisine of Mongolia after the empire remained largely the same; the use of noodles and dough seems to have remained—or at least is commented on by observers. Again, stews and soups with meat predominated, but noodles, fried millet, and flour were added, providing additional substance. Another item that entered the Mongolian palate was tea. Exactly when Mongolians adopted the habit of drinking tea is unknown, but their tea habit was such that a regular exchange of horses for tea took place between the Mongolians and the Ming Empire (1368–1644) for most of the latter's duration. Although tea may have been adopted by Mongolians during their reign over China, it is somewhat doubtful that they drank it regularly before 1300—Marco Polo, who spent seventeen years among the Mongols and in China, never mentions it.

Most likely, their adoption of tea also came with their adoption of Buddhism. The drinking of tea was a part of many ceremonies in Tibetan Buddhism as well as daily life. Combined with the fact that it is served hot and caffeinated, one can only imagine that Mongolians welcomed it wholeheartedly in the midst of cold steppe winters. Yet one should not imagine a Mongolian, at any point, sipping it from a cup and saucer with a pinky out or asking for someone to pass the cucumber sandwiches. While one may easily drink tea anywhere in Mongolia, true Mongolian-style tea is made with milk, salt, and butter. This is known as *suutai tsai*, or "milky tea"—very similar to Tibetan-style tea. In addition, particularly on the steppe, it may not be surprising to find millet in it, as if it were porridge, or even a chunk of meat or fat. Typically, though, one will not encounter this practice, although it is not unknown. Regular tea, as Westerners know it, is *khar tsai*, or "black tea." Perhaps one reason for the creation of *suutai tsai* is that the tea traded during the Ming era was of low quality and often consisted of bits of leaf and stem pressed into bricks. The bricks, however, did make it easier for the nomads to transport.

With Qing domination of Mongolia, Mongolian cuisine was altered again. Previously, meat from hunting formed a major part of the Mongolian diet.

This traditionally had been obtained through large hunts called *nerge,* which also served as military practices. The hunters formed a line that gradually formed a circle and drove all game toward the center. It was a matter of pride to not allow any animal to escape. The animals were then killed in demonstrations of bravery—hand-to-hand combat with tigers or wolves, marksmanship by shooting fleet-footed antelope or hares, and so on. Although Mongols served in the Qing military, the government curtailed military-style hunting exercises. In addition, Buddhist influences reined in some of the hunting. Fishing, which never was a mainstay of the Mongol diet, but rather a supplement, ceased almost altogether under Buddhist influence.[1] While this certainly limited the variety of meats in the Mongolian diet, the herds of the Mongolians provided an ample amount.

While government regulation limited large hunts, the Qing Empire also introduced more staples to the Mongolian diet. With a unified empire, foods from the southern part of the empire now entered Mongolia, in the north, on a regular basis. Thus sugar and rice gradually became ubiquitous. Also, new dishes appeared, such as *bortsog,* which is fried bread; typically, it is fried in animal fat, which was preferred to oil in Mongolia. *Bortsog* became a standard part of the meal. Other dough-based foods also entered Mongolia, and it is difficult to conceive of modern Mongolian cuisine without some of their presences.

Steamed buns and dumplings remain very popular. These include the steamed and leavened bun known as *mantuu,* and *banshi,* which is a dumpling made with a meat stuffing wrapped in dough and boiled in soup. Another popular item is the *khuushuur.* This is flattened dough that is stuffed with meat and then fried. Often, vegetables are also added. Not surprisingly, Chinese-style pancakes also appeared. Undoubtedly, the most popular dumpling-style food in Mongolia is *buuz.*

Buuz is made for holidays and for guests in one's home. The dumplings are stuffed with meat and steam-cooked. The stuffing itself is made from ground mutton, onions, and cabbage and is seasoned with salt and pepper. A hole is poked in the skin of the dumpling so that steam can escape. Typically, when Mongolians make *buuz,* they not only make it for the occasion, but they also freeze extras for future use. In the cities, *buuz* are eaten commonly during the winter but are reserved for special occasions in the summer, probably due to the sweltering process of making them.

Yet foods such as rice and dumplings were not the only items adopted from the Chinese—utensils for eating came, too. Typically, the Mongolians drank their soups from a bowl and used a knife for other purposes. By the Qing era, it was commonplace for everyone to carry a knife on his or her belt in a sheath. In addition, there was space for chopsticks.

Of course, with Russian influence in Mongolia, other foods have entered. One item that has become standard fare in Mongolia is potato salad. As potatoes first originated in the Andes Mountains of South America, a cold and arid setting, they are one of the few crops that can grow well in Mongolia. Naturally, potatoes appear in other dishes.

The urban cuisine of Mongolia changed significantly due to Russian influences. Eating utensils such as forks, spoons, and knives replaced chopsticks. Restaurants and hotels served only European-style food. Indeed, even today, breakfast at a hotel is very reminiscent of the fare found at a Soviet hotel in Moscow—sausages, eggs, toast, and so on. It sounds very American, yet the flavor (though not bad at all) is quite different. Also, because the sausages are made from beef or mutton, they are truly unique. In some ways, it is almost indescribable. One must experience it.

The European preference for beef also entered with the Russians, although mutton remains the favored meat of Mongolia. Chicken is quite rare and pork has yet to come into favor, possibly facing discrimination as being "too Chinese." Chickens, not an animal that one typically herds, are not really native animals. Thus, whereas Americans consume vast quantities of chicken, it is rarely eaten in Mongolia. Of course, mutton is not a commonly eaten meat in the United States, except in the form of lamb, and usually only as chops or racks of lamb. Thus, when one goes to Mongolia, one should expect to eat mutton. And indeed, the author does so precisely because it does not cross his plate often in the States. Oddly enough, at one dinner in an Ulaanbaatar restaurant, a Mongolian friend passed on some delicious mutton *khorkhog* for a grilled chicken breast simply because at home, he rarely sees chicken but eats mutton frequently.

Political change affected Mongolian cuisine in other ways as well. With the Sino-Soviet rift, Mongolia suffered as its millet supply from China ended. Although some millet grew in Mongolia, it was insufficient, and thus fried millet more or less disappeared from Mongolia's collective menu. Yet, at the same time, bread, which simply did not exist in Mongolia prior to the Russian presence, is now a standard part of most meals. One of the achievements of the Mongolian government under Soviet influence was to make Mongolia self-sufficient in producing grain.

Although some cereal farming has existed in Mongolia throughout history, it has not always been successful. Indeed, by 1926, only about seventy-five thousand hectares were under cultivation. Not until World War II did it increase substantially, primarily to help supply the Soviet Union, which lost its Ukrainian breadbasket to the Nazis. In 1959 Mongolia also underwent a "Virgin Lands" experiment, following the lead of Nikita Khrushchev in the Soviet Union. Although millet traditionally has been the preferred cereal crop of Mongolia, surprisingly, the focus was on wheat, barley, and potatoes. At its peak in 1985, 1.24 million hectares came under cultivation. Almost 20 percent of this, however, was also to produce fodder for the animal herds for the winter. For a short period, Mongolia truly became self-sufficient for grains, although the variables of the economic market somewhat undermined the cost-efficiency of this after the collapse of Communism. By 2000 only 497,000 hectares were under cultivation. Now, Mongolia produces approximately one-third of its own flour.[2]

Although bread became a standard part of the Mongolian diet, the grain and potato cultivation actually benefited a new industry, and continues to do so, in producing the materials for distilled alcohol. Although distilled alcohol existed in Mongolia prior to Soviet domination, it was made by distilling milk products like *airag*. The *shimiin arkhi* that is produced through distillation raises the alcohol content from roughly 3 to 12 percent. Russian influences brought in new foods and drink. Perhaps the most regrettable one is vodka due to the high rate of alcoholism. The Mongolians have always been notorious for their love of alcohol. After all, it was Chinggis Khan who said,

If unable to abstain from drinking, a man may get drunk three times a month; if he does it more than three times he is culpable; if he gets drunk twice a month it is better; if once a month, this is still more laudable; and if one does not drink at all what can be better? But where can such a man be found? If such a man were found he would be worthy of the highest esteem.[3]

Airag has always been the national drink of Mongolia. Today, medical authorities have discovered that moderate drinking can help reduce the chances of acquiring, or the effects of, several diseases, and for Mongolians, the benefit may have been even greater. And although Chinggis Khan may have half-heartedly condemned drinking, drinking *airag* also provided vitamins A, B_{12}, B_2, B_1, and C to the diet. Although milk-based alcohol, such as *airag* (koumiss), remains popular, cheap distilled alcohol remains easily available. Vodka (or *arkhi* in Mongolian), in particular, is very popular—and often quite high in quality. What is notable about the alcohol industry in Mongolia is that it has embraced Mongolia's heritage. Brand names range from the popular Hunter to a series of historical motifs ranging across the span of Mongolian history—from Hun and Golden Horde to the ever-popular Chinggis Khan vodka. Of the latter, there are a number of styles and images of Chinggis Khan, from the original Chinggis Khan, with a picture based on a Yuan-era painting, to Imperial Arkhi, which is not only of high quality, but also comes in a leather-clad bottle.

Vodka, while still the most consumed alcoholic beverage in Mongolia, is losing ground to a competitor: beer. German influences have penetrated Mongolia, particularly in the 1990s, and several Mongolian beers have appeared. All of the breweries appear to have followed German standards and styles. In some ways, this is reminiscent of Japan's modernization during the Meiji period (1868–1912), when they brought in the best to teach them how to modernize Japan: for the army, Prussian advisors; for the navy, British. For Mongolian beer, they followed German advice. Some of the top brands are Altan Gobi, Khan Brau (which is also served in a German restaurant), and, of course, Chinggis Khan. In addition, a few Korean breweries have set up bottling plants in Ulaanbaatar.

Despite outside influences, the Mongolian palate still desires the basics of meat and dairy products. They tend to prefer fatty dairy products and meats. Indeed, one of the most prized pieces from the sheep is the tail fat. Often, this is offered to the guest. When eating *khorkhog*, one should expect it to be greasy. In the premodern era, the fatty food not only helped insulate the body, but the grease accrued on one's fingertips from eating could then be smeared onto one's face, providing protection from the cold and cutting wind. Despite this love of fatty food, the vast majority of it comes from animal fat (dairy or meat), and Mongolians tend to have low cholesterol. Still, more vegetables are eaten than ever before—primarily hearty and somewhat bland ones such as cabbages, carrots, and potatoes, although radishes are enjoyed.

In general, Mongolian food is somewhat bland, with little seasoning beyond salt and perhaps black pepper. While in the popular imagination, Mongolian food may be thought spicy, all one has to do is sample it to find that Mongolians do not enjoy spicy foods as a general rule. Finally, while many Chinese restaurants may attempt to entice eaters with an exotic dish called "Mongolian beef," it has little to do with Mongolia. Certainly, while the key ingredients (beef and onions) may evoke thoughts of Mongolia, it is prepared and cooked in an East Asian style. The Mongolian style would be boiled or probably cooked all together in a container.

DRESS

The traditional dress of Mongolia in the past, the present, and the probable future is the *deel*. It is a long, loose robe that comes down approximately to somewhere between the knees and mid-shin level. The front overlaps and is fastened with two buttons on strings on the overlapping side with loops, connecting on the upper right-hand side and then at intervals on the right side. It is usually also fastened with a sash. Underneath, men and women wear trousers and boots as shoes.

Nomads have virtually always worn trousers due to their livelihood: riding a horse all day is much easier with pants than in a toga or dress. As both men and women carried out many of the same jobs, the basic *deel* is unisex. The *deel* is one of the most practical forms of clothing in the world. It can serve as a coat or as a blanket. Also, for the nomad on the steppe, it provides some privacy for bodily functions. At the same time, the *deel* varies with the season. The basic deel is the *dan deel,* which is a plain and unpadded *deel.* One might consider it a housecoat- or work shirt–type garment. These tend to be of a gray or earth-toned color. There are *deels* often referred to as *terleg,* which are padded and worn in cooler weather or even on top of the *dan deel.* In winter, a *deel* lined with sheepskin and wool or stuffed with cotton is worn.

Nonetheless, the *deel* can be quite individualistic and decorative, not only for gender, but also for tribal or familial identity. Indeed, even subtle differences can be determined between the *deels* of men and women, with the male version being slightly wider and made in more conservative colors. Women's *deels* tend to be of brighter or flashier colors. While everyday *deels* for either gender tend to be dull in color, those worn for special occasions or events are often made of blue, green, or deep red silk. Other colors are possible, but these tend to be favored. The collar, sleeves, and breast are often trimmed with brocade, fur, or leather. The buttons and fastening loops vary in material. A long silken sash is tied around the waist.

In the past, the sash served multiple purposes. Not only did it help fasten and add another color to the *deel,* but it also historically served as a corset. This purpose did not arise because the typical Mongol was concerned about keeping a small waist, but rather, it alleviated some of the pounding and bouncing the body took on long horseback rides across the steppe. More mundane uses included holding things, such as the knife and chopsticks, a snuff bottle, flint, a tinder box, and cleaning pipes. The pipe rested in the boots.

Mongolian boots are heelless, with upturned toes. Curiously, they also are almost always uniform in shape for the right and left feet. The boot is high and quite stiff but lined with layers of felt to protect against the cold. Meanwhile, on the foot, one wears a thick, quilted sock made from cotton or felt. The upturned toe also serves as insulation, as the foot warms the air in the empty space. Much like Western cowboy boots, the Mongolian boot is decorated in a myriad of styles and patterns.

Hats and headdresses are also part of the traditional dress. The style varies greatly from region to region as well as by gender and social position. The basic hat in winter is simply a fur hat with sides that can be turned down to protect the ears or kept up in warmer weather. Other, nonwinter hats also denoted social status in the past. These styles are still sometimes worn but more or less no longer carry a meaning. Typically, hats are round and made from felt and dyed in a variety of colors, with upturned brim pieces and a cord knot on top of a peak. The hat is often decorated with patterns sewn on the sides.

The very construction of the hat carries significance. The cone or peak was sewn together with thirty-two stitches to represent the thirty-two Mongolian tribes, and the knot on top represented the unity of the country. The broad brim demonstrated the country's inaccessibility.[4] In the past, red ribbons were attached to the peak and represented the rays of the sun, although today, the ribbons are rarely worn.

Another traditional item is the *tolgoin boolt*, or headdress worn by women. The headdress varies from tribe to tribe and region to region. Prior to the 1921 revolution, most noblewomen wore these. Now one rarely sees them outside of festivals and special occasions. The headdress is made from silver and is usually decorated with a variety of precious and semiprecious stones. For some of the headdresses, an elaborate frame was used along with the equivalent of hair extensions. Combined with ceremonial dresses, often with padded shoulders, it transformed the wearer into a striking image. Americans have seen it as one of the fashions worn by the queen of Naboo, Padme, in the *Star Wars* movie *The Phantom Menace*.

Although the *deel* continues to be the daily form of dress in the countryside for most of the rural population, in urban areas, it is quite different. It is not uncommon to see someone, particularly among the elderly, wearing a *deel* and the upturned boots, but most urban Mongolians wear Western-style clothing. Seventy years of Soviet influence have made Western fashions a common part of Mongolian life. Indeed, shortly after the revolution, traditional fashions were targeted just like any other indication of nationalism. The suit and tie and Western laced shoes became the norm; however, the *deel* did not disappear by any means. For instance, one might see a nomad wearing a *deel* but atop his head a Western-style hat, often a fedora or trilby hat. It is also not uncommon to see younger Mongolians wearing baseball caps.

The most influential source of fashion in Mongolia, however, is not Europe or America, but rather South Korea. The "Korean Wave," as the spread of Korean influence is often called, has had tremendous influence in Mongolia. Thousands of Mongolians study or work in South Korea and then return home to Mongolia, bringing various elements of Korean culture with them. The most apparent, beyond the numerous Korean restaurants in Ulaanbaatar, is fashion. Everything from jeans to shoes is strongly influenced by fashion currents in Seoul.

Nonetheless, some fashions are distinctly Mongolian and have been updated for the twenty-first century. One example of this is the *khurem* jacket. The *khurem* is made from felt and has long sleeves and buttons down the front center of the jacket, with looped buttons similar to those on the *deel*. Typically, it is trimmed with cloth in traditional knot patterns. In winter, it is often worn over a *deel* but is warm enough to wear in early spring through autumn. The *khurem* jacket tends to be worn by young men, and its style has crept into other forms such as sweaters. One can also find leather jackets that follow the *khurem* style or are cut like a *deel* but at jacket length.

Women's fashions are also inspired by traditional Mongolian clothing and materials. The female equivalent of the *khurem* is a coat that extends to just below the knees but in all other aspects resembles the *khurem*, from the cut of the sleeves and the button loops to the knot-pattern trim. Dresses and blouses bear a certain resemblance to the *deel* in that they fasten on the right side.

As Mongolia is the world's second largest producer of cashmere, it is not surprising that high-quality cashmere garments, ranging from short-sleeved sweaters to dresses, are worn by the fashionable. While perhaps odd to the non-Mongolian, garments produced from camel wool are also quite stylish—and very warm. Leading designer labels include Gobi, the largest producer of cashmere in Mongolia.

NOTES

1. Christopher Atwood, *Encyclopedia of Mongolia and the Mongol Empire* (New York: Facts on File, 2004), 184.

2. Tsegmediin Natsagdorj, *Mongolia of Chinggis* (Ulaanbaatar, Mongolia: Monsudar, 2004), 102–3.

3. Valentin A. Riasanovsky, *Fundamental Principles of Mongol Law,* Uralic and Altaic Series 43 (Bloomington: Indiana University Press, 1965), 88.

4. Natsagdorj, *Mongolia of Chinggis*, 187.

7

Gender, Courtship, and Marriage

TRADITIONAL ROLES

UNLIKE IN MANY Asian societies, Mongolia has never been a state in the classical patriarchal mode, with the senior male in the family dominating all aspects of family life. This was probably due to the unique situation of the nomadic household, which often required men to do so-called women's work and women to perform so-called men's work. In the household, women tend to be in charge of the daily affairs of the household and do most of the household labor. Men have traditionally been the breadwinners who support their families. Thus, although the male is traditionally the head of the household, there is much more equality in Mongolia than elsewhere in Asia. Women have always been held in respect; indeed, Chinggis Khan often relied on his mother and wives for trusted advice. Only a few symbolic items really demonstrate any difference between genders, such as where one sits in a *ger*, as will be discussed in chapter 9. This equality has only been increased through Mongolia's experience under Communism. More recently, the situation has changed significantly, primarily due to the economic changes of the 1990s.

Although nomadic women have traditionally enjoyed a high level of equality with men, their status has fluctuated considerably. By the early twentieth century, the rights of Mongolian women had actually eroded, but the arrival of Communism in 1921 transformed the situation through prohibitions on arranged marriages. Later, the government enacted laws that promoted equality in the workplace, in education, and in politics. Nonetheless, it was not a paradise of equality. Although women regained much of their traditional standing, they still received lower pay and benefits compared with their male counterparts. Since 1990, women also have increasingly joined the workforce, partially out of economic necessity, but also out of desire. Several occupations became the domain of women. Most of the doctors and teachers are women, as are those in banking, finance, and insurance. Indeed, in 1990, of the six thousand physicians in Mongolia, 75 percent were female.[1] Unfortunately, a glass ceiling exists and prevents Mongolian women from rising to positions of power, although exceptions always exist. For instance, 70 percent of Mongolia's lawyers are women, but few female lawyers have been able to advance beyond junior positions.

Part of the dominance of women in professional fields stems from women's desire to improve the status and lives of their daughters. Rural women push for education for their daughters. Boys also receive an education, but many do not complete secondary school, as they are needed at home. Many poor urban women also view education as an avenue of escape from poverty for their daughters. The males have more opportunities, simply through physical labor, to gain a sustainable wage.

Despite the fact that more women have entered the workforce, women remain the primary caregivers in the household. Since the advent of capitalism in Mongolia, this has become increasingly difficult for many women, particularly among the lower income levels. Health and welfare benefits promoted by the government have greatly assisted women; for instance, in the countryside, state-sponsored maternity homes for rural women allowed them to adequately recuperate and provided a safe place to stay during the last part of their pregnancies. The importance of this cannot be overstated, considering that many of the families were remote from any medical assistance. In addition, the state provided facilities to assist women with infant and child care when they returned to work. Women with four or more children also received optional early retirement packages. Additional support was also available to widows, as were pensions for the elderly and care for the disabled. As Morris Rossabi has pointed out, "The government's support for such needy groups relieved females of some of these demanding responsibilities."[2]

Of course, not everything was perfect. Birthrates have dropped since 1990 as well, but this is not necessarily a negative change. During the Communist period, the government pushed a pro-natal agenda. Abortion was illegal, even for circumstances in which the mother's life was endangered. In addition, the drive for an increase in population did send the birthrate soaring, but it also meant that contraceptives were scarce due to government planning. As a result, women often had many children too early, too soon between children, or too late, thus endangering their health and lives. Finally, the idea that pregnancy was a civic or even a national duty complicated the issue further. So, despite many of the beneficial health services that the government provided to assist with pregnancy, the government also contributed to an increase in maternal mortality.

After the fall of the Communist regime, the situation reversed—perhaps too much. Although the 1992 constitution did make health care a right, the sudden switch to a market economy undermined its intentions. Rather than being free or inexpensive, medical services were now compensated by a Western-style fee system. Unfortunately, a sizeable percentage of the population could not afford these fees. Also, without state funding, many of the maternity services closed or severely limited their services. Rural women suffered greatly from this reduction. Although promoters of the new-style health care services cited that infant mortality had declined from 57.4 per 1,000 in 1990 to 29.5 per 1,000 in 1994, this had more to do with the fact that the birthrate had dropped.[3] No longer did women feel pressure to have an abundance of children, and thus the average number of children per household declined from four to two.

Women continue to play an increasingly important role in Mongolia's present and future. In addition to remaining the primary caregivers and running the household, increasingly, particularly in urban areas, women are also assuming many of the traditional roles of the male.

Traditionally, men have been the breadwinners. On the steppe, as discussed in chapter 2, pastoral nomads took care of animals but also hunted and manufactured necessary items. While this remains true on the steppe, in the urban setting, the situation has changed. Men still hold most of the higher positions in virtually every field, even those in which most of the workforce, such as medicine, is made up of women. When privatization occurred, many men profited from nepotism, thus securing good deals or a position. Of course, this was limited to the upper segments of society—usually those with connections to the government. The vast majority of men did not see any true benefits.

This also has led to some difficulties. As mentioned previously, male children from the steppe often drop out of school or do not continue to the university level due to responsibilities at home. There is a sense of obligation as well as desire. For many young men (and women) from the steppe, leaving the countryside and attending school in the cities is difficult. While some receive a free education, they are often less prepared than their urban peers, and they struggle. Many give up and either return to being herders or find jobs in the towns as unskilled laborers. Either way, poverty is virtually ensured, although those who return to the steppe have a better chance of living a comfortable and familiar life, rather than dealing with the vagaries of an urban setting. Owing to this, many are incapable of fulfilling their traditional role of breadwinner and thus find it difficult to find a spouse.

As a result, the traditional role of the Mongolian male is declining in society. While it is unfortunate that so many males failed to find economic riches and stability in the market economy, it is not completely unexpected. As their traditional role has been breadwinner, they are expected to take risks that might improve the lot of the family. Unfortunately, statistically speaking, it is to be expected that most would fall short. The reality of the collapse of the planned economy is that few were prepared for the instability of a market-based economy. In addition, many men have ventured out of Mongolia to find steady work, particularly in South Korea, but also in the United States, Japan, and European countries. Nonetheless, this means that there are fewer men present, or many are absent from the household. Furthermore, when they do return home, employment opportunities often are difficult to find.

As men went out to seek their fortunes, women, meanwhile, focused on education and gaining the skills that come with it. In general, Mongolian women have thus become a better fit for the new market-based economy. They have gained not only jobs, but also economic independence.

For the men, the situation has been demoralizing. Unemployment, inadequate skills and opportunities to learn new skills, and the resulting failure to fulfill the traditional role of Mongolian men has rendered many useless due to depression. As a result, alcoholism has increased, as have broken homes. Many of the self-sufficient women choose not to marry or to leave their ineffectual husbands behind for a variety of reasons.

Just as some groups have been organized to deal with the domestic abuse that has arisen from the desultory situation, there are also groups to help the men. One such organization is the Men's Union, which was founded by a woman, D. Badamtsetseg.[4] The purpose is to step in and assist men—breaking the cycle of unemployment, alcoholism, and depression.

Needless to say, not all of the gender relations or roles are in such depressing states. The majority of families are solid and have loving spouses, interacting more or less as families do anywhere. By and large, though, interaction between spouses in Mongolia tends to be more similar to that in Western societies than in many Asian ones.

DATING AND MARRIAGE

Marriage and courtship have changed significantly in Mongolia, although August remains the most favored month for weddings. Traditionally, marriages were often arranged and included a large payment from the groom's family for the bride. The payment included not only livestock, clothes, and household goods, but also items such as saddles or other equestrian accoutrements. The payment was not to purchase the bride per se, but rather the rights to her fertility and offspring, as they would belong to the groom's clan. At age fourteen, daughters were considered of marriageable age and were expected to be married by age twenty. In the time of the Mongol Empire, adultery, committed by husband or wife, carried the death sentence. This also applied to elopement. Over the centuries, this penalty lessened and typically carried a heavy fine of livestock. Divorce seemed to be rare, or perhaps not even an idea held by the Mongols, prior to the nineteenth century. The families of the married couple carried an obligation to mediate any disputes. Only if families failed to resolve the marital dispute did civil officials intervene.

In the nineteenth century, a shift in marital relations occurred. Only the nobility still practiced the exchange of a large payment. The commoners simply could not afford it. In addition, an increasing number of men joined monasteries. This had a twofold effect on Mongolian society. By monastic rule, monks could not marry, thus reducing the pool of available men. The lamas could not marry, although many had wives and children; however, they did not pay a bride price, most likely due to vows of poverty, nor did they have a formal marriage. It became more of a common-law marriage. This may have also played a role in the decline of polygamy. Although it existed among some of the nobility, few others had the economic means to make it feasible.

The twentieth century saw more marriages, even before the 1921 Revolution. For instance, the disappearance of the bride price throughout much of Mongolia became the death knell of the arranged marriage. Added to this was an increased rate of elopement, which also negated the payment of a bride price. As negotiations over the bride price often dictated who could meet the demands of the bride's family, the marriage ultimately was arranged. With no bride price, then, fewer obstacles could block the bride and groom from each other, although family pressures and approval never disappeared.

Also in the twentieth century, the husband and wife shared increasing equality. While some of this shift had antecedents prior to the 1921 Revolution, at least one revolutionary organization, the Mongolian Revolutionary Youth League, took action against husbands who beat their wives or against parents who did the same to their children. In the past, fathers and mothers could physically intimidate their married children, and as a matter of custom, the young husband and wife often submitted.

Following the trends of the nineteenth century, marriage became monogamous. At eighteen, both men and women were deemed old enough to marry. Other legal requirements came into being. Again, most of these followed trends emanating from the late nineteenth century, but they became law.

Arranged marriages ended, at least overtly, as the bride and groom could only marry if mutual consent existed. Prohibitions against paying a bride price or dowry became law. Finally, husbands and wives had the same rights, including the right to divorce.

While romantic love existed prior to the twentieth century, most marriages had been born of economic and social considerations. Now, love and compassion gained emphasis in relationships. This also manifested in literature. The government also effectively denigrated many of the older customs through this. The ideal of formal and long-lasting marriages solidified.

Today, marriages occur relatively early in life, with women marrying around age twenty and men around age twenty-four. The couples usually have known each other and courted each other for a reasonable length of time, ranging from several months to several years. Courtship habits are similar to those found in Western societies. Most will marry someone with whom they attended school or a coworker, as work and school are where most people meet others of the opposite sex. This also has resulted in people generally marrying someone from their own social class; for instance, herders usually marry other herders, educated professionals marry other educated professionals, and so on. Another factor in this may also have to do with Mongolian male pride, which makes men reluctant to marry women who are more educated than them or whose occupation might be more dominant. This also seems to lessen marital strain, resulting in a low divorce rate. Divorces, while available, are rare. While the number has increased since the end of Communism, so has the number of marriages by a larger margin. More recently, however, many men have had difficulty finding women to marry. Many women are reluctant to marry and possibly give up their careers, or, as has happened to many women, not only maintain the household, but also become the primary breadwinner.

Taboos against premarital sex have never been a major component of Mongolian culture. As a result, this sometimes has also been a driving force in marriages, as the responsibility of parents for their children is expected. Indeed, single-parent households make up less than 5 percent of the married population.

Mongolian weddings take two forms: traditional and modern. In the traditional form, the wedding is preceded by an engagement process. This consists of three to four visits by the groom's family to the bride's household. In the first visit, the groom's mother visits the bride's family. She brings with her a *khadag* and some ceremonial gifts. The *khadag* is a silk scarf that is used in most ceremonies and rituals. It is usually made from blue or white silk. The gifts are given on top of the *khadag*. On her visit, the groom's mother inquires about the bride—her health, welfare, and so on.

The second visit is made by a friend of the bride and groom (or their families). Again, the friend carries the *khadag* and a few gifts. The friend is the person who will actually propose marriage between the prospective bride and groom. If the bride consents, then the friend returns to the groom's family, where they consult astrological tables or an expert to make sure all signs are favorable. Then the friend returns to the bride's family accompanied by the father and, if need be, another person known for his eloquence. In the past, it was on this visit that the bride price was negotiated. The final visit is by the groom and was when, traditionally, the bride price was made. At this point, the couple is considered to be engaged.

During the engagement, the bride avoids her fiancé. Considering that the engagement traditionally lasted a year, one may wonder just how rigorously this separation was enforced. Indeed, often, the engagement process has become quite simplified, although many families still appreciate the custom. In the final weeks before the marriage, the bride visits friends and family.

On the wedding day, the groom and his entourage ride to the bride's home. The groom's party always consists of an odd number; thus, when the bride is added, it makes an even number. The entourage includes the groom's mother, the best man, and others, depending on the size of the party, which never is more than nine people but is at least three. At the bride's house they have a feast. Prayers are said if the family is religious, and then the bride and her family ride to the groom's home. Both groom and bride wear their wedding finery. The wedding clothes resemble traditional *deels* but are made from brightly colored silk and have festive designs on them. Red and green are considered auspicious colors for a wedding, but there is no hard and fast tradition that dictates what color the bride or groom wears. Outside the groom's home, the bride's hair is arranged in a style appropriate for marriage, and she puts on her jewelry, which signifies that she is a married woman.

Afterward, the woman enters the groom's home. The couple then bow before Buddha and before the groom's family. A family elder gives a blessing, and then they celebrate with a feast. Throughout the wedding process, members of both families engage in poetic contests, usually with the bride's family questioning the ability of the groom to take care of their daughter. These contests or games involve good-natured teasing, testing the groom's knowledge of folklore and history. The groom is assisted by his best man and any others in his entourage. The groom may even be required to undergo a few trials to demonstrate his worthiness, such as breaking the neck of the sheep that will be served at the wedding feast.

At the *ger* of the groom, additional prayers are said, and usually, the groom receives a new set of clothes from his father, which marks a change in the groom's status. Other rituals exist but vary greatly from region to region. In some cases, there is a ritual that consists of introducing the bride to the family dog. This a rather important ritual, considering the well-known ferocity of Mongolian dogs toward strangers. During this, the groom's father also says a prayer for the bride and dog. At the end of the ritual, the bride's mother then leads her to her new home, where the celebration takes place.

Modern weddings take place in a so-called wedding palace. These are somewhat similar to wedding chapels throughout the United States. Here the bride wears a white wedding dress, while the groom dons a tuxedo. A civil servant performs the service and the marriage is completed with the signing of appropriate forms. Although bride prices and dowries are a thing of the past, weddings in the countryside and in urban areas have replaced these with lavish gifts. Christian weddings have also arrived in Mongolia with the adoption of the new religion. Still, most couples tend to follow the traditional path.

In any circumstance, the wedding ceremony is not as elaborate as American weddings. The emphasis is on the celebration afterward, which is more like a party than an American-style wedding reception. Naturally, this includes drinking vast amounts of *airag*, vodka, and, more recently, beer. Mounds of food are present, with stacks of *buuz*, *khuushoor*, slabs of cheese, boiled mutton, sweets, and other Mongolian foods. This is one reason why August is the most popular month for weddings: the lambing season is over and white (dairy) foods are in abundance, so there is plenty of food to serve.

Often, all of the guests take turns singing songs or making a speech about the happy couple or about marriage in general. While this is going on, a bowl of *airag* is passed around. When the bowl is handed to a person, this signifies that it is his or her turn not only to drink, but also to sing. Everyone is expected to sing, and typically, as almost anyone who has visited a karaoke bar knows, after enough liquor, anyone will sing. Traditionally, the celebration could last three days, although this is rare today.

FAMILY LIFE

While Mongolia historically has been somewhat of a patriarchal society, matriarchal households were not uncommon. In certain periods, such as in the nineteenth century, when approximately 45 percent of the male population were lamas, matriarchal households became quite common. In the twentieth century, women also entered the urban workforce, even though the Communist government idealized the idea of motherhood and raising children. Part of the problem was the simple lack of an adequate labor supply. Women simply could find work if they so desired. Also, socialism had conflicting messages about the status of women. While the government promoted motherhood, it also told women that they were equals to men in society in all areas. Thus traditional ideas of being a homemaker and mother fell apart. Other issues have appeared, as described in the previous section.

One of the most difficult problems facing young urban couples is finding living space. Apartments can be tough to find. Those coming from the countryside into the city simply erect a *ger*. Another issue is child care. If one member, usually the wife, stays at home, then it is not a problem; however, for single mothers or mothers without relatives nearby, child care must be found. During the Communist period, child care was more accessible and free or inexpensive. The market economy has changed that. For many Mongolians, it is simply too expensive, and some are forced to leave their children at home alone while they work.

In the countryside, family life remains more traditional than in the urban centers, with women taking care of the household as well as caring for young children. Rural couples rarely have difficulties in establishing a household with a *ger* but do face other problems. The foremost include education and health services, as they often can be quite remote from any town centers. Although wind and solar power generators have alleviated the problem, obstacles in communication also exist. Most families live fairly close together. It is not uncommon to see two or three *gers* together, which helps immensely. Typically, elderly family members will live with or near their children, helping with some of the tasks as well as teaching the others.

As noted earlier, the Communist government greatly promoted having children. Birth in any society is a momentous occasion, but unlike in many countries, Mongolians do not do much to prepare for the newborn, such as a holding baby shower: it is considered bad luck. Mongolians are born with a blue spot at the base of the spine. It resembles a bruise but fades over the course of the child's first year. Infants spend much of the first few months of their lives tightly swaddled. Although this practice has become customary, it is primarily due to necessity because of the cold. Breast-feeding is the most common form of nourishment for infants. The father also cuts the shape of a fox from felt and hangs it above the baby's bed as a charm against evil spirits and nightmares. Although this is derived from old shamanistic practices, it remains a time-honored tradition. Naming the child often is an esoteric practice. The parents, if religious, visit a lama to select an auspicious name. The father will then whisper it three times, three being a lucky number, into the infant's ear. The naming of the child and his or her first haircut are momentous occasions, as discussed in detail in chapter 9, as they are derived from time-honored traditions.

As in most societies, divorce is frowned on but permitted. Much like in the rest of the world, poverty tends to be a pivotal factor in divorces or the breaking of a home. Although not a cure-all, if one family member has gained a well-paying job, he or she then shoulders the responsibility of supporting the family or sharing the wealth. In many ways, this is a carryover from tribal society, in which one of the responsibilities of the wealthier members of the tribe was to assist the less fortunate. Still, the rate of divorce has increased due to unemployment, alcoholism, and domestic abuse.

Since the fall of Communism, Mongolia has undergone a number of changes. The transition to a market economy has not been easy. Indeed, it has undermined educational, medical, and a number of other services. Probably the group that has lost the most due to capitalism is women. A curious side effect of this is that among Christian converts, women comprise the majority. As discussed before, many convert simply because they find the missionaries to be sober, employed, and not abusive—a common theme for many of Mongolia's ills.

A few moments are life changing for a family. These moments are typically birth, marriage, and death. In Mongolia, nomadic, Buddhist, and Western traditions all play a part. Prior to 1950, the most common method of funerary practice was exposure—simply taking the body onto the steppe and leaving it for animals. In 1955 the government banned the practice as a holdover of Buddhist influence.

The 1921 revolution and Soviet influences introduced the Western practice of burial to Mongolia. Although officially an atheist state, the Soviet Union could not break from centuries of Christian practice of burying the dead. In the 1920s, a cemetery was opened outside Ulaanbaatar to bury key members of the revolutionary government, including Sukhebaatar. Sukhebaatar, however, was later exhumed and entombed with Choibalsan on the edge of Sukhebaatar Square. Choibalsan was to be embalmed and displayed like Lenin in Moscow, but the process failed. Overall, the burials followed Russian practice in terms of form and aesthetics (i.e., styles of headstone). This changed in the 1970s as headstones of natural stone came into vogue. Vertical script inscriptions and traditional symbols adorned the headstones. Some people also place small metal *gers* on the tombstone as well.

While the government could regulate the form of burial, it could not eliminate other traditions that carry on today. Many burials involved consulting a lama or the use of astrology (which the government also frowned on as superstition) for determining when and where the body should be buried or left—exposure, despite government prohibitions, continued.

With the end of Communism, the ban on exposure of the dead ended. Herders returned to exposure, though in truth, many never abandoned it, despite government prohibitions. Most urban citizens, however, continue to bury the dead. Grave sites today are more uniform in their headstones but with more variation in the inscriptions on the stone. In addition to the name and dates of the deceased's life, symbols of the person's life adorn the stone. These can be Buddhist symbols, secular markings such as ones associated with the person's occupation, or even a Christian cross.

NOTES

1. Morris Rossabi, *Modern Mongolia: From Khans to Commissars to Capitalists* (Berkeley: University of California Press, 2005), 151.

2. Ibid.

3. Ibid., 152.

4. Nomin Lhagvasuren, "Uniting for Men," *Transitions Online*, June 23, 2003. http://www.tol.cz/look/TOL/article.tpl?IdLanguage=1&IdPublication= 4&NrIssue=47&NrSection=2&NrArticle=9883.

8

Festivals and Leisure

FESTIVALS

NAADAM IS THE biggest festival in Mongolia and is held on July 11 and 12. It consists of the three so-called manly sports—wrestling, horse racing, and archery. *Naadam* literally means "game," and thus the Naadam is often referred to as the National Holiday Naadam to distinguish it from local *naadams*, which can have from one hundred to one thousand participants. Unless specified otherwise, in this discussion, the term *Naadam* will always refer to the National Holiday Naadam.

The origins of Naadam date back to the seventeenth century, when the *eriin gurwan naadam*, or "three manly games," took place at the completion of summer religious ceremonies. The first one took place in honor of the Jebtsundamba Khutukhtu in 1697. Since then, it has become a major event in Mongolia.

Originally, the games did not have a set date, but in 1912, after Mongolia gained independence from the Qing Empire, the games were moved to the last lunar month of the summer (July–August). The games also came to symbolize an honor not only for the Jebtsundamba Khutukhtu, but also for the state. After the 1921 Revolution, the symbolism of the games changed again. The Communists filtered out much of the religious content and finally abandoned all of it in 1923. Naadams connected with religious celebration, however, continued until the government purge of religion in the 1930s.

In 1922, Sukhebaatar began a new *naadam*, the army games that took place on July 11 to commemorate the anniversary of the revolution's success. This date also marked the separation of the secular and religious calendars, as the army games and anniversary of the revolution were now tied to a Western calendar rather than the religious lunar calendar. By 1924, July 11 became an official national holiday, and the army games became the National Holiday Naadam.

Prior to World War II, most of the games took place in the countryside outside Ulaanbaatar and other cities. With the building spree after the war, the games were moved into stadiums, for the most part. Athletes still wore traditional dress during the ceremonies and often during the games themselves. During the Communist period, the games were also used not only to commemorate the revolution, but also to honor great leaders. Thus, rather than the original honor given to the Jebtsundamba Khutukhtu, now Marx, Lenin, and Sukhebaatar received veneration as the participants marched through Sukhebaatar Square. It also had a similar feel to Soviet parades in which military equipment paraded past leaders, in addition to the athletes.

Although the athletes still proceed past Sukhebaatar and Choibalsin's tombs through Sukhebaatar Square, the Communist symbolism has vanished. Instead, an honor guard in costumes from the period of Chinggis Khan parade past along with a white horsehair banner. The white banner symbolizes peace. Actors also carry out skits from Mongolia's history. Although the stands are still filled for the games, many people now watch it on television, a stark contrast with the Communist period, during which attendance was mandatory.

The other important Mongolian holiday is Tsagaan Sar, literally the "White Month," or New Year's Day, which has been celebrated since the time of the Mongol Empire. Although Mongolia uses the Gregorian calendar, the lunar calendar is also used due to tradition and religious practice, and thus Tsagaan Sar usually falls in February or early March. As with most New Year celebrations, Tsagaan Sar focuses on happiness and an optimistic future, and the color white is considered an auspicious color in Mongolian tradition. During the holiday and days preceding it, offerings are made to ancestral spirits or in honor of their memories. Blessings are made. Owing to Communist oppression of the holiday and a decline in religiosity, the holiday has changed considerably over the years. Now, in addition to being a holiday that is both a thanksgiving and a looking forward to a good year, it has become a holiday for visiting family and friends.

A central part of the celebration is food and *buuz*, devoured in great quantities, followed by liberal doses of vodka. The *buuz* serves another purpose: families often put a silver coin in one *buuz*, and according to tradition, whoever finds it will have prosperity in the coming year. At family gatherings in the countryside, the largest sheep in the flock, or in the city, the largest a family can buy, is cooked and eaten. It becomes, like the Thanksgiving turkey, a point of pride. The importance of food is marked in the preparations for the holiday, which often begin a month before the holiday.

During the Communist period, Tsagaan Sar came under attack. During the religious purges, the celebration of Tsagaan Sar was criticized, although during some years the criticism decreased. During World War II, herders received government approval to celebrate the holiday—perhaps because Josef Stalin, occupied with the Nazis, was too busy to notice or to care. In 1954 the holiday was declared a workday and the government again began a crackdown against it. Nonetheless, their efforts failed. While not willing to admit defeat, the government found a solution by making Tsagaan Sar "Collective Herders' Day" in 1960. Not until 1988 did Tsagaan Sar receive official recognition as a national holiday.

Overall, Mongolia does not have an abundant number of holidays or fes- tivals, but there are several that merit attention. One of the most important festivals is Maidar Ergekh, which is usually held in August. The exact date varies due to the lunar festival. Maidar Ergekh is a Buddhist festival that drew thousands of lamas and spectators before the 1921 Revolution. After the rise of the Communist government, the festival was banned. Since 1990, though, the festival has made a modest comeback, and the celebration takes place at a different monastery every year. During the celebration, monks perform *tsam* dances and parade a statue of the Maitreya Buddha (the future or messiah Buddha) through the monastery grounds. Another Buddhist holiday is Ikh Duichin, the Buddha's birthday, which takes place on May 18. Although it is celebrated at all of the monasteries, the main celebration takes place at Gan- dantegchinlen Khiid in Ulaanbaatar.

Some new festivals have also appeared, primarily as tourist attractions for both national and international tourists. While many appear close to anniver- saries of the Mongol Empire, some more permanent regional festivals have appeared. These include the Yak Festival, held in Arkhangai Aimag in early August; the Eagle Festival in the Bayan Olgii Aimag, held in early October; and the Camel Festival in Omnogov Aimag, held a week after Tsagaan Sar (February–March). The Eagle Festival is a Mongolian Kazakh festival in which displays of hunting with eagles are performed. In addition, there are tradi- tional horse races and archery contests as well. Another interesting one is the Airag Festival in Dundov Aimag, held in late August.

THE THREE MANLY GAMES

The main sports in Mongolia traditionally have been the manly sports— wrestling, horse racing, and archery. These all are performed at the Naadam festival but are also conducted at other points in the year. Sports have always played an important role in Mongolia in providing an identity. Sports clubs and organizations can be found everywhere, and Mongolia, despite its small population, has performed quite well in world competitions. It joined the International Olympic Committee in 1962 and has participated in several Olympic Games as well as in Asian and regional events. Although Mongolian athletes have done well in a variety of events, most of the medals that come back to Mongolia are awarded in wrestling.

Wrestling

Wrestling is the primary sport of Mongolia. During televised competitions, traffic can literally come to a halt. Unlike in other parts of the world, there are no weight divisions. Thus contestants could be the same weight or separated by a hundred pounds. The wrestlers, known as *bokh*, begin all rounds of a match in a standing position. The objective is to force one's opponent to lose his balance and fall or force him to touch the ground in some manner, and only the feet and the palms of the hand may touch the ground. Although kicking and punching are illegal, a wrestler may use his feet or legs to gain leverage or trip his opponent. Traditionally, the matches go on until someone falls or another part of the body, other than the legal parts, touches the ground. Thus it is conceivable for the match to last for hours. Recently, however, some thirty-minute time limits have been imposed on Naadam matches and elsewhere, such as at the Wrestling Palace in Ulaanbaatar. If the match is not settled within the time limit, then it goes into overtime, with the leading wrestler able to take a better position. The matches do not take place in a defined ring, but always in a grassy area. As there is no ring, the contestants have considerable latitude in their movements, although wrestlers tend to always have their hands on their opponents.

Unlike Western wrestlers, Mongolian wrestlers do not wear singlets or tights. Typically, Mongolian wrestlers wear a *zodog*, which is a tight-fitting jacket or open shirt. It basically looks like two sleeves with cloth running across the upper back and shoulders, attaching them. A rope ties the *zodog* together in the front. The purpose of the *zodog* is to give the wrestlers something to grip on an otherwise bare upper body. The wrestlers also wear a *shuudag*, or the equivalent of trunks or briefs. The outfit is completed by the standard upturned Mongolian boots. Before the match, the wrestler wears a conical hat, often with a ceremonial scarf of *khadag* attached to it. Their coaches hold this for them during the match. Owing to the wrestling garb, women have traditionally been excluded from participating. Some legends promote the idea that the use of the *zodog* and *shuudag* was a deliberate choice to exclude women. Today, however, some women wrestle by wearing a shirt underneath their *zodog*.

Before and after the matches, there are standard rituals that the wrestler must perform. He circles the field where the matches take place in a clockwise fashion and makes a libation of milk to the gods and local spirits. There is also a ceremonial dance called the "eagle," or *garuda*, a bird from Buddhist mythology, that the wrestler performs after his coach chants words of praise for the wrestler. The dance is performed by hopping and flapping the arms. This is usually performed around a flagpole topped with a tribal or national flag. The dance must be performed before the wrestler touches the ground with his hands.

After a match is completed, the losing wrestler passes under the winner's arms. The winner also slaps the loser on the buttocks, retrieves his hat, and tips it to his opponent. He then performs the eagle dance again. Then he goes to his coach and retrieves a bag holding bits of cheese, which the wrestler flings. This serves as an offering to the spirits and gods and also as a thank-you to the fans.

The tournaments are single elimination and are organized based on seeds. Thus lower-ranked wrestlers face the top ones. Winners of their matches move to the next round. These tournaments vary in size, but the Naadam matches have had up to 512 wrestlers in the match.

The wrestlers receive ranks that are centuries old and based on their performance, although two ranks—hawk and *garuda*—were added recently in 2003. The tournaments can last for eleven or twelve rounds, although fewer rounds are more common, with winners of some rounds receiving a rank. The winner of the fifth receives the *nachin*, or "falcon," title. In the sixth round, one can win the *khartsgai*, or "hawk," title. In the seventh and eighth rounds, the winners are awarded with the *zaan*, or "elephant," rank. The ninth-round winner receives the *garuda* rank—this is a mythical bird from Buddhist mythology. The winners of the tenth and eleventh rounds are awarded the *arslan*, or "lion," rank. The highest rank obtainable is that of *avarga*, or "titan"; however, one must win a tournament twice. Afterward, the titan title may become more elaborate, with tournament victories at Naadam or other national tournaments. Thus one may see an "invincible titan," and so on. The highest possible rank is the *ulsyn avarga*, or "titan of the state"—the national champion. Owing to the popularity of Mongolian wrestling, the best wrestlers, like most sports heroes, are also immortalized in posters on the walls of their fans.

Mongolian wrestlers have excelled in other forms of wrestling. Mongolia's first Olympic medal came in 1968, when J. Monkhbat took the silver for his weight class in freestyle wrestling in Mexico City. This success has carried over into other martial arts such as sumo wrestling, which will be discussed later, and judo. In the latter, Tuvshinbayar Naidan, known as Tuvshee, won Mongolia's first Olympic gold medal in the men's 100 kilogram weight class during the 2008 summer Olympics, causing fireworks and celebrations as Mongolians poured into the streets in Ulaanbaatar.

Horse Racing

Horse racing in Mongolia is quite different from races elsewhere, as they range from five to thirty kilometers (3.1–19 miles). For the race, the horses are divided into five age categories: two-year-olds, four-year-olds, five-year-olds, over fives, and stallions. Most of the horses are geldings; mares never race. The categories of horse run different lengths of race courses. The two-year-old horses ran a five-kilometer course, while only those horses that were over six years old ran the full thirty-kilometer race. Since 1997, however, during Naadam, the horses over six years old run a twenty-five-kilometer race (15.5 miles). Prior to 1997, the Naadam race for the older horses was twenty-eight kilometers (17.3 miles). The five-year-old horses race for twenty-two kilometers (13.6 miles), while the four-year-old horses race for eighteen kilometers (11 miles). The three-year-old horses race for sixteen kilometers (10 miles), and the two-year-old horses race for twelve kilometers (7.5 miles). Although horse racing is one of the three manly sports, the jockeys are almost always children, boys and girls. Adults occasionally race, but these races attract little attention, while hundreds of family members and fans anxiously await the conclusion of the other races.

The jockeys sit atop felt pads, rather than a normal saddle. Usually, these do not have stirrups. The choice in riding equipment focuses more on the comfort of the horse than of the rider. Still, over the long distance, the pads offer more comfort than the leather and wooden saddle that most Mongolians use for normal riding. During the Naadam races, however, regular saddles and stirrups are used. The jockeys also wear appropriate uniforms—colored shirts and hats. During the Naadam races, well over a thousand horses take part.

After some rituals of procession and song, the races take place through the steppe, rather than on a track; thus the riders must contend not only with the distance, but also with hills, rivers, and uneven ground. In addition, the horses run at full speed, approximately thirty-five kilometers (21.7 miles) per hour, the whole race. Even though children ranging from five to twelve years old participate, it is a dangerous sport for both horse and rider. Riders have fallen from horses, and horses have collapsed from exhaustion. For this reason, some race officials also ride along to take care of or prevent injuries as well as to locate runaway horses. Ultimately, while speed is necessary, endurance is the prized feature of a horse. The length of the race demonstrates that the race is more about the horse than about the skill of its rider, and this is reflected in the awards. Indeed, as long as the horse crosses the finish line, the race is considered completed—the jockey need not be present. As a horse crosses the line, the judge sings a song praising it, anoints the head and flanks of the horse with *airag*, and gives the rider some cheese crumbles. The judge then sips some of the *airag* and passes it to the jockey. The winning horse receives the title of "Forehead of the Ten Thousand Race Horse." Medals are awarded to the five runners-up, who also undergo the ritual that the winner undergoes. Oddly, the person who finishes last also receives a medal and is honored as "Rich Belly" in word and song.

Archery

Archery is the final manly sport and is performed by men and women. Although the old techniques of Mongolian bow-making have been lost, and thus bows are not as powerful as those used in the time of Chinggis Khan, the composite bow, constructed from layers of horn and wood, is still used. Nonetheless, even in the Qing period, bows had a pull weight ranging from 80 to 130 pounds. The bows of the Mongol Empire had a maximum pull of 160, although most probably fit in the same range as the Qing period. A few artisans can still replicate the process used in the Qing period.

The bow itself usually is about four feet in length, although some extend to six feet when strung. Unstrung, the bow takes on more of a C or crescent shape. Made from horn and layered with wood and glue, the bow is then wrapped in tendons, which not only hold the bow together but, as they dry, shrink, and further compress the layers. The bowstrings are made from silk or leather wrapped in tendons. The archer shoots arrows normally constructed of pine, birch, or willow, with fletching made preferably from eagle or falcon feathers.

Mongolian archery techniques are quite different from Western styles. The arrow is placed on the right side of the bow and is held in place by the thumb and forefinger, unlike in the West, where the arrow is held by the forefinger and middle finger. Whereas in the West, the string is pulled by the forefinger, middle finger, and ring finger, Mongolians pull the string with their thumbs with the aid of a thumb ring. This device is made from either polished stone or leather. When performed properly, the string slides off of the thumb with little friction.

Mongolian archery contests also have another unusual feature: singing. As the archers take aim, their coaches and the umpires begin to hum. Rather than being a distraction, the archers find that it helps them concentrate. Then, when the arrow hits the target, the umpires yell "*Uukhai!*" and raise their arms in a circular motion, with hands pointed to the sky.

Rather than shooting at an upright target, Mongolian archery contests focus on shooting at a target that is flat on the ground, perhaps a carryover from the medieval period, when a common tactic was shower shooting. This consisted of shooting at a specific location rather than at a target, thus creating a kill zone.[1]

The targets consist of small, upright cylinders placed in groups several meters across. They are usually painted white, yellow, or red, each with a point value, with red being worth the most. The key for the archer is determining the trajectory of his or her shot. Men shoot from about seventy-five meters (82 yards), while women shoot from sixty meters (65.5 yards). The men shoot forty arrows and must score at least fifteen points to advance to the next round, while women shoot twenty arrows and must score at least thirteen points. Curiously, men and women use the same type and draw of bow, although women only began participating in the sport in the 1960s. The winner receives the title of *Mergen*, or "Sharpshooter."

Another game that exists today, but that used to be part of *naadam* games in the nineteenth century, also takes place from a standing position. In this game, the archers shoot at a target consisting of a pyramid or line of targets, usually made of leather cylinders. The idea is to knock the targets over, much like shooting at cans with a pellet or BB gun. This contest is known as the *khana tsuvaa* and can be performed by teams. Usually, a team consists of ten or twelve archers. The archers begin at a set range, but if an archer fails to knock down any of the targets, the team must take another step backward for each failed attempt.

While not part of Naadam, other archery games exist and are derived from older practices associated with military drills. Rather than standing and firing, these involve shooting arrows from the back of a horse. One such contest used today in Mongolia is the *bombog namnakh*, or "ball shooting," in which three leather balls are mounted on poles in intervals. The mounted archer attempts to hit the first one while advancing on it, then the second as he rides by it. The final ball is targeted after the archer has ridden past it using the Parthian shot, which is performed by turning the torso backward and shooting. The most difficult part of the exercise is controlling the horse solely with the knees, as both hands are occupied with the bow and the reins are tied to the saddle.[2] Other games also consist of firing at sheepskins or bull skins stretched over a frame. This is known as *sarampai kharvaa*.

Curiously, the Communist government both revived and also ended the revival of archery as a sport. With the spread of firearms in the nineteenth century, the use of bows in hunting dwindled. As a result, archery contests suffered. In 1922 the military held a *naadam* and included an archery contest as one of the competitions. This began the revival of archery in Mongolia. In the 1940s, however, it was discouraged and even banned from the Naadam festival. It was still practiced, but often covertly. It was not until the 1950s that archery regained government approval.

NEW SPORTS

Other sports have gained popularity in Mongolia, although none of them rivals the three manly sports. Although soccer, or rather, football, is still the most popular sport in the world, it has not gained the same popularity in Mongolia. By far, the so-called new sports that have gained adherents primarily have been martial arts. Judo, boxing, and particularly sumo wrestling have grown in popularity not only in participation, but also as spectator sports. In judo and boxing, Mongolian athletes have performed exceptionally well and are competitive at all levels. In sumo wrestling, however, Mongolian athletes are emerging as a dominant group, comprising approximately half of the foreign sumo wrestlers.

Sumo Wrestling

Although sumo wrestling is the traditional sport of Japan, foreigners have participated since 1970. Prior to the 1990s, however, few enjoyed great success. Akebono, a Hawaiian-born wrestler, attained the rank of *yokozuna*, the highest rank, in 1993, becoming the first foreigner to do so. Since then, others have become *yokozuna*, a difficult task because promotion to the highest rank requires not only winning two consecutive championships, but also demonstrating power and skill while wrestling. In addition, there is a more subjective and sometimes contentious issue of *hinkaku*, which translates roughly as "dignity and grace." Quite simply, the wrestler maintains the proper decorum befitting the title of *yokozuna*. As a result, some sumo wrestlers have failed to gain the title of *yokozuna*. In the past, there have been allegations that some wrestlers did not achieve *yokozuna* status because they were foreigners. This is no longer the case, although only four have been granted the status of *yokozuna*. Two of them are Mongolian—Asashoryu and Hakuho, as they are called in Japan—and they are the only active *yokozuna*.

Mongolians entered the sumo world in 1991, when Japanese sumo trainers ventured into Mongolia to look for someone who might be suitable for training. The Japanese scouts observed almost two hundred Mongolians and selected six to take back to Japan. Most of them failed to make it due to a variety of problems, including homesickness. Davaagiin Batbayar, however, stayed, although he almost returned home as well after only six months of training. In Japan, he adopted the name of "Kyokushuzan" and became the first successful Mongolian sumo wrestler. He retired in 2006 but has contributed much to Mongolia. He was the inspiration for many other Mongolians to seek a career in sumo wrestling. Indeed, the origins of Mongolia's amateur sumo tournaments are probably due to his success in the late 1990s.

After Chinggis Khan, the best-known Mongolian outside Mongolia is likely Asashoryu. Dolgorsürengiin Dagvadorj, as he is known in Mongolia, entered the sport in 1999 and was not the first Mongolian to try to transfer his Mongolian wrestling skills into a new medium. Two other Mongolians had achieved a respectable level of success in Japan. Asashoryu's success, however, dwarfs that of most wrestlers. By 2002 he obtained the rank of *ozeki*, the second highest rank, and by the end of January 2003, Asashoryu won the rank of *yokozuna*. By 2008 Asashoryu had won twenty-two tournaments and remains one of the most dominating competitors in the history of sumo.

Asashoryu's career has not been without controversy, as indicated by the sobriquet of the "Bad Boy of Sumo." The fact that he is not Japanese and yet is so dominant, and that he refuses to adopt Japanese nationality, irritates some Japanese fans. Yet his habit of not conforming to the code of conduct that is expected from not only the *yokozuna* but from all sumo wrestlers, has caused him trouble. This included some conduct both in the ring and outside the ring. Early in his career, he violated the sensibility of *bushido*, chivalrous notions in Japanese martial arts, by raising his fist in victory. In addition, he gained a reputation as a womanizer and is seen frequently at nightclubs. In public, he typically appears in a Western-style suit, rather than in the traditional kimono that sumo wrestlers wear. The key moment that cemented his notoriety occurred in Mongolia. In July 2007 the Japan Sumo Association (JSA) granted Asashoryu permission to miss an exhibition tour to recover from elbow and back injuries. Unfortunately, he was spotted on television playing soccer in a charity tournament in Ulaanbaatar. The JSA suspended him from the autumn tournaments and cut his pay by 30 percent, along with that of his trainer. As one report put it, the JSA effectively put him under house arrest.[3]

Considering that Japan and Mongolia have established very warm relations since 1990 and that Japan is one of the largest donors to and investors in Mongolia, what happened next is a bit surprising. After the news of Asashoryu's suspension reached Mongolia, protests occurred outside the Japanese embassy, and diplomats from both countries talked. Asashoryu's success now represented more than an athletic contest. Some Japanese businesses worried that their investments in Mongolian minerals and other areas might suffer from a backlash. Some also accused the JSA of trying to eliminate Mongolian wrestlers, who recently had begun to dominate the sport. In August 2007 the JSA reinstated him, but it is likely that punishment for future transgressions, like Damocles' sword, hangs over Asashoryu's head. The JSA did grant Asashoryu permission to return to Mongolia, however, to deal with severe depression. In his absence, the other Mongolian *yokozuna*, Hakuho, has continued the trend of Mongolian sumo domination.

Hakuho, or Monkhbatyn Davaajargal, comes from a line of successful wrestlers. His father, Jigjid Monkhbat, won the silver medal in freestyle wrestling in the 1968 Olympics. Davaajargal joined the sumo ranks in 2000 only with the help of fellow Mongolian sumo wrestler Kyokushuzan. He needed intercession due to being grossly underweight, at only sixty-two kilograms (136 pounds) at age fifteen. With the help of Kyokushuzan, Davaajargal entered sumo training and took the name of "Hakuho" while steadily growing in size and skill. By 2001 he entered his first professional tournament and, by 2006, attained the rank of *ozeki*. In 2007 he became the sixty-ninth *yokozuna*. One of his major victories included defeating Asashoryu in 2008.

Owing to the success of these wrestlers, sumo wrestling has gained popularity in Mongolia. Amateur bouts are held, and Kyokushuzan Batbayar, as Kyokushuzan is called in the Mongolian press, is now the president of the Mongolian Sumo Wrestling Federation. While it is doubtful that it will replace wrestling in the hearts of Mongolians, it is possibly the most popular nonnative spectator sport.

Basketball

Although soccer, or football, is the most popular team sport in the world, it has not risen to the same level of popularity in Mongolia as elsewhere. Although Mongolia fields a team to keep at the international level, a different team sport is on the rise: basketball. Even in the countryside, one can find a basketball hoop attached to a solitary pole and children playing the sport, with their family's *ger* and livestock in the background. There is even a Mongolian Basketball Association (MBA), and one player, Sharavjamts "Shark" Tserenjanhor, a seven-footer, played for the world-renowned Harlem Globetrotters in 2002 and 2003 as their first Asian player. Before being signed by the Globetrotters in 2001, he played in the MBA for four seasons and is known as the "Michael Jordan of Mongolia."

He was discovered by Dale Brown, who also discovered a then-thirteen-year-old Shaquille O'Neal on a military base in Germany. When Brown saw Tserenjanhor play in a game, the seven-footer's ball handling impressed him. Brown immediately envisioned him attending a National Collegiate Athletic Association (NCAA) Division I school in America, but to his chagrin, Tserenjanhor was twenty-seven years old, past the age limit for NCAA eligibility.[4] As a result of his age, it was unlikely that Tserenjanhor could develop to play at the National Basketball Association (NBA) level. Still, Brown called Mannie Jackson, the owner of the Harlem Globetrotters, who allowed him to try out. The Shark made the team. Although he no longer plays professional basketball, it was still quite an adventure. When asked by a reporter for the magazine

Sports Illustrated if it was his dream to play in the NBA or on the Globetrotters, the modest Tserenjanhor replied, "My dream was to someday watch the Globetrotters."[5]

NOTES

1. Timothy May, *The Mongol Art of War* (Yardley, PA: Westholme, 2007), 72.

2. "Old Songs of Arrows," *Mongolia Today* 7 (2002), http://www.mongoliatoday.com/issue/7/archery.html.

3. "The Masher from Mongolia," *The Economist*, August 29, 2007.

4. Albert Chen, "The Mongolian Shark," *Sports Illustrated*, November 5, 2001, http://vault.sportsillustrated.cnn.com/vault/article/magazine/MAG1024192/1/index.htm.

5. Ibid.

9

Social Customs and Lifestyle

WHILE THE PASTORAL nomadic lifestyle defines much of the character of Mongolia, Mongolia's nomadic population is shrinking. Although roughly half of the population lives in a traditional *ger*, many are not nomads, and the *gers* can be found in the cities as well as the countryside, particularly on the outskirts of the cities. Gradually, these are being replaced by homes. The other half of the population tends to live in apartments, although since 1990, individual Western-style homes have become popular. The rearing of children and many other customs remain very traditional in the countryside, and certain customs still permeate Mongolian culture, whether in the countryside or in the city.

RURAL TRADITIONS

Many of the day-to-day Mongolian customs ultimately are derived from living on the steppe. One such custom is hospitality. In most instances, one can visit a *ger* and find a warm welcome. This is common with most nomadic traditions often in such remote areas simply because of the rationale that if you help others, you will find help when you need it. While these customs are alive and well in the countryside, many of them are still practiced in the towns. Many of the rural traditions also include eating protocol.

Anyone invited into a *ger* can expect to be fed something and, at the very least, served some tea. Guests should always accept food or drink with the right hand. It is assumed that the left hand is usually involved with bodily functions. One should use the left hand with food only to support the right hand, but it should never touch the bowl or food. With tea, one should sip it first before setting it down. It is expected that the guest eat or drink at least a small amount. Not to do so would offend the host. Once a meal starts, an individual sits with his or her feet together or underneath him or her but never with the feet sticking out or with legs crossed. One also should never point with a knife or pass it with the blade first. It is also considered bad luck, and rude, to step on the doorstep when entering or exiting a *ger* (or anywhere). This tradition can be found in reports left by travelers in the Mongol Empire.

Another tradition related to the *ger* is the practice of many Mongolians of keeping a handsaw tucked between the wooden poles that support the roof and the felt. The saw is to ensure that an evil person does not enter the home. A second tradition related to protecting the home is the so-called wolf snout rope. This is a rope wound underneath the roof poles, and one end is tied into a knot that resembles a wolf's head. The snout of the wolf faces the door. According to tradition, if any evil enters the *ger*, the spirit of the wolf will destroy it. Not all Mongolians truly believe that the saw or the rope protects the *ger*, but they have become such strong traditions that many maintain the practices just because they and their parents have always done so.

There is also protocol for sitting in a *ger*. The doorway of the *ger* always faces south, and the husband traditionally sits on the western side facing the doorway, while the wife's side is on the east. The wife is also near the hearth, which is in the center, to tend the fire and make tea. Children sit closer to the door. Guests are often allowed to sit at the northern end of the *ger*, which is considered the most honored place. It is also where there is often a small shrine with a statue of Buddha, or perhaps sutras wrapped in silk. At the very least, there are pictures of friends and families as well as a few prized possessions on display. More often, though, guests will sit on the western side of the *ger*, and the family will sit on the eastern side.

There are several traditions associated with pregnant women and young children. For instance, one social taboo is to frighten a pregnant woman, utter any curse words, or speak loudly in her presence. Also, when walking, one should never cross in front of her. After the child is born, it is common not to cut the child's hair until he or she is three years old or even older. This idea stems from shamanic practice. In shamanism, illness is thought to be caused by evil spirits. There are certain spirits who target children; however, they are gender-specific. In other words, certain spirits can only harm boys or girls, but not the other. Thus, by allowing the hair to grow, all of the children look similar, which confuses the evil spirits. Further steps are also taken by calling the child a name like *Nerguai*, or "No-name." Again, the spirits are confused and will leave the child alone.

The first haircut for a child occurs at different ages—for boys, from age three to five, and for girls, from age four to six. This is an important rite of passage and thus involves an elaborate ceremony. Before the ceremony can even be organized, an astrologer is consulted to find an auspicious day, usually in the summer or autumn. Once the day is chosen, the ceremony is prepared. The child will wear his or her best clothes and attend the ceremony with friends and family. During the ceremony, each guest cuts a small lock of hair from the forehead. Should an important relative be absent, a lock will be saved for that person at another time. By the end of the ceremony, only a small lock on the forehead remains. The mother then takes all of the cut hair and places it in a silk cloth. This serves not only as a memento, but is also thought to be a charm to give the child a long and joyful life. After the hair-cutting ceremony ends, the child receives some presents and the guests sing songs praising the child. The child also receives a major gift in the form of a young animal such as a lamb or colt.

The importance of hair does not end at childhood. In Mongolia, one does not touch the head or hair of other people without permission. It is viewed as a major offense. Indeed, many people (rural or urban) do not get their hair cut until they check astrological tables to see if it is an auspicious day.

Children are taught to be respectful and to have good manners as well as to take care of livestock, as depicted in chapter 2. While nomadic children attend school, they also gain another education at home. Beginning at about age two or three, children learn seasons, colors, directions, and the names of common objects. Gradually, they also play games to improve memorization. Girls will also learn to sew, while boys learn carpentry and how to repair the *ger* and other items used by the family, such as wagons, or other gear used with the horses.

URBAN LIFE

Most of the population lives in the city, mainly in high-rise apartments. These are typically two- to three-room affairs. Like many apartments in America, many of these, since 1997, are not privatized as condominiums. Although more people are purchasing single-family homes, there are also plenty of people who live in the so-called *ger* districts, which will be discussed later. Modern conveniences, such as televisions, radios, kitchen appliances, and laundry appliances, are commonplace for most urban households, except among the poor.

Life in the countryside may be difficult, but in urban areas, difficulties are compounded simply by the number of people living in a relatively small space. Even almost twenty years after the collapse of Communism, the transition to the new market economy and life has been difficult. Many have succeeded and become quite wealthy. As a result, many have flocked from the countryside to the towns, particularly Ulaanbaatar. Unfortunately, not everyone is successful. A sizeable portion of the population is mired in poverty and lives in shantytowns of *gers* or small houses slapped together out of scrap wood and brick on a plot of enclosed land. Many remain in their *gers* simply because its felt covering makes it much warmer in the winter. Others live in the house during the other seasons and erect their *ger* for the winter months. Many of these districts lack basic utilities, and people live much like they would on the steppe. In the *ger* districts, it is not uncommon to see livestock wandering the streets. Families still use dried dung for fuel. Water is a different matter, as one cannot simply go to a river or well. One must purchase ration cards, usually at the State Department store, and then turn them in at another location to fill up containers of water.

Pensions that have carried over from the Communist government are insufficient in the new economy. Unemployment tends to be high, especially for those with a low level of education. One of the largest issues is alcoholism, which often leads to other difficulties such as domestic abuse and other violent crimes. While alcoholism existed prior to the fall of Communism, it increased in the 1990s, as did the crime rate. Fortunately, since 2000, the statistics show that the situation is improving, but only moderately. Nonetheless, this has led to an increase in female-headed households in urban areas.

When discussing urban life beyond just daily life, the focus is the "UB," as Ulaanbaatar is often called. Approaching 1 million people, it is truly the only place in Mongolia that can be viewed in the same manner as one might view New York, Chicago, London, or any other sizeable city.

Mongolia has numerous museums and a burgeoning restaurant scene. Finding a restaurant that serves Mongolian food can be tricky, though. The ever-pragmatic argument is that if you are going to a restaurant, why eat something you can eat at home? A few Chinese restaurants exist, but Korean restaurants are much more numerous, especially on "Korea Street." In addition, a German restaurant/brew pub offers German food, but with mutton substituting for beef. South American cuisine can also be found. Curiously, one can also go to one place that serves Mexican food on one side and Indian food on the other. By and large, though, the primary visitors to the restaurants tend to be the elite, not due to any social proscription, but rather because of simple economics. While the prices may be low by Western standards, they are still beyond the reach of much of Ulaanbaatar's population. Most Mongolians who eat out tend to frequent a *guanz*—essentially, a canteen with food of varying quality.

As evinced in chapter 5, Ulaanbaatar also has a thriving music scene. Indeed, in many ways, the music scene is stranded in Ulaanbaatar simply because of space limitations and cost factors for the music groups. Music clubs of varying sizes and venues are scattered throughout Ulaanbaatar. These include everything from the aforementioned German-style brew house to discotheques.

Although privately owned cars are more common now, public transportation is abundant, with both buses and taxis. Foreigners are well advised to take advantage of the taxi service simply because driving in Mongolia requires one to understand the rules of the road—which at times seem to be nonexistent.

EDUCATION

Prior to the 1921 Revolution, education and literacy were not widespread. Although the Buddhist monasteries offered an education, only a small percentage of the population had access to it. Thus only monks and government officials truly could be considered literate. Mongolia endured many atrocities and hardships during the Communist period, but it also enjoyed many benefits. One was a free and universal system of education, which was subsidized by 20 percent of the state's budget throughout most of the Communist period.

By the 1930s, a nationwide school system existed in the urban areas. The government also created boarding schools and dormitories within the town centers to accommodate the children of nomadic families. The switch from the old vertical Mongolian script to the Cyrillic alphabet also allowed for the government to standardize the curriculum across the country during the 1940s. The switch in alphabets also caused an education dilemma, as it led to the possibility that the older generation might be rendered illiterate. Thus the government sent teachers into the countryside and set up schools to educate all of the population to read and write in the new system. In addition, by 1983, ten thousand Mongolian students studied annually in the Soviet Union in a variety of fields. Most postsecondary education, particularly among the elite (socially and academically), took place in the Soviet Union and other Eastern Bloc countries. In short, the Communist period produced a population with a high literacy rate and an impressive educational system. This achievement continues today, as Mongolia possesses a literacy rate of 97.8 percent, one of the highest in the world.[1]

Mongolian children begin school at age seven, although preschool opportunities are available from ages two to seven. Primary and secondary education lasts for eleven years and is universal, enrolling over five hundred thousand children, although it is compulsory for eight to ten years. In addition to the primary and secondary schools that provide general education, there are also specialized schools. These include not only vocational or technical schools, but also schools for students who excel in academics.

Approximately one hundred twenty thousand students are enrolled in higher education, ranging from universities to postsecondary vocational schools. The majority of students in higher education, however, tend to be female. Indeed, males from the countryside typically do not last long at the universities, even though many are given scholarships or fellowships to attend. Although steppe children in the secondary schools have a high dropout rate, most of their schools are in local towns. Once in Ulaanbaatar, other distractions appear: not only the new and somewhat exotic experience of living in a large city, but also simply culture shock. Most of the students from herder families grew up in a *ger* under an open sky. Then they attend a university in a very busy city with a severe pollution problem from not only automobiles, but also coal-fired power plants and furnaces. One may liken it to similar situations in America in which children from small rural schools then go to the major state university. The difficulty of adjusting from a school of three hundred to a university, where there are classes that could fit more than one's entire high school, is immense. Many American rural students fail to adjust and do poorly, drop out, or transfer to another, smaller university.

Oddly, the end of Communism threatened Mongolia's educational successes. In the 1990s, donor agencies insisted that the government play a less visible role in society and, as with medical services, create a fee-based system. As a result, the percentage of the budget devoted to education shrank even as the budget shrank. The funding reductions carried over to the classroom. Class sizes increased, particularly in the primary grades. Basic materials such as textbooks were lacking. Often, several students had to share one book. Some schools even lacked utilities, including heat during the winter. At times, educational funding was so insufficient that teachers did not receive their pay. And when they received their pay, with the rampant inflation of the 1990s, it was insufficient as a livable wage. As a result, many teachers abandoned their careers in education due to the dire financial situation.

Teachers were not the only ones to abandon the schools. The dropout rate increased as well, particularly among boys, due to the reasons given previously. Compounding the issue, as many people returned to herding animals, they pulled their children from school to assist them. Their parents did not help, as they deemed that academic education would not really train the children for the jobs they did as nomads. In the cities, similar rationalization was also used in that education did not necessarily lead to better jobs or wages—perhaps disillusionment from the parents, as they saw the old Communist cliques still benefiting in the capitalist economy. This led to a decline in enrollment not only in primary, secondary, and higher education, but also in vocational and technical schools. Over a decade, the enrollment in vocational and technical schools plummeted from 26,400 in 1990 to 14,900 in 2001.[2] Fortunately, the government's budget has now stabilized, and so has the educational sector of Mongolia.

A major issue since the collapse of Communism has been maintaining the physical structures and equipment of the schools. In many areas where international aid has been misused or misguided, often by the foreign bureaucrats who run the programs, aid to schools has been moderately successful. The Asian Development Bank has assisted in renovating rural schools and providing computers for one hundred forty secondary schools and has provided funding for teacher training workshops as well as assisted in the creation of new, updated textbooks. Higher education has also benefited, as the Asian Development Bank assisted in the building and renovation of university science labs.[3]

Higher education in Mongolia has exploded since the 1990s, which is particularly reflected in the number of opportunities available within and outside Mongolia. Founded on May 5, 1942, the Mongolian State University, originally named Choibalsan University, has grown into the principal university in Mongolia and has spawned other universities. In 1951 the Department of Teacher Education became a separate institute (State Pedagogical Institute), but then it became a full university and was renamed the State Pedagogical University. The university's engineering departments also followed this line by becoming a separate entity known as the Polytechnic Institute in 1983. Whereas the Mongolian State University teaches the sciences, math, the social sciences, and the humanities, the Polytechnic Institute focuses on engineering and mining. Similar changes occurred within other branches of the Mongolian State University, resulting in ten state universities by the 1990s.

In the 1990s, a number of private institutions came into existence as well. Many of them were created at the urging of international donors, particularly in the instance of vocational and technical schools.[4] Most of the private colleges and universities, however, came into existence through the will of individual Mongolians. Initially, many of these suffered from the same lack of funding and materials that the public universities experienced. In addition, they also faced a very skeptical public, who criticized their admission and evaluation standards as being too low. The public also was not impressed with the quality of their teachers. Many simply viewed these institutions more as profit machines than as an ivory tower. While some schools floundered, others improved and are now viewed as providing a high-quality education. As the private schools stabilize and become more reputable, they are increasingly viewed as an alternative path for an education.

Their entry standards are still generally deemed less stringent than those of other schools, and they often offer less academic, but more practical and limited, fields of study such as intensive English, tourism-related studies, or business courses. Another reason for their appeal is that the public schools usually gave priority to the children of the elite. Although others gained admittance to the public universities, it was not uncommon for someone to lose his or her slot to a less-qualified but better-connected individual.

Considered to be one of the best private colleges in Mongolia by Mongolia's National Council for Higher Education Accreditation, Ikh Zasag is a model of success for private universities. The name refers to the Great Laws of Chinggis Khan. Originally established in 1994 with forty students and three instructors, the university has grown to five thousand students. The university is the dream of its president and founder, Namsrain Nyam-Osor. According to its president, what separates it from the public universities is that it focuses more on personal over professional education: students have more of an opportunity to immerse themselves not only in a regular education, but also in the history and culture of Mongolia.[5] He also has set stringent policies. Students can be expelled for missing more than thirty-six hours of classes. Also, his faculty members are not permitted to moonlight at other institutions, and thus they are not overworked and are able to focus on their students at Ikh Zasag. Adjuncting at other schools is a fairly common practice in Mongolia due to simple economics, allowing instructors to often effectively double their salaries.

Another well-regarded institution is Chinggis Khaan University, which, surprisingly, did not come into existence until 1999 with twenty faculty members and 130 students. It became a fully accredited university in 2004 and increased to eight hundred students and forty-five faculty members by 2008. It is probably the only place in the world where one can major in Chinggis Khan studies. The focus, as one might gather from the name, is only on Mongolia and the recovery of Mongolia's heritage. This focus is particularly emphasized in the graduate programs, which include a PhD in Chinggis Khan studies as well as shamanism studies. Other majors and courses of graduate studies focus on tourism and diplomacy.

Nonetheless, the decline of government support for education has had a tremendous impact on Mongolia. Although Mongolia still maintains a high literacy rate, it has seen a dramatic change in the quality of education. In addition, due to privatization, declines in government funding, and the closure of some schools, education, especially at the university level, has become inaccessible for many, not only in terms of tuition, but also simply due to geography.

The tragedy of it is that many cannot learn new skills to improve their situations. In addition, the basic level of education has dropped not just because of funding, but also because many teachers have not returned. As they already possessed many of the skills necessary for the new economy, they could find new jobs.

Another issue with the financing of education in Mongolia is one that chaffs public universities in America. The government has limited the funding of the universities but then retains control of the universities' budgets, despite the fact that the majority of funding comes from other sources. The problem is much more acute in Mongolia than the United States, though; for instance, expenses must meet the approval not only of the Ministry of Education, but also the Ministry of Finance. As a result, some purchases are delayed for months. Professors then lack the funds to attend conferences or conduct research, the physical structures suffer, and equipment for science laboratories and libraries deteriorates. Some organizations, such as the American Center for Mongolian Studies (ACMS), have made efforts to mitigate the lack of library resources by opening their reading rooms to students and scholars. In addition, the ACMS is working with Mongolian libraries to catalog their collections and also to create a consortium to gain access to online journal collections—a common practice among American universities.

It is hoped that the situation will right itself, and it has the potential to do so. At no point in Mongolia's history have there been as many universities as there are now. As of 2008, there were thirty-one public universities, three vocational-technical colleges, fifty-five accredited private colleges and universities, and many more unaccredited schools.

NOTES

1. United Nations Development Programme, *Fighting Climate Change: Human Solidarity in a Divided World*, United Nations Human Development Report 2007/ 2008 (New York: United Nations Development Programme, 2007), 231.

2. Morris Rossabi, *Modern Mongolia: From Khans to Commissars to Capitalists* (Berkeley: University of California Press, 2005), 163.

3. Ibid., 107.

4. Ibid., 163.

5. Jen Lin-Liu, "Discipline and Devotion at Ghenghis Khan U.," *Chronicle of Higher Education* 51 (2005): A40.

10

Legacy of Chinggis Khan

TODAY IN MONGOLIA, one cannot avoid the legacy of Chinggis Khan. To the Mongolians, he is the father of their state and nation, and to outsiders, he is easily the most identifiable figure in Mongolian history. This became even more so in 2006, which marked the eight hundredth anniversary of the founding of the Mongolian state and Empire by Chinggis Khan in 1206. His face and presence are everywhere.

Indeed, when one travels to Mongolia, one arrives at the Chinggis Khan Airport in Ulaanbaatar, catches a taxi and rides down Chinggis Khan Avenue, exchanges money at the Chinggis Khan Bank, sleeps at the Chinggis Khan Hotel, dines at the Chinggis Restaurant, and quenches his thirst with Chinggis beer—a fine, German-style lager. If a traveler is tired, he or she can get reenergized with a Chinggis Khan energy drink—if Red Bull gives Americans "wings" and another drink enables them to "party like a rockstar," one might wonder what happens if one drinks this beverage. For a nightcap, one can select from a variety of vodkas that carry Chinggis Khan's visage. And by now, one would have also noticed that one has paid for all of these activities with currency bearing the icon's face. All currency notes, from five hundred togrogs and above, display Chinggis Khan's visage.

Furthermore, his face adorns a hillside overlooking Ulaanbaatar, and a new display on Sukhebaatar Square overshadows the statue of the city's namesake. The five-meter-high statue sits in the middle of an open palace surrounded by statues of his successors and a couple of exquisitely sculpted Mongol warriors; indeed, it is quite impressive. The size of the palace and statue clearly demonstrates Chinggis Khan's significance and the country's direction for the future. As it is significantly larger than the tomb and statue of Sukhebaatar, the hero of Communist Mongolia, it signifies that the Communist period is merely a part of the past. It is not surprising that in 2006, one politician proposed renaming the city after Chinggis Khan.

The use of Chinggis Khan as a historic symbol of national pride is one of great importance. At the same time, since the fall of Communism in Mongolia, the Mongolians have also been quick studies in advertising. While American basketball star Michael Jordan may have been the most recognizable face in America during the 1990s, his exposure pales in comparison with the Chinggis Khan advertising spree.

Unsurprisingly, this has led to some concern over exactly how the Chinggis Khan "brand" should be used. While Chinggis Khan vodka is somewhat amusing, what should one do about Chinggis Khan toilet paper? Furthermore, who should be allowed to use it? Other states, such as Russia, Kazakhstan, and China, have also attempted to tap into the legacy of Chinggis Khan, for reasons to be discussed later. Thus, in 2006, the Mongolian legislature, the Ikh Khural, discussed the nature of this problem as well as how to control it.

Nonetheless, the importance of Chinggis Khan to Mongolia cannot be overlooked. Indeed, in many ways, he embodies and symbolizes the ideas and hopes of Mongolia, as does Britain's legendary "Once and Future King," Arthur; however, how did he reach this status? Considering his significance in history, it is not surprising that Chinggis Khan would have his admirers and would be recognized in his rightful spot as the founder of the Mongolian state. Yet one cannot help but question how he obtained such an elevated status that his image may be even more ubiquitous than Lenin's during the existence of the Soviet Union. And the reasons are partially divided into events that occurred shortly after his death.

CULT OF CHINGGIS

Although his importance as the father of the Mongolian people and founder of the Mongol Empire was not forgotten, during the Qing period, the focus of the attention and reverence toward Chinggis Khan was not on the historical Chinggis Khan, but rather on the religious Chinggis Khan.

One of the practices used to ensure that Buddhism took root was syncretism. The lamas, to ensure conversion and popular acceptance, adapted some elements of Mongol popular folk beliefs. One way the lamas did this, and also followed their own beliefs, was to adapt the practice of worshipping ancestors as protective spirits. In the seventeenth century, Chinggis Khan became part of the Buddhist pantheon as a protective god, and lamas wrote prayers to use in the worship of Chinggis Khan. This transformation of Chinggis Khan was not a difficult one, as Mongolians already worshipped him in several forms of folk religion.

There are three aspects to the deification of Chinggis Khan. The first, which is shamanistic, portrayed him as an ancestral spirit who served as a protective deity for the whole Mongolian people. In the second form, Chinggis Khan entered the Mongolian Buddhist pantheon as a low-ranking local guardian deity. In folk religion, Chinggis Khan appears in many forms that incorporated the shamanistic and Buddhist versions; for instance, in the folk religion, Chinggis Khan has traits of an initiatory god. Among some of the things he initiated were marriage customs and seasonal festivals. Of course, many of these were traditional beliefs with little to substantiate them, but as Chinggis Khan's prestige as a mortal, and then as a god, grew incrementally over time, so did the number of customs attributed to him. Eventually, many of the true origins were soon forgotten.

His transformation as a shamanistic protective deity occurred not long after his death. In shamanism, all ancestors receive some veneration, but Chinggis Khan's larger-than-life actions and his role in creating a complete Mongolian identity raised him to a level beyond simple ancestor veneration. It is clear that the Chinggisid princes of the royal family venerated him, but there are also indications that this practice extended beyond the royal family. It is uncertain, however, just to what extent the commoners worshipped him.

The idea of a protective spirit or guardian stemmed from the practice of ancestor worship. This was symbolized in the Mongolian war standard of *tuq*. The white *tuq* also symbolized the protective spirit of the tribes. The traditional *tuq* consisted of nine yak or horse tails, with each tail representing one of the original tribes. Coincidentally, nine is also viewed as a lucky number. Many believed that when he died, Chinggis Khan became the *sulde*, or "genius," of the Mongolian people and that he entered the standard of the Mongolian people, thus becoming the guardian genius of his people.[1]

Another appearance of Chinggis Khan occurs during the period of the Qing Empire and involves the living Buddha, or *khubilgan*, of Batogar Sume. According to the early-twentieth-century Mongolian expert and adventurer Owen Lattimore,

There is a story...about a Living Buddha of Batogar Sume who once went on a pilgrimage to Lhasa. In his train there was a man who looked just like him. On the Yellow river this man plotted with several others, seized the Living Buddha, pushed him through a hole in the ice to drown and went on to Lhasa, impersonating him.

The Living Buddha did not drown but floated under the ice until he came to another hole. There a smallish, thinnish, somewhat Chinese-looking man with a small round black cap and a thin, slight, long mustache came riding by on a chestnut horse with white points. He stooped over, seized the Living Buddha, drew him out of the water and then rode away and disappeared; and who should this man be but Jenghis [*sic*] Khan. The Living Buddha then started to wander, a poor and homeless man, working as a shepherd and moving on from time to time. After many wanderings he came at last to the camp of his own mother who recognized him. "I have heard that you were thrown into a hole and drowned," she said, "and I have heard that you were on pilgrimage in Lhasa, and I did not know which was the true story and which the false; but now I recognize you as my own son."[2]

Owen Lattimore never heard the end of the story, but the false living Buddha apparently failed to make a good impression on the Dalai Lama, who then looked into the affair. Lattimore believed that in the end, the living Buddha was vindicated. Of more significance is that we have an example of Chinggis Khan rescuing a living Buddha.

In addition, a prevalent belief among Mongols at various points in history was the inevitable return of Chinggis Khan. This belief has taken several different forms. In some legends, Chinggis Khan has returned in the form of an incarnated body. In other legends, Chinggis Khan never died, but rather is just resting. The most common legend is that Chinggis Khan returns, but only briefly, and only in times of need. The millenarian movement of Chinggis Khan came to a peak in the early twentieth century when Mongolia became a theater of the Russian civil war with the arrival of Baron Ungern von Sternberg. One refugee from the chaos of the war in Siberia, Paul Ossendowski, fled through Mongolia to escape the Bolsheviks. Along his route, Ossendowski met some Mongolians, who told him about von Sternberg:

From the North a white warrior came and called on the Mongols to break their chains of slavery which fell on our freed soil. This white warrior was the Incarnated [Chinggis] Khan.[3]

Another legend points to the eventual return of Chinggis Khan, which was recorded by Owen Lattimore. The legend is mixed with historical events. After the kingdom of Xixia rebelled against the Mongols, Chinggis Khan went to crush the rebellion. Finally, only the capital city remained. Historically, Chinggis Khan died in 1227 from internal injuries suffered from falling from his horse while hunting, but the legend tells a slightly different story.

According to the legend, Chinggis Khan dreamed of red blood on white snow. After consulting with his shaman and other advisors, it was determined that the dream concerned the most beautiful woman in the world. After gathering reports from throughout the empire, it was discovered that the fairest maiden was the daughter of the king of Xixia. Chinggis Khan made a simple demand to the king: surrender her or face destruction. The king consented, but also made his own plans to deal with the Mongol ruler.

Secretly, he gave his daughter a knife and instructed her to hide it. When Chinggis Khan came to her in the night, she cut him in the groin. At his cry, guards and others entered the room. Chinggis Khan's only words to them were, "Take this girl away, I wish to sleep." Supposedly the girl escaped and drowned herself to avoid capture and execution. Meanwhile, Chinggis Khan went to sleep and did not wake, but did not die. He was laid to rest in a safe place. Tradition says that an honor guard kept watch over the burial spot. Chinggis Khan was even at times considered to be Chinggis Bogdo, or "Holy Chinggis," a virtual god. His followers believed that he would heal himself and return. One saying goes, "They say he is dead, but he never died; he is only asleep, and he will awake."[4]

This legend corresponds with a belief common in many cultures that entails a tradition dubbed the "sleeping warrior" by Lord Raglan.[5] The idea is that the hero, resting in a cave on some remote mountain, is a national hero who will come to the country's defense in a time of great need. Of course, no one knows what this time of need is, but it will be one of dire consequences. In Mongolia, the warrior is Chinggis Khan. The corresponding figure in Wales is King Arthur; in Scotland, it is Robert Bruce; in Germany, it is Frederick Barbarossa, Charlemagne, or Siegfried; and in Spain, it is El Cid.

Legends like this only boosted the image of Chinggis Khan. Thus it is not surprising that he was viewed as a demigod. According to tradition, the Mongolians erected shrines for the worship of Chinggis Khan in the thirteenth century. Of the four known shrines, only the one known as Ejen Khoroo, in the Ordos region of Inner Mongolia, remains. It fell out of use at one time but came back into service at the command of the Qing dynasty. In 1863 the Khalkha prince Toqtaqutoru built another shrine in northern Mongolia, thus demonstrating some form of veneration carried into the late nineteenth century. This image of Chinggis Khan did change over time, and after the 1921 Revolution, it took a different turn.

SOVIET REPRESSION

In the twentieth century, views of Chinggis Khan changed once again. In Mongolia, as a fledgling state trying to gain independence, Chinggis Khan once again emerged as a national symbol. He once again became the symbol of the Mongolian people. His role as a world conqueror gained new life. Nationalism has never been an approved sentiment in Communism, but the veneration of Chinggis Khan in Communist Mongolia did not become an issue until 1949. As tensions between the Soviet Union and the People's Republic of China intensified, Chinggis Khan suddenly became a pawn in cold war politics.

Mongolia was not the only country to consider the historical role of Chinggis Khan. While Westerners read Harold Lamb's biography on the great Mongolian leader in the 1930s and 1940s, Chinggis Khan became a matter of patriotism in East Asia as Japan, China, and Russia attempted to gain the support of Mongolians. Although Japan and China vied for the attention of the Inner Mongolians, much of what they did had the potential to influence sentiments in Mongolia.

Both Japan and China supported Inner Mongolian efforts to honor Chinggis Khan. During the 1931–1945 Japanese occupation of much of Inner Mongolia, the Japanese supported the building of a large temple (more than 2,500 square feet) to Chinggis Khan in Ulanhot. At the same time, the Nationalist Chinese (Guomingdang) government tried to maintain Inner Mongolian support by protecting the sacred relics of Chinggis Khan held at Ejen Khoroo in the Ordos region of Inner Mongolia. These were moved from the Ordos to Gansu. Not to be outdone by his rivals, the Nationalists, or by his enemies, the Japanese, Mao Zedong, as leader of the Chinese Communists, also used Chinggis Khan. Mao attempted to gain Inner Mongolian support by calling on them to resist Japanese occupation and aggression in the spirit of Chinggis Khan.

Although this did not impact Mongolia directly, the use of such an iconic figure demonstrated how important not only Chinggis Khan, but also the Mongolian people, were to all sides. If Japan had monopolized the support of the Mongols and the relics of Chinggis Khan, one might wonder how they would have used them in propaganda in Mongolia—especially as they periodically espoused a pan-Mongol movement, much to the chagrin of the Soviets.

During World War II, Chinggis Khan remained important in Mongolia. Just as the Soviets used national heroes, such as Aleksandr Nevsky, in propaganda to build patriotic fervor against German invaders, they endorsed the process for Mongolia. Indeed, Stalin had no objections to the use of Chinggis Khan, even as part of governmental symbols. Historical studies on Chinggis Khan also increased during this period.

The end of World War II, however, meant a change in perspective for the Soviet leadership. With the defeat of Germany, patriotism that was focused through a lens of nationalist heroes lost favor, particularly when focused on non-Russian heroes. Part of this arose from the fear that these heroes, real and mythical, could potentially serve as rallying figures against Communist rule. Thus, in 1949, the Mongolian government followed suit. Chinggis Khan was condemned as a feudal and reactionary lord. His campaigns were deemed nothing more than plundering expeditions that exploited the people.

The rhetoric turned milder after the death of Stalin in 1953 but did not cease altogether. Mythical heroes, such as Geser, received less criticism, but Chinggis Khan and other national figures still received their share of condemnation. This was true not only in public speeches, but also in the work of historians. Quite simply, unless one wrote in an anti-Chinggis tone, the manuscript could not be published.

Chinggis Khan's condemnation in Mongolia was relatively short-lived due to events outside Mongolia. Once again, Inner Mongolia played a factor. In the long run, it was the Chinese Communist efforts to harness the aura of Chinggis Khan that played a role, albeit minor, in the Sino-Soviet split. The Communist defeat of the Nationalists allowed them to gain the relics of Chinggis Khan. In 1954 these were returned to Ejen Khoroo with pomp and grandeur. Then, in 1956, the government constructed an immense mausoleum (almost 5,000 square feet) to house the relics. Furthermore, the Communist government also restored the Japanese-built Temple of Chinggis Khan in Ulanhot. Thus, while one Communist condemned the Mongolian leader, another promoted him. As China renewed relations with Mongolia, this had potential for swaying public opinion.

In the 1960s, Mongolia's government began to reconsider its position on Chinggis Khan, especially as 1962 marked Chinggis Khan's eight hundredth birthday. No one is positive of the date; Western scholars mark it as either 1165 or 1167, but in Mongolia, 1162 remains in vogue. Although Tsendenbal, Mongolia's leader at the time, did not fully endorse it, the government allowed the Mongolian Academy of Sciences to study the issue. The first effort comprised simply commemorative stamps, an academic conference, and an editorial in the state newspaper, *Unen*. The final touch was the creation of a stone monument, topping thirty-six feet, with Chinggis Khan's portrait. The government erected this near the birthplace of Chinggis Khan at Gurwan Nuur in the Khentii Aimag.

Mongolia normally followed the Soviet lead in most matters, but in this, Mongolia did not consult the Union of Soviet Socialist Republics. Soviet historians criticized the academic conference. In China, the reaction was quite different. Although some Chinese historians criticized Chinggis Khan, others praised him. Yet they did not criticize him or praise him in the context of Mongolia, but rather in the context of his role in Chinese history—particularly as a unifier. Also in 1962, Inner Mongolians held their own conference on Chinggis Khan. New tensions arose between the Soviet Union and China because at this conference, some scholars suggested that Mongolia be reunited with China. Naturally, the Soviets complained vociferously. Not only did they continue their criticism of all of the 1962 events, but they also took offense at the Mongolian scholars who dared to criticize Soviet historical studies of Chinggis Khan. The fact that the Mongols conquered Russia in the late 1230s and then dominated it for two hundred years certainly played an unspoken role in Soviet policy. In the end, Tsendenbal defused much of the situation by naming and dismissing Daramyn Tomor-Ochir, a party official, as the scapegoat for the whole affair.

Mongolian scholars also felt Soviet wrath. X. Perlee, one of the greatest Mongolian scholars, refused to play by Soviet rules. As a consequence, he was imprisoned, and when he was not in jail, he was refused permission to perform research outside Mongolia. The fact that he was Tomor-Ochir's teacher also placed a target on his back. Relatives of scholars also came under scrutiny by the government. Many faced demotions or the loss of their jobs. Meanwhile, the territory around Chinggis Khan's birthplace became a Soviet tank base under restricted access.

Nonetheless, Chinggis Khan continued to be one of the subplots in the Sino-Soviet split. From 1963 to 1964, the Soviets denounced Chinese scholarship favorable to Chinggis Khan. It is difficult to blame them, though, as Chinese scholars insinuated that the Russians would have remained ignorant savages had the Mongols not bestowed some elements of Chinese civilization on them.[6]

In 1975 Tsendenbal also chimed in and ridiculed the Chinese obsession with the Mongolian leader. He also linked it back to ideas expressed at the Inner Mongolia 1962 conference, where some advocated reunifying Mongolia with China. Thus honoring Chinggis Khan placed Mongolia's independence in peril. Neither side truly favored Chinggis Khan's role in its history. While the Chinese promoted his image in the 1950s and early 1960s, overall, outside Inner Mongolia, the Chinese held little interest in the topic. The Cultural Revolution of the late 1960s and early 1970s then reversed the situation completely, as Inner Mongolian scholars and others associated with studying or praising Chinggis Khan found themselves targets of persecution. The temple at Ulanhot and the mausoleum both suffered extensive damage.

REVIVAL AND REHABILITATION

Not until the period of glasnost and perestroika did government attitudes toward Chinggis Khan change. Although government attitudes toward Chinggis Khan were unfavorable, the populace maintained a favorable impression of the Mongolian leader. Yet, until the government ideology altered, making favorable statements about the Mongolian leader was done at one's own risk. Once official sanction ended, though, Chinggis Khan became the symbol of Mongolia. As discussed in chapter 5, a rock group and song named after Chinggis Khan vividly demonstrated the separation between state and popular views.

Considering Chinggis Khan's achievements, it is not surprising that his popularity is on the rise. After all, Chinggis Khan is the founding father of Mongolia. The Mongolian nation lasted longer than the empire itself. What is notable is that most Mongolians rarely speak of Chinggis Khan's deeds outside Mongolia, but rather of his statesmanship, vision, and laws. To them, the importance of the conquests is secondary to the institutions that he gave to the Mongols. This is not because they are apologetic for the brutality of the conquests, but rather, they realize the importance of Chinggis Khan's other activities. As a result, since 1990, he has become the ultimate symbol of Mongolian nationalism. Furthermore, Chinggis Khan is not only the father of the country, but many—including academics and politicians—view Chinggis Khan as the reason why Mongolia has successfully transitioned into a democratic state. In the eyes of many Mongolians, the framework for democracy was created by Chinggis Khan through the tradition of having his successors elected.[7]

While the historical validity of this belief is rather dubious, as only the descendents of Chinggis Khan could rule, it does demonstrate a rationalization and justification for why democracy has taken root. By tracing it back to Chinggis Khan, it justifies the experiment and makes it part of the customs and culture of Mongolia.

During the Communist period, the national flag flew over the Naadam games. Now, the primary symbol is the white *tuq*, or battle standard, consisting of nine horse tails. In addition, the regular army troops have been replaced with a special military unit dressed as warriors from the period of Chinggis Khan.

The revival of Chinggis Khan is perhaps most apparent in the realm of education. Not only is there a Chinggis Khaan University, but there is also Ikh Zasag University, which is named after Chinggis Khan's law code. Both schools place an emphasis on the great Mongolian leader, from the universities' names to the portraits that adorn their walls. Whereas in the past, Chinggis Khan was viewed as an oppressor of the common people and as a feudal lord in Marxist dogma, he is now associated with being an emancipator of the people from the fetters of ignorance.

In many ways, this is not surprising. Ikh Zasag University's founder, Namsrain Nyam-Osor, had a childhood education that was relatively devoid of any reference to Chinggis Khan. He only learned about the founder of Mongolia when he stumbled across a statue of Chinggis Khan on the steppe that had been overlooked by Soviet troops. Fascinated by the image, Namsrain began to pursue the study of the Mongolian leader.[8]

In Mongolia, he is rarely viewed in the same way he is in the West. Rather than as a ruthless conqueror, he is viewed as a promoter of peace. Indeed, when examining the situation of Mongolia prior to the rise of Chinggis Khan, one can understand why this view dominates. The Mongolians also want to link the present with the past. Just as Chinggis Khan's empire made Mongolia the center of the world and a broker in terms of trade, ideas, and technology, modern Mongolians want to see Mongolia's role and status increase. There are no false illusions of being a major power. Poverty and a small population prevent that in the modern age. Nonetheless, they seek a fully independent Mongolia that no longer has to modify its policies according to the fears and desires of its larger neighbors.

This more benign view of Chinggis Khan is becoming less of an oddity to Westerners. Although scholars of the Mongolian Empire have known the complete picture of Chinggis Khan for decades, such a view has not carried over into the public perception. One reason is due to the success of American scholar Jack Weatherford's book *Genghis Khan and the Making of the Modern World*, which sat high on the *New York Times* Best-Seller list for several weeks.

Chinggis Khan's importance to Mongolia cannot be overemphasized, nor can it be ignored. Throughout its history, he has been a constant symbol for Mongolia, even though his image has changed throughout time. He has been venerated, denigrated, and made a national symbol as well as an advertising emblem. Not all Mongolians hold him in the same esteem, but even those who simply view him as a pivotal historical figure still appreciate his importance to Mongolia. In this context, it is not surprising that Inner Mongolians still look to Chinggis Khan and that even in Kazakhstan, there are some who look to Chinggis Khan as a national hero, as evinced by the 2008 movie *Mongol*.

In a sense, Chinggis Khan, historical figure, sleeping warrior, and demigod, has returned. With the collapse of the planned economy and Communist government, Mongolia was thrown into upheaval. While Americans generally assume that capitalism and democracy are good things, they are also concepts that are taken for granted. To be sure, there are many benefits to them, but learning how these ideas work is not easy. Westerners grew into these modes and today have little concept of the hardship and confusion that can arise out of the turbulence that market economies or democracies can cause in areas where they never before existed. In a sense, Chinggis Khan has returned not in a physical sense, but as a symbol to unify the country and restore a sense of nationalism, grandeur, and even stability to an independent Mongolia.

NOTES

1. B. Y. A. Vladimirtsov, *The Life of Chingis Khan*, trans. Prince D. S. Mirsky (New York: Houghton, Mifflin, 1930), 65.

2. Owen Lattimore, *Mongol Journeys* (New York: Doubleday, 1941), 83.

3. Ferdinand Ossendowksi, *Beasts, Men, and Gods* (New York: E. P. Dutton, 1922), 203.

4. Lattimore, *Mongol Journeys*, 27.

5. Lord Raglan, *The Hero: A Study in Tradition, Myth, and Drama* (New York: Oxford University Press, 1937), 41–42.

6. Jack Weatherford, "A Scholarly Quest to Understand Genghis Khan," *Chronicle of Higher Education* 46 (2000): B10.

7. Paula Sabloff, "Why Mongolia? The Political Culture of an Emerging Democracy," *Central Asian Survey* 21 (2002): 19–36; also see Andrew F. March, "Citizen Genghis? On Explaining Mongolian Democracy through 'Political Culture,'" *Central Asian Survey* 22 (2003): 61–66.

8. Jen Lin-Liu, "Discipline and Devotion at Ghenghis Khan U.," *Chronicle of Higher Education* 51 (2005): A40.

Glossary

aarts   A soft and slightly fermented cheese.

aaruul   A hard, dried cheese curd.

ail   A nomadic camp, usually consisting of a few *gers* belonging to the same family.

aimag   An administrative unit in modern Mongolia, comparable to a province.

airag   Fermented mare's milk with a low alcohol content.

amban   Title of a provincial governor during the Qing period.

arat   Common herdsmen during the Qing period. It has also come to mean "the people."

arkhi   Vodka.

banshi   A meat-stuffed dumpling boiled in soup.

bielgee   A dance performed with the upper body.

bodhisattva   Someone who has attained enlightenment but remains on earth to help others.

Bogd Khan   The "Holy King"; the title originally referred to Chinggis Khan but was later a title that the Qing came to adopt. The Jebtsundamba Khutukhtu ruled an independent Mongolia under this title.

boo   Shaman.

boodog   A style of cooking in which the animal carcass serves as the vessel. Hot rocks are placed inside and the outside is cooked with a blowtorch.

borts   Wind-dried meat, similar to beef jerky.

bortsog   Fried bread.

buuz   Meat-stuffed steamed dumplings.

Chinggisid   A descendent of Chinggis Khan. Most of the Mongolian aristocracy were Chinggisids.

Da Lama   "Great Lama"; this was a political position within the monasteries. The Qing appointed the Da Lama to track the wealth of the monastery and to inform the government of any suspicious activity.

deel   The traditional Mongolian caftan-like garment.

eriin gurwan naadam   The "three manly games" of the Naadam: wrestling, horse racing, and archery.

five snouts   The animals that are herded in Mongolia. Although they are not always used by all nomads, some combination exists. The Five Snouts are horses, sheep, goats, cows (or yaks), and camels.

Gelukpa   The Yellow sect of Tibetan Buddhism. It is called the Yellow sect due to the color of the monks' robes and hats.

ger   The round, felt-covered tents used by the nomads. Also known by its Turkic name, yurt.

gobi   A gravelly desert. The Gobi Desert is the largest of many *gobi* areas in Mongolia.

Han   Ethnic Chinese. The ethnicity name is derived from the Han dynasty.

Ikh Khural   The legislative body of Mongolia and the equivalent of a parliament or congress.

Jebtsundamba Khutukhtu   The highest-ranking incarnate lama in Mongolia. Also considered to be the third-highest-ranking incarnate lama in the Yellow sect of Buddhism.

joochin   Dulcimer.

Jujuan   Possibly the forerunners of the Mongols. The confederation that dominated Mongolia from the fourth to the sixth centuries. When they appeared in eastern Europe, Europeans called them "Avars."

Kereits   A Turkic tribe that dominated central Mongolia in the twelfth century.

khainag   The result of cross-breeding cows and yaks. The *khainag* thrives in areas of altitude ranging from sixteen hundred to twenty-five hundred meters.

Khamag Mongol Ulus   All-Mongol nation or state. The name of the initial state created by Chinggis Khan after unifying Mongolia.

khan   A title equivalent to "king."

Khitans   A proto-Mongolian group that established the Liao dynasty and dominated much of Mongolia from 960 to 1125 CE.

khoomii   Throat-singing.

khorkhog   A style of cooking using hot rocks and a large can or other metal container. The rocks and food are placed in the container.

khubilgan   Lesser incarnate lama.

khurem   A traditional Mongolian jacket.

khutukhtu   An incarnate lama of high prestige, or a lama who has been reborn.

khuurshuur   A meat-stuffed pancake.

koumiss   Fermented mare's milk, known in Mongolia as *airag*.

lama   A Buddhist monk.

Manchus   A Tungusic people from what is now northeastern China, also known as Manchuria. They were semi-nomadic and dominated China from 1644 to 1912. Included in their empire were virtually all Mongolian groups.

mantuu   A steamed bun.

morin khuur   A two-stringed instrument with a carved horse head topping it.

MPRP, Mongolian People's Revolution Party   Created along the line of Leninist revolutionary ideology, it became the dominant political force in Mongolia in the twentieth century.

naadam   Literally, "games"; it became an annual sporting event focused on the "three manly games": wrestling, archery, and horse racing.

negdel   A Mongolian collective introduced during the Communist period.

nokhoi khorio   Literally, "please restrain the dogs!" It has also become a casual greeting.

nokhor   A companion or vassal during the pre-Mongol Empire period.

oboo   A cairn or pile of rocks. The rocks are placed as an offering to shamanistic spirits. Khadags or prayer scarves are also placed on the *oboo* by Buddhists.

Oirats   Western Mongols. Their leaders were typically not Chinggisids.

ongghot   A felt doll used in shamanism. The doll represents a protective spirit, usually an ancestor. The *ongghot* is kept in the *ger*.

orom   A sweet cream.

samsara   The cycle of birth and death and rebirth in Buddhism.

Second Conversion   The arrival of Buddhism in the sixteenth century. It is called the Second Conversion because Kublai Khan's preference for Buddhism is usually considered the first period of Mongolian Buddhism.

shabinar   The *arats* who tended the herds and flocks of the monasteries. They were tied to the monastery almost like serfs.

shang   The treasury of an incarnate lama. This consisted primarily of portable goods and was separate from the monastery's treasury.

shanyü   The title used by a Xiongnu ruler, equivalent to "king" or "emperor."

shimiin arkhi   Distilled *airag*.

shuul   Soup. Sometimes served with food and becoming a stew.

suutai tsai   Tea with milk.

Tengri   Heaven. The sky god of the medieval Mongols.

thangka   A Buddhist style of painting.

togrog   Mongolian currency.

tsagaan sar   "White Month"; the Mongolian New Year.

tsam   A papier-mâché mask used in a Buddhist exorcism dance.

Uighurs   Tribal confederation that dominated Mongolia from 744 to 840 CE.

Urga   The city of the Jebtsundamba Khutukhtu. Now known as Ulaanbaatar.

urtyn duu   The "long song."

uurga   The long pole lasso used by Mongolian herders to control their animals.

Xianbei   Tribal confederation that succeeded the Xiongnu and dominated Mongolia from approximately 150 to 528 CE. Members of the Xianbei also established the Northern Wei dynasty in China (386–528 CE).

Xiongnu   A tribal confederation that dominated Mongolia from roughly 300 BCE to 150 CE. In the West, they became known as the Huns.

yatga   A stringed instrument, similar to a zither but possessing a movable bridge.

Yuan dynasty   Dynastic name of the Mongols during their domination of China and East Asia.

zhos   The treasury of a monastery that included movable property, such as herds, as well as fixed property, such as the monastery and shrines.

zhud   A winter storm or blizzard with an intensity that devastates the herds of nomads.

Zungars   The Oirat confederations of the seventeenth and eighteenth centuries that challenged the Qing dynasty.

zurag   Literally, "painting," but more specifically, a contemporary, secular style.

Bibliography

Academy of Sciences, MPR. *Information Mongolia: The Comprehensive Reference Source of the People's Republic of Mongolia (MPR).* Oxford: Pergamon Press, 1990.

Allsen, Thomas. "Mongolian Princes and Their Merchant Partners, 1200–1260." *Asia Major* 2 (1989): 83–126.

Amitai, Reuven, and Michal Biran, eds. *Mongols, Turks, and Others: Eurasian Nomads and the Sedentary World.* Leiden, Netherlands: Brill, 2004.

Amitai-Preiss, Reuven, and David O. Morgan, eds. *The Mongol Empire and Its Legacy.* Leiden, Netherlands: Brill, 1999.

Atwood, Christopher. "Buddhism and Popular Ritual in Mongolian Religion: A Re-examination of the Fire Cult." *History of Religions* 36 (1996): 112–39.

———. *Encyclopedia of Mongolia and the Mongol Empire.* New York: Facts on File, 2004.

Avery, Martha. *Women of Mongolia.* Seattle: University of Washington Press, 1996.

Badarch, Dendeviin, Raymond A. Zilinskas, and Peter J. Balint. *Mongolia Today: Science, Culture, Environment, and Development.* London: Routledge Curzon, 2003.

Bamana, Gaby, ed. *Christianity and Mongolia.* Ulaanbaatar, Mongolia: Antoon Mostaert Enter, 2006.

Bartold, V. V. *Turkestan down to the Mongol Invasion.* New Delhi: Munshiram Manoharlal, 1992.

Batbayar, Tsedendambyn. *Modern Mongolia: A Concise History.* Ulaanbaatar, Mongolia: Mongolian Center for Scientifica and Technological Information, 1996.

Bawden, C. R. *An Anthology of Mongolian Traditional Literature.* London: Kegan Paul, 1969.

————. *The Modern History of Mongolia.* New York: Praeger, 1968.

————, trans. *Tales of an Old Lama.* Tring, UK: Institute of Buddhist Studies, 1997.

Becker, Jason. *The Lost Country: Mongolia Revealed.* London: Hodder and Stoughton, 1992.

Berger, Patricia, and Terese Tse Bartholomew. *Mongolia: The Legacy of Chinggis Khan.* San Francisco: Thames and Hudson, 1995.

Bergholz, Fred W. *The Partition of the Steppe: The Struggle of the Russians, Manchus, and the Zunghar Mongols for Empire in Central Asia, 1619–1758.* New York: Peter Lang, 1993.

Bira, Shadaryn. *Studies in Mongolian History, Culture, and Historiography.* Tokyo: Institute for Languages and Cultures of Asia and Africa, 1994.

Bira, Shadaryn, and John R. Krueger, trans. *Mongolian Historical Writing from 1200–1700.* Bellingham: Center for East Asian Studies, Western Washington University, 2002.

Bold, Bat-Ochir. *Mongolian Nomadic Society: A Reconstruction of the "Medieval" History of Mongolia.* New York: St. Martin's Press, 2001.

Bruun, Ole. *Precious Steppe: Mongolian Nomadic Pastoralists in the Age of the Market.* Lanham, MD: Lexington Books, 2006.

Bruun, Ole, and Ole Odgaard, eds. *Mongolia in Transition: Old Patterns, New Challenges.* Surrey, UK: Curzon, 1996.

Buell, Paul D. *Historical Dictionary of the Mongol World Empire.* Lanham, MD: Scarecrow Press, 2003.

Buell, Paul D., and Eugene N. Anderson. *A Soup for the Qan.* London: Kegan Paul International, 2000.

Bulag, Uradyn E. *Nationalism and Hybridity in Mongolia.* Oxford: Clarendon Press, 1998.

Chen, Albert. "The Mongolian Shark." *Sports Illustrated,* November 5, 2001, http://vault.sportsillustrated.cnn.com/vault/article/magazine/MAG1024192/1/index.htm.

Choijamts, Abbot. "An Interview with His Eminence Abbot Choijamts." Interviewed by Andrew Shimunek. *Mongol Survey* 20 (2007): 10–12.

Cleaves, Francis W., ed. and trans. *The Secret History of the Mongols.* Cambridge, MA: Harvard University Press, 1980.

Craven, David, and Molly Curtin. *Environmental Profile of Mongolia.* Bethesda, MD: Development Alternatives, 1998.

Dawson, Christopher, ed. *The Mongol Mission.* New York: Sheed and Ward, 1955.

Elverskog, Johan. *The Jewel Translucent Sutra: Altan Khan and the Mongols in the Sixteenth Century.* Leiden, Netherlands: Brill, 2003.

Ertel, Manfred. "Mongolia's New Nomads: High Heels in the Desert." *Spiegel Online,* December 20, 2007. http://www.spiegel.de/international/world/0,1518,524714,00.html.

Ewing, Thomas. *Between the Hammer and the Anvil? Chinese and Russian Policies in Outer Mongolia, 1911–1912.* Bloomington: Indiana University Press, 1980.

Frederick, Jim. "Guess Who's Taking Over the Sumo Ring." *Time*, November 20, 2005.

Gilmour, James. *James Gilmour of Mongolia: His Diaries, Letters and Reports*. Edited by Richard Lovett. Kila, MT: Kessinger, 2007.

Haslund, Henning. *In Secret Mongolia*. Kempton, IL: Adventures Unlimited Press, 1995.

Heissig, Walther. *A Lost Civilization: The Mongols Rediscovered*. Translated by D. J. S. Thomson. New York: Basic Books, 1966.

———. *The Religions of Mongolia*. Translated by Geoffrey Samuel. Berkeley: University of California Press, 1980.

Humphrey, Caroline, and Urgunge Onon. *Shamans and Elders*. Oxford: Clarendon Press, 1996.

Jagchid, Sechin, and Paul Hyer. *Mongolia's Culture and Society*. Boulder, CO: Westview Press, 1979.

Jerryson, Michael K. *Mongolian Buddhism: The Rise and Fall of the Sangha*. Suthep, Thailand: Silkworm Books, 2007.

Juvaini, Ata Malik. *Genghis Khan: The History of the World Conqueror*. Translated by J. A. Boyle. Seattle: University of Washington Press, 1997.

Jûzjânî, Minhâj Sirâj. *Tabaqât-i-Nasirî*. 2 vols. Edited by Abd al-Habibi. Kabul: Anjuman-i Tarikh-i Afghanistan, 1964–1965.

———. *Tabakât-i-Nasirî: A General History of the Muhammadan Dynasties of Asia*. 2 vols. Translated by H. G. Raverty. New Delhi: Oriental Books, 1970.

Kaplonski, Christopher. *Truth, History and Politics in Mongolia: The Memory of Heroes*. London: RoutledgeCurzon, 2004.

Khazanov, Anatoly. *Nomads and the Outside World*. London: Cambridge University Press, 1984.

Lattimore, Owen. *Mongol Journeys*. New York: Doubleday, 1941.

———. *The Mongols of Manchuria*. London: Kimble and Bradford, 1935.

———. *Nomads and Commissars: Mongolia Revisited*. New York: Oxford University Press, 1962.

Lhagvasuren, Nomin. "Uniting for Men." *Transitions Online*, June 23, 2003. http://www.tol.cz/look/TOL/article.tpl?IdLanguage=1&IdPublication=4&NrIssue=47&NrSection=2&NrArticle=9883.

Lin-Liu, Jen. "Discipline and Devotion at Ghenghis Khan U." *Chronicle of Higher Education* 51 (2005): A40.

Liu, Xiaoyuan. *Reins of Liberation: An Entangled History of Mongolian Independence, Chinese Territoriality, and Great Power Hegemony, 1911–1950*. Stanford, CA: Stanford University Press, 2006.

Lord Raglan. *The Hero: A Study in Tradition, Myth, and Drama*. New York: Oxford University Press, 1937.

Man, John. *Genghis Khan: Life, Death, and Resurrection*. London: Bantam Press, 2004.

———. *Gobi: Tracking the Desert*. New Haven, CT: Yale University Press, 1999.

March, Andrew F. "Citizen Genghis? On Explaining Mongolian Democracy through 'Political Culture.'" *Central Asian Survey* 22 (2003): 61–66.

Marsh, Peter. "Mongolia Sings Its Own Song." http://mongoluls.net/ger/sing.shtml.
———. *Mongolian Pop-Rock Unleashed.* Ulaanbaatar, Mongolia: UN Development Programme, 1999.

Martelle, Scott. "Horse Race of a Different Color." *Los Angeles Times,* March 15, 1998.

"The Masher from Mongolia." *The Economist,* August 29, 2007.

May, Timothy. *The Mongol Art of War.* Yardley, PA: Westholme, 2007.

"Missionaries, Democrats in Fight for Mongolian Souls." *Asian Political News,* July 29, 2002.

"The Mongolians Are Coming to China! With Heavy Metal!" *New York Times,* November 26, 2004.

Mooney, Paul. "Orphans of Change." *Asia Now.* http://cgi.cnn.com/ASIANOW/asiaweek/98/1127/feat5.html.

Morgan, David O. *The Mongols.* 2nd ed. Oxford: Blackwell, 2007.

Moses, Larry W. *The Political Role of Mongol Buddhism.* Bloomington: Indiana University Press, 1977.

Moses, Larry, and Stephen A. Halkovic Jr. *Introduction to Mongolian History and Culture.* Uralic and Altaic Series 149. Bloomington: Indiana University Press, 1985.

Murphy, George G. S. *Soviet Mongolia: A Study of the Oldest Political Satellite.* Berkeley: University of California Press, 1966.

Namjim, T. *The Economy of Mongolia: From Traditional Times to the Present.* Edited by William Rozycki. Bloomington, IN: Mongolia Society, 2000.

Natsagdorj, Tsegmediin. *Mongolia of Chinggis.* Ulaanbaatar, Mongolia: Monsudar, 2004.

Noerper, Stephen. *Mongolia Matter.* Brookings Northeast Asia Commentary, October 17, 2007.

O'Donnell, Linda. "Mongolia: The Last Frontier Buddhists Are Battling Christians for Market Share in Post-Communist Mongolia." *World Tibet Network News,* December 4, 1999.

"Old Songs of Arrows." *Mongolia Today* 7 (2002). http://www.mongoliatoday.com/issue/7/archery.html.

Onon, Urgunge, ed. *Mongolian Heroes of the Twentieth Century.* New York: AMS Press, 1976.

Onon, Urgunge, and Derrick Pritchatt. *Asia's First Modern Revolution: Mongolia Proclaims Its Independence in 1911.* Leiden, Netherlands: Brill, 1989.

Ossendowski, Ferdinand. *Beasts, Men, and Gods.* New York: E. P. Dutton, 1922.

Pegg, Caroline. *Mongolian Music, Dance and Oral Narratives.* Seattle: University of Washington Press, 2001.

Perdue, Peter. *China Marches West: The Qing Conquest of Central Eurasia.* Cambridge, MA: Harvard University Press, 2005.

Petech, Luciano. *Central Tibet and the Mongols: The Yuan-Sa'skya Period of Tibetan History.* Rome: Instituto Italiano Per Il Medio Ed Estremo Oriente, 1990.

Polo, Marco. *The Travels of Marco Polo.* Translated by Henry Yule. New York: Dover, 1993.

Poppe, Nicholas. *The Heroic Epic of the Khalkha Mongols.* 2nd ed. Bloomington, IN: Mongolia Society, 1979.

Pozdneev, Aleksei Matveevich. *Mongolia and the Mongols.* Bloomington: Indiana University Press, 1971.

de Rachewiltz, Igor, ed. *The Secret History of the Mongols.* Brill's Inner Asian Library 7. Leiden, Netherlands: Brill, 2004.

de Rachewiltz, Igor. "The Title Cinggis Chan/Chaghan Re-examined." In *Gedanke und Wirkung: Festschrift zum 90. Geburtstag von Nicholaus Poppe,* edited by W. Heissig and K. Sagaster, 281–99. Wiesbaden, Germany: Harrassowitz, 1989.

Riasanovsky, Valentin A. *Fundamental Principles of Mongol Law.* Uralic and Altaic Series 43. Bloomington: Indiana University Press, 1965.

Rossabi, Morris, ed. *China among Equals.* Berkeley: University of California Press, 1983.

Rossabi, Morris. *Khubilai Khan: His Life and Times.* Berkeley: University of California Press, 1988.

———. *Modern Mongolia: From Khans to Commissars to Capitalists.* Berkeley: University of California Press, 2005.

Rupen, Robert. *How Mongolia Is Really Ruled: A Political History of the Mongolian People's Republic 1900–1978.* Stanford, CA: Hoover Institution Press, 1979.

———. *The Mongolian People's Republic.* Stanford, CA: Hoover Institution Press, 1966.

Sabloff, Paula. "Why Mongolia? The Political Culture of an Emerging Democracy." *Central Asian Survey* 21 (2002): 19–36.

Sandag, Shagdariin, and Harry H. Kendall. *Poisoned Arrows: The Stalin-Choibalsan Mongolian Massacres, 1921–1941.* Boulder, CO: Westview Press, 2000.

Sanders, Alan J. K. *Historical Dictionary of Mongolia.* 2nd ed. Lanham, MD: Scarecrow Press, 2003.

Schiling, Mark. "Sumo Still Socko." *Variety,* September 3–9, 2007.

Schwarz, Henry. "Otrâr." *Central Asian Survey* 17 (1998): 5–10.

Severin, Tim. *In Search of Genghis Khan.* New York: Atheneum, 1992.

Shagdar, Enkhbayar. "The Mongolian Livestock Sector: Vital for the Economy and People, but Vulnerable to Natural Phenomena." http://www.erina.or.jp/en/Research/db/pdf2002/02160e.pdf.

Sneath, David. *The Headless State: Aristocratic Orders, Kinship Society, and Misrepresentations of Nomadic Inner Asia.* New York: Columbia University Press, 2007.

———. "Mobility, Technology, and Decollectivization of Pastoralism in Mongolia." In *Mongolia in the Twentieth Century: Landlocked Cosmopolitan,* edited by Stephen Kotkin and Bruce A. Elleman, 223–36. Armonk, NY: M. E. Sharpe, 1999.

Tsultem, N. *Mongolian Zurag.* Ulaanbaatar, Mongolia: State Publishing House, 1986.

United Nations Development Programme. *Fighting Climate Change: Human Solidarity in a Divided World.* United Nations Human Development Report 2007/2008. New York: United Nations Development Programme, 2007.

Urnaa, Vaanchig, Masashi Kizuki, Keiko Nakamura, Akie Kaneko, Tomoke Inose, Kaoruke Seino, Takehito Takano. "Association of Swaddling, Rickets Onset and Bone Properties in Children in Ulaanbaatar, Mongolia." *Public Health* 120 (2006): 834–40.

Vladimirtsov, B. Y. A. *The Life of Chingis Khan.* Translated by Prince D. S. Mirsky. New York: Houghton, Mifflin, 1930.

Weatherford, Jack. *Genghis Khan and the Making of the Modern World.* New York: Crown, 2004.

———. "A Scholarly Quest to Understand Genghis Khan." *Chronicle of Higher Education* 46 (2000): B10.

Wingfield-Hayes, Rupert. "Mongolia's Return to Religion." BBC News. http://news.bbc.co.uk/1/hi/world/asia-pacific/3113839.stm.

Index